D0821822

Order of
Fifinella
© Walt Disney

COOLANT

WASPs

Women Airforce Service Pilots of World War II

Vera S. Williams

PACIFIC HISTORIC PARKS
Remember • Honor • Understand

Dedication

To the first Woman Warrior in my life—my mother, Eleonora (Macziola) Stone

---

Published in 2011 by Pacific Historic Parks
1 Arizona Memorial Place
Honolulu, Hawaii 96818 USA

Pacific Historic Parks is a non-profit cooperating association that supports National Park Service educational programs at four pacific region parks. For more information, please visit our website at www.pacifichistoricparks.org

Library of Congress Cataloging-in-Publication Data
Williams, Vera S.
WASPs : women airforce service pilots in World War II / Vera S. Williams.
p. cm.
Includes index.
ISBN 0-87938-856-0
1. Women air pilots—United States. 2. World War, 1939-1945—Aerial operations, American. 3. Women's Air Service Pilots (U.S.) I. Title.
D790.W493 1994
940.54'4973—dc20 93-39573

On the front cover: Members of a group of WASPs who have been trained to ferry the B-17 Fortress: Frances (Green) Karl, Class 43-W-5; and Margaret (Kirchner) Stevenson, Ann (Waldner) Currier, and Blanche (Osborn) Bross of Class 43-W-6. They stride confidently along in front of the B-17 *Pistol Packin' Mama. USAF (neg. no. 160449 AC)*

On the frontispiece page: Fifinella, the WASP's mascot, was created by Walt Disney. She was a female gremlin blamed for mishaps such as maps flying out of cockpits and missing airfields in the fog. *© Disney Enterprises, Inc.; photo by Hans Halberstadt*

On the title page: Two WAFS and an Army pilot with an early-model P-51 Mustang. The girls got to pilot a variety of aircraft including the P-51s. Barbara Jane (Erickson) London is on the left. The first group of women to fly for the United States Army Air Force were the WAFS—the Women's Auxiliary Ferrying Squadron. This group of highly experienced female pilots was headed by Nancy Love. The first twenty-eight WAFS were known to later WAFS and WASPs as the "Originals." *Courtesy of US Air Force Photo Collection (USAF neg. no. K 619)*

On the back cover: Top, two WAFS chat with an Army pilot near a P-51 Mustang. *Courtesy of US Air Force Photo Collection (USAF neg. no. K 619).* Left, WASP Mildred "Mickey" (Tuttle) Axton in 1943. *"Mickey" Axton.* Right, three WASPs play in the snow beside an AT-6 trainer aircraft. *Special Collections, Texas Woman's University*

Printed and bound in China

Contents

(Top) President Barack Obama signs S.614 in the Oval Office July 1 at the White House. The bill awards a Congressional Gold Medal to Women Airforce Service Pilots. Official White House photo by Pete Souza. (Bottom left) Betty Wall Strohfus, a Women Airforce Service Pilot from Minnesota, displays her copy of the Congressional Gold Medal at the Capitol March 10, 2010. The audience, which Speaker of the House Nancy Pelosi noted was one of the largest ever in the Capitol and too large to fit into Emancipation Hall, also included their families, as well as the families of those who have since died or couldn't travel. U.S. Air Force photo by Staff Sgt. J.G. Buzanowski (Bottom right) Betty Wall Strohfus, a Women Airforce Service Pilot from Minnesota, sings the "Star-Spangled Banner" during the Congressional Gold Medal ceremony at the Capitol March 10, 2010. More than 200 WASPs attended the event, many of them wearing their World War II-era uniforms. U.S. Air Force photo/Staff Sgt. J.G. Buzanowski.

Foreword

Pacific Historic Parks working with the National Park Service has created a new series of publications that reprint works of history documenting unique World War II experiences and stories. It is with that spirit that we are proud to offer Ms. Vera Williams' celebrated book "WASPs".

At the conclusion of hostilities of the greatest war the world had ever known the records of a unique organization of women were sealed for 35 years. They were the aviators of the Women Airforce Service Pilots... WASPs.

Prior to Pearl Harbor in 1941 aviator Jackie Cochran and, at the beginning of 1942, Nancy Love had submitted proposals to use female pilots to ferry aircraft from factories to military airfields. This would free up their male counterparts for combat service.

These women served the nation with heroic loyalty and dedication. Despite discrimination and a pointed lack of military recognition, over one thousand earned their wings and became the first women to fly military aircraft. During World War II, thirty-eight WASPs lost their lives in accidents related to training or to the ferrying of aircraft.

Nearly three decades passed before they were recognized officially by Congress. In 1977 the GI Bill Improvement Act granted WASPs full military stature and in 1984 were awarded the World War II Victory Medal.

Ms. Vera Williams was one of the first authors to research and chronicle the amazing history of the WASPs. Her dynamic photographs and descriptive text allow the reader insight into the remarkable achievements of American women who dared to serve the nation during its greatest crisis, World War II.

During the process of creating the first photo essay of the WASPs she met and interviewed many of the women who participated in the unique flying service. Relationships were developed and friendships created that endure to this day. The author's journey to create this magnificent book is a salute to the fading generation of women who served this country.

In July 2009 President Barack Obama signed the bill that authorized the Congressional Gold Medal into law. Three of the almost three hundred surviving WASPs were present at the White House to witness this historic recognition. During that ceremony the President stated..

"The Women Airforce Service Pilots courageously answered their country's call in a time of need while blazing a trail for the brave women who have given and continue to give so much in service to this nation since. Every American should be grateful for their service, and I am honored to sign this bill to finally give them some of the hard-earned recognition they deserve. As you read and look upon their story, pause for a moment and think of their remarkable experience and the perseverance of the women who served."

Against all odds the WASPs succeeded in carving out a significant page in American history. During World War II 25,000 women applied to be members of the WASPs; 1,830 were accepted and 1,074 passed flight training... this is their story...

Daniel A. Martinez, Chief Historian
WWIII Valor in the Pacific National Monument
National Park Service

Jan Nicolai holds a photo of Helen Jo Anderson Severson, a deceased pilot from South Dakota who flew with the Women Airforce Service Pilots during World War II, during a wreath-laying and remembrance ceremony for all WASPs pilots at the Air Force Memorial in Arlington, Va., March 9, 2010. The ceremony was part of a two-day event in which all pilots received the Congressional Gold Medal at the U.S. Capitol for their service. *DoD photo by Linda Hosek*

Preface

"Here's Looking at You Kid"

Reminiscing with the Fly Girls of World War II

I love the 1940s. I wasn't alive back then, but my parents were, and photographs of them have always intrigued me. I love the men's double-breasted suits and fedoras, the women's shoulder pads and straight, slim skirts. I love the music: Tommy Dorsey, Glenn Miller, and even the Andrews Sisters. The movies were fabulous. The best was *Casablanca.* That scene where Humphrey Bogart says farewell to Ingrid Bergman is perfect. The mist is swirling around them; her face is luminous. Watching, I wonder what it might feel like to do something wonderful and noble for my country.

It seemed that everyone in America in the 1940s had captured that sense of duty. Everyone was patriotic. We were at war, but it was such an easy war to grasp. The bad guys were so very bad, and we were going to win because we had God and good on our side. Everybody wanted to be a part of the winning team. So they bought war bonds. They gave scrap metal, rubber, rags, and paper to salvage depots. They rationed meat and sugar. They took binoculars and stared into the sky to spot airplanes. They watched their "loose lips." They united for the common cause, and the more they sacrificed, the better they felt.

The young people offered the most heroic gift—their lives. To die in service for one's country, for democracy, for freedom, was true splendor. So the young men joined the Army, the Navy, and the Marines and were kissed good-bye by their sweethearts. Their sweethearts made a remarkable sacrifice too; they put on trousers and went to work in factories. If they were really patriotic they joined the WAVES (Women Accepted for Volunteer Emergency Service) or the WAC (Women's Army Corps) and typed and filed for their country, or maybe nursed.

Perhaps the most glamorous image in the 1940s was the pilots—those fly boys. Young, handsome men piloted B-17 bombers or screamed off the decks of carriers in Hellcats to engage in dogfights with Japanese Zeros. They were something, those Hot Pilots, those H.P.s!

A Miss H.P.? Is this a typographical error? A WASP trainee? What the heck is a WASP?

Well, men weren't the only pilots in World War II. There was a group of women, of fly girls, ready and willing to do their part too. They flew bombers and fighters and everything else, and they were called WASPs—Women's Airforce Service Pilots. The WASPs were started in 1942, and for the next two years they filled an important gap with courage and determination. They were the first American women to fly military planes. In fact, after they were deactivated, no more women flew in the military until 1977. Unfortunately,

A portrait of World War II pilots. Four Women Air Force Service Pilot (WASPs) walking into history wearing their Santiago Blues. ***Special Collections, Texas Woman's University***

I wanna be a Miss HP

I wanna be a Miss H.P.
H'mmmmmmm and a little bit more,

I wanna be a WASP trainee,
H'mmmmmmm and a little bit more,

I wanna be a graduate, and then I'll ask no more
For I'll have all that's coming to me,
H'mmmmmmm and a little bit,

H'mmmmmmm and a little bit,
H'mmmmmmm and a little bit more!

© Disney Enterprises, Inc.

The cover of the *WASP Songbook*. Some of the songs were quite racy—so racy, in fact, that Jackie Cochran had the song "Rugged But Right" banned at the training field.
Florence (Emig) Wheeler

they were deactivated in 1944, before the war was over and before the need for them was over.

There was a need for more pilots to do noncombat duties at home, freeing the men to fight overseas. Twenty five thousand women applied to become WASPs. Only 1,830 were accepted for training, and 1,074 won their wings. Qualified women pilots ferried planes from the

WOMEN PILOTS SET RECORD

Wasps Fly 3,000,000 Miles for Each Fatal Accident

Washington, Jan. 5—(AP)—A new safety record in military flying has been set by the Wasps, the civilian women pilots with the Army Air Forces who recently rounded out their first year of activity.

They flew the equivalent of 3,000,000 miles for each fatal accident, the War Department disclosed. Their present rate is .05 fatal accidents for each 1,000 hours of flying while the over-all fatality rate in the United States for the air forces is .07.

There now are 900 Wasps in the service.

factories to air fields. They towed targets so young men with guns could learn to shoot at bad guys. They test-flew new planes and planes just back from the repair shop.

They were patriotic like everyone else in the country, so they joined to help the war effort. But they also loved to fly. This was their chance to fly every day, to fly big planes and little planes, to fly cross country, or to fly tricky aerobatics to throw off other pilots using them for target practice. Some of these women were wealthy and could afford to visit Piper Aircraft and buy planes of their own. But others scrimped and saved for flight time in rented two-seaters at small air fields. The WASP organization was a pot of gold at the end of a rainbow for all of them. It was a chance to fly while serving their country.

This book is my pot of gold. I got the chance to interview many of these women (most of them now in their seventies) about the days when they did something wonderful and noble for their country.

"The thing about memories," said Rita (Davoly) Webster, Class 43-W-6, "is that looking back on your old home town you want to remember the good things. I keep remembering our porch in the front, with pillars, where we would sit in the summer time. It was so nice. We would watch the people go by. But when I went

Twenty-five thousand women applied to the WASP program. They wanted to do their duty for the war effort. Only 1,830 were accepted, and 1,074 completed flight training. *Gene (Shaffer) FitzPatrick.* Previous page, right, This January 5, 1944, Associated Press story lauds the WASPs for their safety record. *Associated Press*

The WASPs proved women could do it. They flew through snow and dark and menstrual periods. They flew planes as fast and as far as the men (but safer!).

These are some of the first American women to fly military aircraft. They came from diverse backgrounds, from all over the country, but they all had a desire to fly and to help their country in a time of need.
Gene (Shaffer) FitzPatrick.
Next page, Rita (Davoly) Webster, Class 44-W-6.
Rita (Davely) Webster

back, I realized I had forgotten all about the mosquitoes."

This is their story, told in their words, in their way. If they sometimes neglect to tell us about the mosquitoes, well I guess we can forgive them.

It's an opportunity to get to know them as they were fifty years ago and as they are today—vibrant, accomplished women. They have generously shared their memories of the glamorous 1940s, when they were young and inexperienced, scared to be away from home for the first time, but exhilarated to be part of an adventure.

Bettie Mae Scott, Class 44-W-3, had adventure. She was test-flying a BT-13 for the cadets. The plane crashed on takeoff, and Scott was killed instantly. Turns out the tail assembly was unstable and there was nothing WASP Scott could have done. Thirty-eight WASPs were killed in the line of duty, but their stories are here too. It was a dangerous adventure, but the camaraderie and friendships they experienced proved to last as long as they would live.

The WASPs proved women could do it. They flew through snow and dark and menstrual periods. They flew planes as fast and as far as the men (but safer!). They strutted their stuff with appropriate songs to boost morale and energy. These songs provide the structure for this

Two "Miss H.P.'s."
Jeanne Robertson

Twenty five thousand women applied to become WASPs. Only 1,830 were accepted for training, and 1,074 won their wings.

WASPs were trained in the military way—and that meant strenuous calisthenics every day. *Jeanne Robertson*

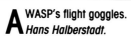

A WASP's flight goggles.
Hans Halberstadt.

A WASP trainee in flight suit, helmet, and goggles. *Jeanne Robertson.* Left, WASPs Elizabeth (MacKethan) Magid (Class 44-W-2), Mildred "Milly" Davidson (Class 44-W-4), Eloise Huffhines (Class 44-W-4), and Clara Jo (Marsh) Stember (Class 44-W-3) on the tail of a B-29 Superfortress at Maxwell Army Air Base, Alabama. These girls were copilots on B-24 Liberators. They flew slow-time and engineering-test missions. Only Dorothea (Johnson) Moorman, (Class 43-W-4), and Dora (Dougherty) Strother, (Class 43-W-3) got to check out in the B-29 Superfortress. *Special Collections, Texas Woman's University.*

book. They are bawdy, funny, and angry, like much popular music.

A word about words: The women in this story were living in the 1940s. The men who went to war were called "the boys," and the pilots, "fly boys." This was not meant in a pejorative way. The women were called gals, girls, and ladies. None of these terms were pejorative. In this book I will refer to the WASPs as gals, girls, ladies, and occasionally women. They will refer to themselves in these terms as well. Please don't take offense, they don't.

"We were called girls, the men were called boys," said Barbara Jane (Erickson) London, WAFS. "It never bothered us. It was natural. Why not? We *were* girls."

A word about names: Ask any woman and she'll tell you how difficult it is to look up old friends. When a woman marries and takes her husband's name, she is much more difficult to find. Most of the women whose names appear in this book were not married when they were WASPs, but many have been married in the years since. Throughout this book, I refer to the women by the names they use today. Maiden names are given in parentheses, and nicknames are enclosed within quotation marks.

So here's to those inspiring Miss H.P.s with the Right Stuff, and to their children, grandchildren, and families. I hope you find their story as inspirational as I have.

Chapter 1

"Yankee Doodle Pilots"

Wheeling and Dealing to Start a Women's Flying Program

The story starts with Jacqueline "Jackie" Cochran. She had learned to fly in the early 1930s, and flew in her first major air race in 1934. In 1937, she was the only woman to compete in the prestigious Bendix race. In that year she also began an unprecedented streak of breaking aviation records by setting a new national speed record for women.

In September 1940, with war raging throughout Europe and with Americans slowly awakening to the realization that sooner or later they would have to join the fighting, Jackie Cochran wrote to Eleanor Roosevelt to introduce the idea of starting a women's flying division in the Army Air Forces. She felt that qualified women pilots could do all of the domestic, noncombat aviation jobs necessary in order to release more male pilots for combat. She was driven by a wish to help her country in a time of need but also a desire to see her own ambitions fulfilled. She pictured herself in command of these women, with the same standing as Oveta Culp Hobby, who was then in charge of the Women's Auxiliary Army Corps (WAAC). (The WAAC was given full military status on July 1, 1943, thus making them part of the Army. At the same time, the unit was renamed Women's Army Corps [WAC].)

Two things made this ambition complicated. First of all, no one in the military felt that the United States was ready for women flyers or that women were ready to fly in the military. The second problem was that at the time, there was no *Air Force*—there was the Army and within the Army was the Army Air Corps—so Jackie Cochran, as head of the women flyers, would have Oveta Culp Hobby as her commander. This did not sit well with Cochran, for professional but also personal reasons.

Also in 1940, Cochran wrote a letter to Colonel Robert Olds, who was helping to organize the Ferrying Command for the Air Corps at the time. (Ferrying Command was the air-transport service of the Army Air Corps; the command was renamed Air Transport Command in June 1942). In the letter, Cochran suggested that women pilots be employed to fly noncombat missions for the new command. In early 1941, Colonel Olds asked Cochran to find out how many women pilots there were in the United States, what their flying times were, their skills, their interest in flying for the country, and personal information about them. She used records from the Civil Aeronautics Administration to gather the data.

WAFS Barbara Jane (Erickson) London and Evelyn Sharp. London prepares to take off in the P-51 Mustang—the Army Air Forces' hottest fighter plane. Sharp wears the gabardine WAFS uniform. The WAFS were disappointed when they had to exchange their uniform for the Santiago Blues worn by the WASPs. ***Courtesy of US Air Force Photo Collection (USAF neg. no. K 621)***

Yankee Doodle Pilots

We are Yankee Doodle Pilots,
Yankee Doodle, do or die!
Real, live nieces of our Uncle Sam,
Born with a yearning to fly.

Keep in step to all our classes
March to flight line with our pals.

Yankee Doodle came to Texas
Just to fly the PTs!
We are those Yankee Doodle gals.

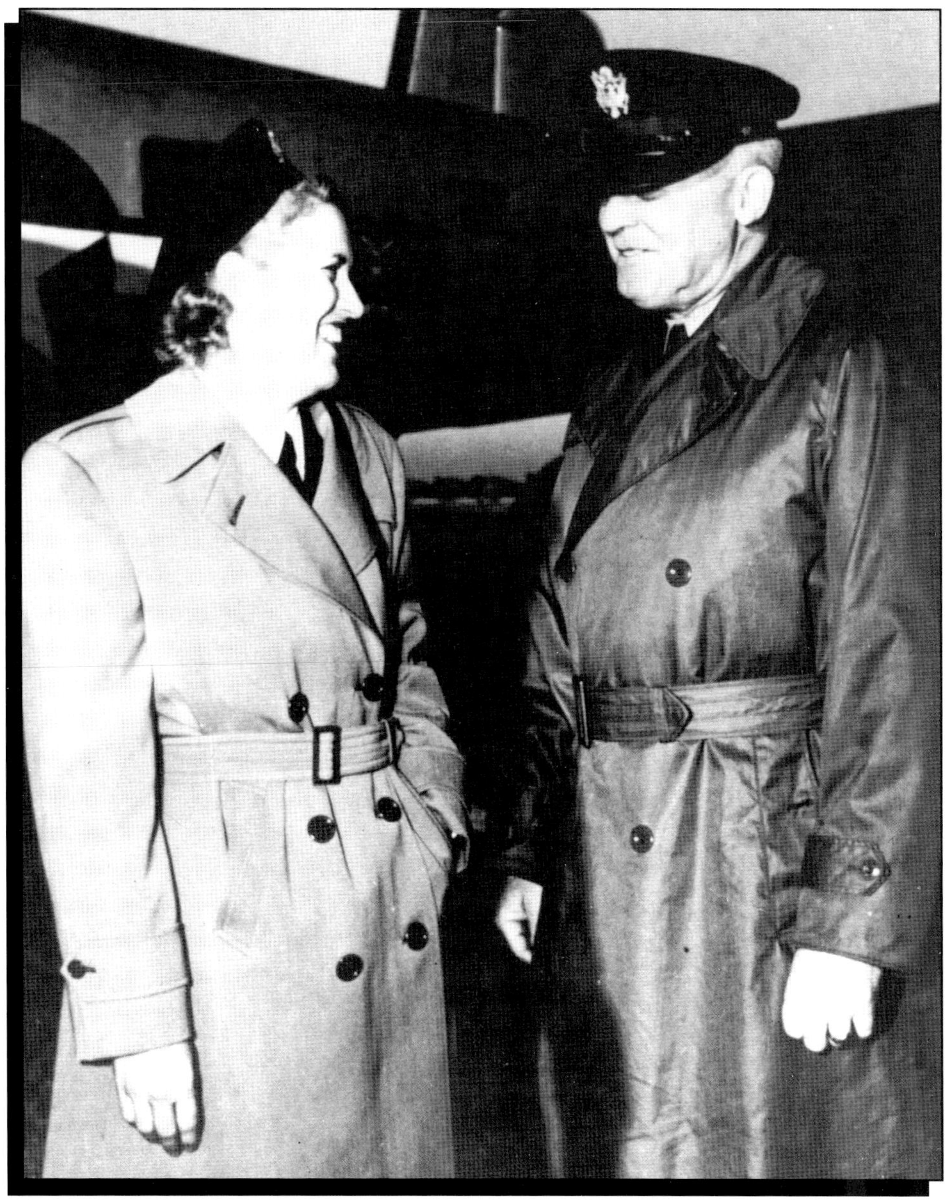

General Henry H. "Hap" Arnold, who wanted to create a separate Air Force from the Army, and Jackie Cochran, who wanted to create a separate women's division of his Air Force. ***Special Collections, Texas Woman's University***

General Henry H. "Hap" Arnold (who had been taught to fly by Wilbur and Orville Wright in 1911 and who was one of the first US Army aviators) was placed in command of the Army Air Forces when it was created from the Army Air Corps in June of 1941. He also had a plan. He wanted to prepare the Army Air Forces to fight the coming war. He felt that the next war would be fought more in the air than had any other, so he wanted an Air Force that would be a strong separate organization, fully funded and fully staffed.

There were a number of obstacles to his desires. One basic obstacle was staffing. There just weren't that many qualified pilots to draw upon and there weren't many more being produced each year. "Hap" Arnold, true to his maverick nature, made a number of precipitous decisions, one of which was starting the Civilian Pilot Training Program (CPT) in 1939 to produce more pilots. The program was offered through universities and allowed one woman for every ten men in each class. This turned out to be a pool from which to recruit flyers, for "Hap" Arnold and for Jackie Cochran. But even with the CPT program in place there were not enough pilots to do all the jobs.

In spite of the pilot shortages, "Hap" Arnold was the person who needed to be convinced that women pilots were the solution to his staffing problems. He knew that women were being used successfully in the Air Transport Auxiliary (ATA) in England. In June 1941, Arnold suggested that Cochran take a group of qualified female pilots to see how the British were doing it. He promised her that no decisions regarding women flying for the Air Corps would be made until she returned.

Even though she agreed to General Arnold's plan, Jackie Cochran continued working toward her goal of a women's flying corps within the American military. Cochran and her husband, Floyd Odlum, were friends with Franklin D. and Eleanor Roosevelt, the president and first lady. Cochran finally convinced the president to support her idea for using women pilots in the Army Air Forces. Eleanor Roosevelt broached the idea of using women pilots to help with the war effort in an August 1941 installment of her "My Day" newspaper column. Shortly thereafter, President Roosevelt asked Cochran to research a plan to train and organize these pilots.

Flying for Britain in the ATA

When General Arnold asked Cochran to go to Britain to study the ATA, she asked seventy-six of the most qualified female pilots—identified during the research that she had done earlier for Colonel Robert Olds—to come along and fly for the ATA.

Qualifications for these women were high—at least 300 hours of flying time, but most of the ladies had over 1,000 hours. Their dedication was high as well—they had to foot the bill for travel to New York for an interview and to Montreal for a physical exam and flight check.

Those that made it to Canada found out that the washout rate was also high.

Skill was not a problem for these women, so perhaps it was attitude that contributed to their washout rate. Those who washed out may not have wanted to fly the "Army way" or put up with Army "sensibilities." And their male check pilots may not have wanted to accept the women as pilots. Finally, though, twenty-five of the women passed the tests, and two months later, in March of 1942 they went to Britain with Cochran to join the ATA.

Betty Jane "B. J." Williams, WASP Class 44-W-6, was a stewardess with Canadian Colonial Airlines when the girls who were soon to be sent to the ATA were in Canada being tested and trained. When she was at Dorval Airport in Montreal, she could stand between the pilot and copilot and listen to the women talk on the radio. The women were flying bright yellow Harvard trainers (the North American AT-6 Texan was designated Harvard by the British and Canadians). As she remembers: "I'd be up in the flight station of a DC-3 as a stewardess looking down at these gals. I knew who they were because I kept track of the program, and that's where I wanted to be."

The American women who flew in the ATA were a little reluctant to go because they wanted to be flying for (and in) the United States, but those that went became the first American women to fly military aircraft.

They were strangers in a strange land, made stranger by war. They were expected to fly over unfamiliar terrain, looking for landmarks that had been obscured or camouflaged, and avoiding the balloon barrages that had been erected to deter the enemy. They flew in silence (no radio traffic was allowed), and the fog blanketing the countryside contributed to the eerie loneliness of the job they were doing. Physically, it was demanding; they made as many as five flights a day, delivering planes from the factories to Britain's Royal Air Force. They had no experience flying many of the aircraft types, but they would read the pilot's manual for the plane and do their best. In fact, they did a splendid job.

They flew the Royal Air Force's front-line aircraft—Spitfires, Typhoons, Hurricanes, Hudsons, Mitchells, Blenheims, Oxfords, Walruses, and Sea Otters—in a non-combat role but in combat-like conditions. Enemy aircraft frequently attacked England, so the possibility of being bombed or shot down was ever-present.

Occasionally, they got to fly something really unusual: Opal Anderson once ferried a German Junkers Ju-88 that had been stolen by a POW while escaping from a German prison camp.

Most of these women served the war in the ATA. In fact there were only three members of the ATA who made it back to the US to participate in the WASP program: Hazel Raines (Class 44-W-3), Myrtle Allen (Class 44-W-8), and Emily Chapin (Class 44-W-10).

Nancy Love and the WAFS

While these women were flying in combat-like conditions in England, back in the states a pretty, very self-effacing woman by the name of Nancy Love was impressing the head of the Air Transport Command, General Harold George. Nancy Love, although working in a strictly administrative capacity for the command's Ferrying Division, was commuting to work in her own airplane, sixty miles back and forth every day. (The Ferrying Division flew planes from the factories where they were built and depots where they were made ready for service to the Army Air Force squadrons.)

In April 1942, Love suggested to Colonel William Tunner, commander of the Ferrying Division that he use experienced women flyers to help ferry planes. Tunner liked the idea, so he took it upstairs to General George.

Tunner suggested that women be added as civilians to the existing ferry pool. These women would be expected to meet the same requirement as the men in the ferrying pools—a high-horsepower rating and a commercial flying license. Tunner wanted to start with twenty-five women at New Castle Army Air Base, near Wilmington, Delaware (probably because the flying distances from factories to field are shorter than for some of the other bases), and he wanted Nancy Love to be in charge.

Love and Tunner, like many in the Ferrying Command, did not want Jackie Cochran involved with setting up a women's flying program. They felt Cochran's ideas were too ambitious to implement in the short term. They wanted things up and running before Cochran got back from England.

Earlier, in March of 1942, "Hap" Arnold had suffered a heart attack and was slowly recuperating, so he was paying little attention to the memos originating from the Ferrying Command and Air Transport Command concerning the women pilot's program.

Nancy Love had an impressive lifetime of flying achievements. It was her idea to have women ferry planes from the factories to the fields.
Jeanne Robertson

"The first time I went up in a plane I was absolutely petrified, but when I got on the ground I said, 'Man! I want to learn how to fly!'"

—Nina K. "Cappy" Morrison, Class 44-W-10

Former WASP Dorothy "Dot" (Swain) Lewis, Class 44-W-5, at her home in California. Lewis was an instructor for the WASPs before she became a WASP. After the WASPs were deactivated, she became a daredevil flyer, a teacher, and an artist. She designed and executed the statue of a WASP trainee that was dedicated at Avenger Field in May 1993.

Then in September of 1942, when rumors of Cochran's impending return from England made the rounds, a memo was sent that practically demanded that the program to hire women pilots as civilians be started and started within twenty-four hours! The memo was also very specific about the person who would head this organization. The requirements were a commercial license, a high-horsepower rating, and at least 1,200 hours of piloting experience. The person must also have been employed by the Air Transport Command in perhaps an administrative position so that she would have full knowledge of its procedures and organization. If they had added "and her initials must be N. L. not J. C." they could not have been more specific.

On September 5, 1942, while Cochran was stalled in England, trying to return home, General Arnold's office (remember Arnold himself was ill) directed immediate action to recruit women pilots. Nancy Love had the telegrams all ready to go and sent them out the same day. Later that day, General George announced the forming of the new Women's Auxiliary Ferrying Squadron (WAFS), with Nancy Love as its director of pilots.

"WHAT!!???"

Or at least that's what I imagine Jackie Cochran said when she heard about this end run.

Cochran met with Arnold and forcefully reminded him of her plans. Arnold realized that Cochran had been treated unfairly, and prudently passed the buck back to General George, since he'd created the ruckus to begin with.

George proposed a two-pronged solution. The WAFS would remain with Nancy Love in charge, and Jackie Cochran could head up the Women's Flying Training Detachment (WFTD), *training* being the key word, based in Houston, Texas. Cochran would take less experienced pilots and train them the military way to eventually join the WAFS. Well, Cochran let them win this battle but planned ultimately to win the war. She had grander schemes for the ladies.

Are you with me so far?

There is the Army, then within the Army is the Army Air Forces. Within the Army Air Forces is the Air Transport Command. A division within the Air Transport Command is the Ferrying Division, and within the Ferrying Division is the WAFS. Then way off in Houston is the WFTDs, a group of gals led by Jackie Cochran who are being trained to fly the Army way so that they can ultimately be a part of the WAFS.

The WAFS were the first women to fly for the US military. They flew their first mission taking Piper Cubs from Lock Haven, Pennsylvania, to Mitchel Field, New York in November of 1942. They completed their very first delivery on the day Class 43-W-1 entered training at Houston. Betty (Huyler) Gillies flew on that first WAFS mission. She told me that the hardest part was flying such light, tiny planes after flying the larger planes they were used to. The tiny planes would float like balloons, and getting them to stay on the ground after they had landed was tough.

The first women who were recruited for the squadron were some of the same women that Cochran had tried to recruit for the ATA. Many of them had not wanted to leave the country, but they were happy to have the opportunity to ferry planes for the United States. The WAFS recruits were required to have a minimum of 500 flying hours.

Barbara Jane (Erickson) London was one of the first group of WAFS, but she did not have the kind of background you would expect from such a highly qualified pilot. "You know, I had never really thought about flying. I never was the kind that went out on Saturday to airports from the time I was twelve and decided I want to fly; I never was exposed to it to ever get that feeling. But once the opportunity was there and I started to fly, then there was never any question about it.

"Like a lot of the girls, I learned in CPT at the University of Washington, in Seattle in 1939. I was in their first class. They divided the class up between land planes and sea planes, so I got mine on water. I went through five of the CPT classes, got my instructor's rating, and went back and instructed in the program while I was going to school. If it hadn't been for the government, I probably wouldn't have started to learn how to fly.

"It was a pretty fast program. We flew almost every day. We went to ground school every day. I can remember the excitement of the first time I flew but then it melds right in with the next one. Within the next two weeks, I was out there by myself. Before long, in the next year or so, I was up there doing it with a student myself. It happens pretty fast.

"Once I was up there, I saw the world from a completely different angle than anybody else was seeing it. Then when I began to instruct, I realized that I was giving that same feeling to other kids and exposing them to flight. It's a great fraternity. There are wonderful people, otherwise I wouldn't have stuck with it for fifty years. It's just a different world. I have always said that anybody that hasn't seen the world from up there hasn't really seen it."

Yeah, but what were *WASPs*?

Jackie Cochran knew that WAFS was an unsuitable designation because the women would soon be doing jobs other than ferrying. She proposed the following titles to General Arnold:

Women's Auxiliary Pilots
Women Supplementary Pilots
Women's Army Support System

Arnold rejected these as having no catchy acronym. He came up with Women's Airforce Service Pilots (WASP) and in August 1943, this title became official. From then on, the WAFS and the WFTDs were to be referred to as WASPs.

During all this maneuvering, Cochran made a tactical move that turned out to be a strategic disaster. All along, her methods were based on producing results within or without the rules. She went to Britain figuring that she'd show them what women could do, and she agreed to head the WFTDs with the same idea. Both the WFTDs and the WAFS, though, were not militarized. The girls were civilians being (minimally) paid by Civil Service. This allowed the programs to get started without congressional approval, and it suited most of the women in the WAFS, who were, for the most part, well-off and liked knowing that they could quit whenever they wanted to. But this wasn't what Cochran had in mind. She wanted her girls militarized with all the benefits but also the drawbacks. She wanted this opportunity for women, to prove that they were capable of making a significant contribution to the war effort and to give women a place in aviation. When the girls were first being used, the country was desperately in need of pilots. If Cochran had insisted then that Congress militarize, they might have. But she was impatient with rules and correct channels. She wanted to show what her girls could do, so she agreed to hold off militarization, assuming that the women's record would assure Congress' approval. By the time Cochran chose to put her foot down—"either militarize us or else"—the war was winding down. There was not such a desperate need for pilots, while there was a great need for ground troops, which were invading all over Europe. The Army was starting to draft male pilots who weren't qualified to fly in combat for duty as ground troops. Well, these guys didn't want to be ground troops, they wanted to fly. So they lobbied Congress that they could be better used doing the jobs the WASPs were doing. So Congress deactivated the WASPs and ended (temporarily) the issue of women flying for the military.

Mildred "Micky" (Tuttle) Axton, Class 43-W-7. She was a daredevil from her adolescence on. ***Hans Halberstadt***

"I always wanted to learn to fly. . . . I got that fearlessness from my family. . . . back in the days when it just wasn't the thing for young ladies to ride a motorcycle, my mother was riding a motorcycle. If she'd known about airplanes, she would have wanted to fly."

—Mildred "Mickey" (Tuttle) Axton, Class W-43-7

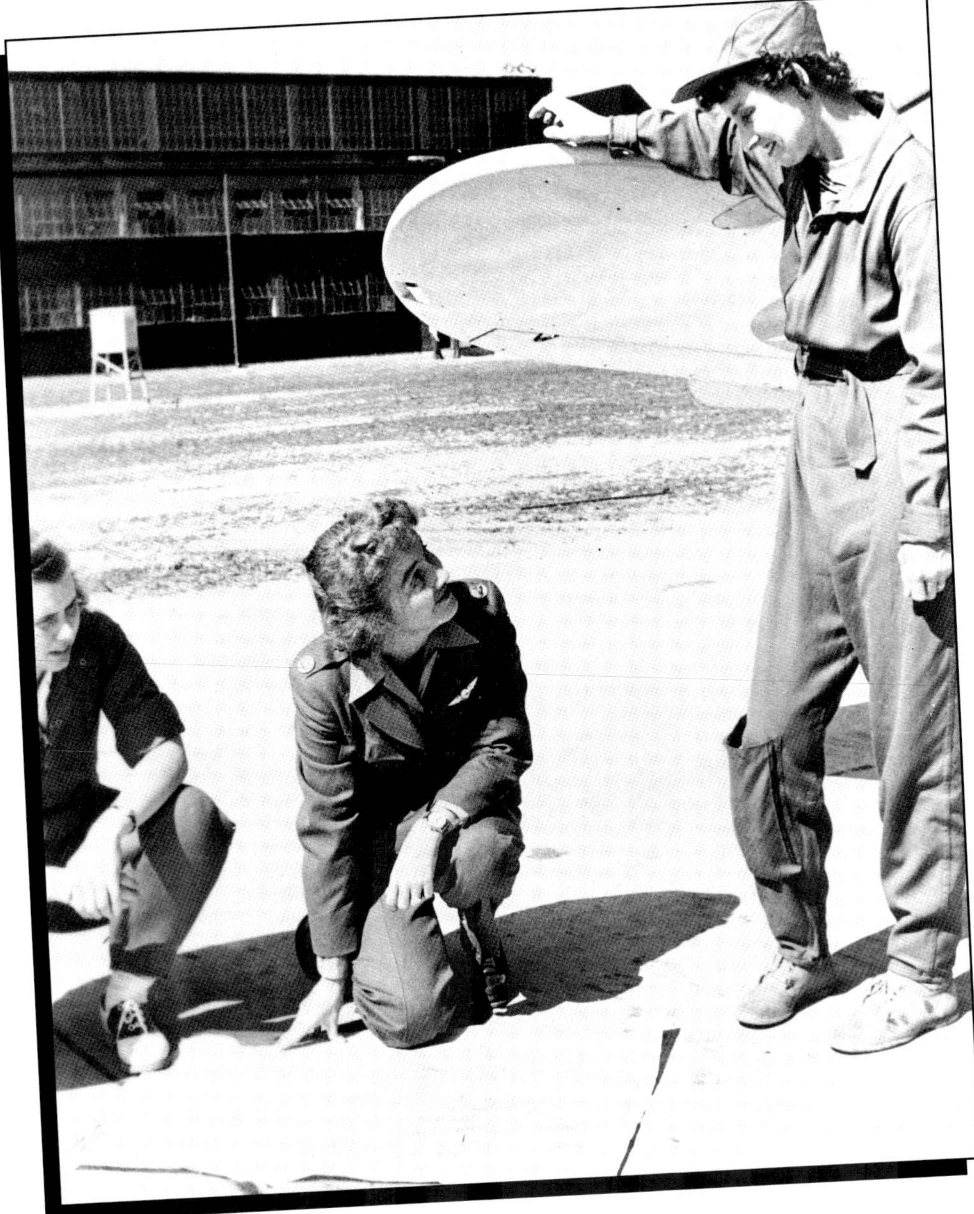

WAFS Nancy Love (center), Gertrude (Meserve) Tubbs (left), and Adela Scharr (right) studying for ferrying operations. Love wears the gabardine gray WAFS uniform. ***Special Collections, Texas Woman's University***

Born With A Yearning to Fly

So, *who* were those "Yankee Doodle Pilots"? Of the women I spoke with, many seemed to have been "born with a yearning to fly" like Nina K. "Cappy" Morrison, Class 44-W-10, who said, "I didn't realize how deeply interested in flying I was for practically all my life. But when I was six to nine years old a black man who worked for my father had gone for a ride in a Jenny [the JN-4, manufactured by Curtiss and nicknamed the Jenny], and he made me an airplane model. I had a little doll that I could put in the cockpit and this hung on my porch. That was one of my earliest memories of airplanes. I used to save my money and buy popular aviation magazines, and I had a scrapbook and collected Wing cigarette cards with airplanes. They had all this information about these planes, and I'd cut it out and study it.

"The first time I went up in a plane I was absolutely petrified, but when I got on the ground I said, 'Man! I want to learn how to fly!'"

Alyce (Stevens) Rohrer, Class 44-W-4: "I always wanted to fly. I was born with the desire, and my family in Utah lived near a small airport. As soon as I got old enough, I used to hang around beside the fence and beg the pilots for rides. I got them a lot of times."

Margaret "Maggie" Gee, Class 44-W-9: "I thought at that time that everyone wanted to fly. We used to go out to Oakland Airport all the time to watch the flyers."

Mildred "Micky" (Tuttle) Axton, Class 43-W-7: "I always wanted to learn to fly. When I was about eleven or twelve we lived on the same block with Rolly Inman who was one of three brothers that owned the Inman's Flying Circus barnstormer pilots. I had my first ride in a Curtiss Jenny, and I just loved it. And so they told us, my brother and me, they'd pick us up when they were there. And if we'd help sell tickets and do little jobs, they'd take us flying. We were so lucky. They'd take us up first, with the townspeople watching. They'd do all kinds of interesting acrobatics, and then when they came down, these people would see that little kids had been doing loops and spins. We sold tickets for a dollar, and we really helped them. So for about four or five years, my brother and I got a lot of rides and I loved it. I always wanted to be a pilot but couldn't afford to.

"I got that fearlessness from my family. My mother was a daredevil. My grandfather was the chief of police at Coffeeville, back from 1906 to 1917, when Coffeeville, Kansas, was a tough border town. All the bank robbers came down there to go over into Oklahoma to hide in the hills. I don't know if you've heard about the Daltons and all. He was the chief of police during this time. Later, he had a big Harley-Davidson motorcycle instead of a Ford, and mother's brother wanted to ride too. So he bought another one for her brother, and she insisted on riding it, too. So back in the days when it just wasn't the thing for young ladies to ride a motorcycle, my mother was riding a motorcycle. If she'd known about airplanes, she would have wanted to fly."

"B. J." Williams had a humanitarian impulse that led her to a cockpit. "'Well Dad, I'll tell you, sometime I may be in a situation where somebody's very ill, an emergency situation, and the only way they can be saved and get to a doctor is you have to fly them there. I want to be able to say, "Hey, I can do that!"'"

"That was my honest reaction when my dad asked

me why in the world I would want to learn to fly. And I knew from the very first lesson I had, that I had found my home. There was a feeling in my stomach that I have yet to ever experience again, it is such a feeling when you know you're right."

For Katherine "Kay" (Menges) Brick, Class 43-W-3, it was fear that sent her up in the air: "I was afraid I was going to be old-fashioned. My grandmother didn't like *this* and didn't like *that*, and I wondered what was going to make a difference in my life. I had been out of college and already had my masters degree and I wondered what was next. Then I saw a sign on the bulletin for adult education classes on aerodynamics and engines, and it hit me that maybe flying was going to be the future!"

At that time Charles Lindbergh and Amelia Earhart were the celebrities, kind of the Madonna and Harrison Ford of the 1920s and 1930s. (Don't panic! I'm not suggesting that the accomplishments or personalities of these four people are in any way comparable. I'm merely equating their name recognition.) Many of the WASPs cited these and other flyers of the day as role models.

Gene (Shaffer) FitzPatrick, Class 44-W-1: "I remember when Lindy came to Oakland; that was 1927. There was going to be a race from Oakland to the Hawaiian Islands. The Dole Race. My mom, dad, my two sisters, and I went out to the airport. I might have been less than ten years old. I remember walking up and down the lines of airplanes. They were refueling them with five-gallon cans, and they're splashing all over, and you could smell the

Front row, left to right: WAFS Esther (Nelson) Carpenter, Barbara Jane (Erickson) London, Teresa James, Esther Manning, and Bernice Batten. In the back are a captain and stewardesses from American Airlines. After ferrying the planes from the factories to the airfields for transport to overseas battle areas, the WAFS sometimes returned by way of commercial airlines. *Special Collections, Texas Woman's University*

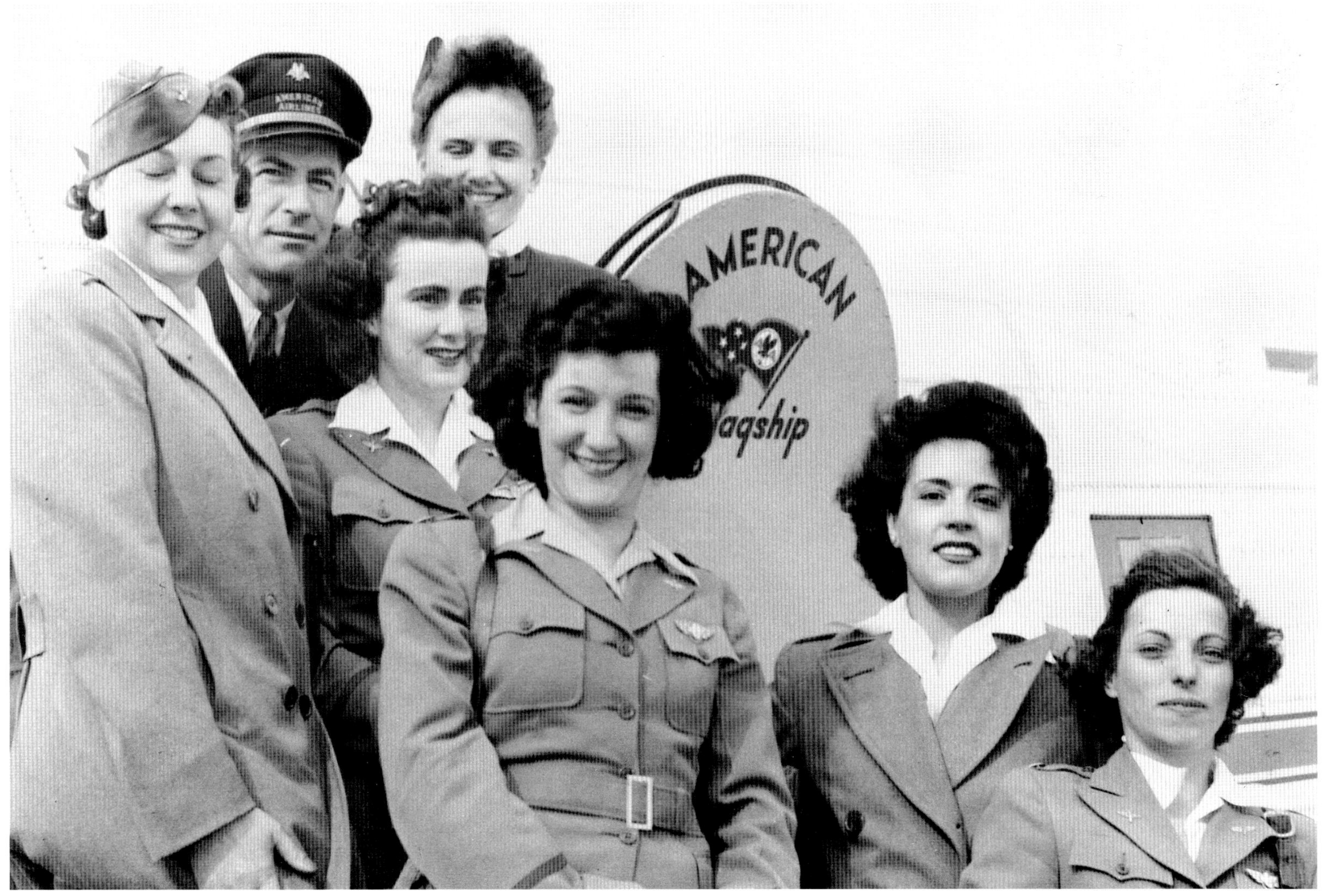

Miss Dorothy Davis Stops Sailing To Fly

Avenger Field, Sweetwater, Tex.—Miss Dorothy Hilliard Davis, 27, formerly of Toronto, Canada, and Richmond, Va., has given up sailing for flying. The former sailing instructor at Taylor Statten Camps, Canoe Lake, Ontario, during summers from 1937 to 1943, has been enrolled in the newest class to begin WASP training to release male pilots in the United States for combat duty.

She is the daughter of Mr. Oscar Harris Davis, retired, of Warrenton, N. C. Miss Davis, whose brother, Maj. W. W. Davis, is overseas with an Aviation Ordnance unit, received her private pilot

From Dorothy "Dottie" Davis' photo album covering her years as a WASP. Davis was in Class 44-W-10, the last class of WASPs to graduate before the WASPs were deactivated. ***"Dottie" Davis***

fumes from the gas. I remember watching them as they took off. The Golden Gate was there, but not the bridge, and we watched them fly low through the Golden Gate.

"In my senior year of high school, I worked on the paper and met and got to interview Amelia Earhart over at the Oakland Airport. Big, big thing in my life. And she was so casual about everything.

"My mom kept a scrapbook of memories, and way back when I was seven, my wish was to fly. So between ambition and wish, it was always flying."

Dorothy "Dot" (Swain) Lewis, Class 44-W-5: "I always wanted to fly from the time I was a little kid. When I was twelve, I put my Sunday School dollar into one of those flights where we went up in one of those old Jennys, which crashed about a week or so later. I read all those old flying stories about World War I. I used to swap airplane stories and the drawings by Clayton Knight with a friend of my brother's."

Some of the ladies weren't born with "prop wash" in their veins.

Florence (Emig) Wheeler, Class 44-W-10: "I wouldn't have learned to fly without the urging of my father. I wouldn't have done it. Not on my own. I'm a very timid person. I was not adventuresome particularly."

Wheeler also figured it was a good way to meet men. "I wasn't a person who dated a lot in high school. I had friends who every time you turned around there was a guy looking to go out with them. That wasn't my luck. I thought maybe another way to meet men would be to be where men were. And so that was sort of an incentive."

Rita (Davoly) Webster, Class 43-W-6, also got her start with a couple of men: "I grew up in suburban Philadelphia. So in the winter time, my friend Franny and I saved up our money and decided that we were going to Florida on vacation. When we were down there, we met this young man, and he said, 'You can't say that you have explored a city until you have seen it from the air.' That's how he talked us into taking this airplane ride. It was probably an old Stearman. It was open cockpit and biwinged. And of course we squealed and so forth and so on. But, anyway, it was really very pleasant. And I never thought more about it. We came home and life went on.

"Then, in 1939 or '40, I was working for Kemper Insurance Company. I was a secretary to the manager of the Fire Insurance Department. A young engineer in the company, Bill Wood, was interested in aviation, and he had many aeronautical magazines come through the mail in the office. These went through my hands, and so I brought them back to Bill, and asked him about his interest in aviation. Well, we talked about that for a while. And I said, you know, I wasn't really thrilled by my airplane ride, but it was interesting.

"A while later, Bill said that there was a program being given in New Jersey, just across the river. It was called Civilian Pilot Training Program. It was competitive and the top ten would receive flying scholarships. I thought, Well, that sounds great, but what chance do I have? I only took a ride in an airplane once. Oh, well, what did I have to lose? So, I went.

"I believe there were about ninety in the class. It was a large class. There was myself and two other gals in the class. I thought these people probably used to hang around the airport, you know, and probably did whatever chores were there just to be around the airplanes. And I was completely green. The first lesson was the history of aviation. I looked around the class, and I thought, You people don't know any more about that than I do, so I stayed. Then the next class was theory of flight. And I thought, They don't know any more about that than I do, so I stayed for that. And so it progressed that way.

"Finally, the last subject was engines, and I thought, This is where they get me. I mean it was just assumed that every man knew everything there was to know about engines because in those days, the cars broke down very readily. A tool kit came with every car and the men were supposed to fix it.

"My instructor was explaining something, and he said, 'And this is actuated by a cam.' Then he went on and on and on, but I stopped right there and thought, Cam, now what in the world do you think a cam is? And I never heard another thing he said because I just puzzled over this cam bit.

"In the meantime, my father found out that I was taking this course in aviation, and he hit the ceiling. He just wouldn't talk to me, you know, but he would talk to my mother in quite a loud voice so I would be sure to hear it, and he would tell her, 'Your daughter really needs to see a psychiatrist because I never heard of a girl getting into aviation.' So, he was no help at all. But I tell you, I never studied so hard as I did then. Certainly never in school.

"That weekend I went to the library, and I must have gotten five or six books on engines. I was thumbing through them, trying to figure out what a cam was. My father happened to pass by and he glanced at my books and said, 'Well, how are you doing?' These are the first words I've gotten (to me, personally) in six weeks. I said, 'Well, I thought I had a pretty good chance up until now, but now we're on engines, and I just don't understand it.' 'Well,' he said, 'what don't you understand? I know something about engines.' I said, 'What is a cam?' And he just took a pencil and he drew one. So he explained that to me, and then there were a few other questions, which he answered.

"Later, I took my test. I came in eleventh, and I missed by one-tenth of a point. It's strange about competition. I didn't think I had a chance. I really didn't. But I

The day in August 1940 when "Micky" (Tuttle) Axton received her private pilot's license at Water-Works Hill Airport, Coffeyville, Kansas. Shown are Axton, Beatrice Tuttle (her mother), Hale Fletcher (her grandfather), and Hulda Fletcher (her great-grandmother). ***"Micky" Axton***

Gene (Shaffer) FitzPatrick, Class 44-W-1, and a high school classmate interviewing Amelia Earhart. At the time, Earhart was a celebrity, and flying was a glamorous and admired endeavor. ***Gene FitzPatrick***

thought, Well, I'm here, you know; I'll keep going. So when it came down to the nitty-gritty, I was devastated because I hadn't won. My family was delighted.

"Monday morning, we went in to work and this was the worst of all. Bill's desk and my desk were all decorated with flags. They had a little airplane suspended from the ceiling and a big sign on Bill's desk, 'Our Tailspin Tommy,' and on mine was 'Flying Jenny.' And I thought, Oh, God, how embarassing, because I didn't even make it. But one day I received this call at work and the voice said that he was the manager of the Palmyra Airport in Palmyra, New Jersey, and that one of the fellows was disqualified for whatever reason. He said, 'You're next.' And he said, 'I'd like to make some appointments with you to take you flying.' So that's how I got started. Really, almost unintentionally."

No matter how they got started, "B. J." Williams tells us what they all had in common: "I don't know of a WASP that really truly didn't love flying or she never would have been able to go through the rigors of training and take some of the conditions under which we had to fly afterwards. And the ability to do something you love and to do it at a time of need for your country—nothing is better than that if you have much patriotic blood in your system."

The women who joined the WASPs were happy to be there.

Gene (Shaffer) FitzPatrick: "It was really very wonderful to be given airplanes and told you could fly them—and they paid you to do it!. We didn't care what they paid us. I would have paid them if they had just let me keep flying."

For all the talk about women being teased or bothered by men in the aviation industry or by family members, there were also many women who received much support and encouragement.

"Micky" (Tuttle) Axton, Class 43-W-7: "During the war, everybody did what they had to do. That's why grandmothers were taking care of kids, so that the women could work in the factories or do other things to help the war effort. Everybody you knew was doing something. And when the telegram came saying women flyers were needed, you can understand that I had to go.

"I think all of my friends thought I was crazy. Some even thought my husband and I weren't having a good marriage, but we had the best marriage in the world. And my mother, without my asking, said, of course, she'd take care of my daughter Carol. And my husband also backed me, and he still does."

The women had some interesting experiences while learning to fly and while gaining the hours to join the WASP program.

"B. J." Williams: "I started to learn how to fly in winter time in eastern Pennsylvania, near the Susquehanna River, so my first takeoffs and landings were on skis. In the wintertime, the perspective's different because everything's white. I had to be careful because if the snow was too wet, the plane might get stuck in it when I was taxiing out. That happened on my second or third lesson.

"I was taxiing out in a J-3 Cub, and the instructor said to me, 'Be very careful. When you check the mags, don't really come to a stop because the snow's very wet, and if you do, we'll get stuck.' Well, of course this being only my third lesson and my not being an expert, we got stuck.

"So he got out of the airplane and shook the wings up and down. I moved the throttle back and forth in order to try to shake the plane loose, but it didn't work. So he said, 'Now I'll get in and move the throttle, and you get out and move the wings up and down.' So he's blastin' the throttle and I'm out pushing the wings when, suddenly, the plane started to move. He says to me, 'Hop in!' and he guns the throttle. We're accelerating down the runway, and half of me is out of the airplane. The plane was at least 200 feet off the ground before I got myself totally inside."

Mary Jane (Lind) Sellers, Class 44-W-10: "Civilian flying was not allowed within 100 miles of the coastline during the war, so I had to take my flying lessons in Winnemucca, Nevada, and Alturas, Colorado. To help pay for my flight training ($8 per hour), I worked at the Win-

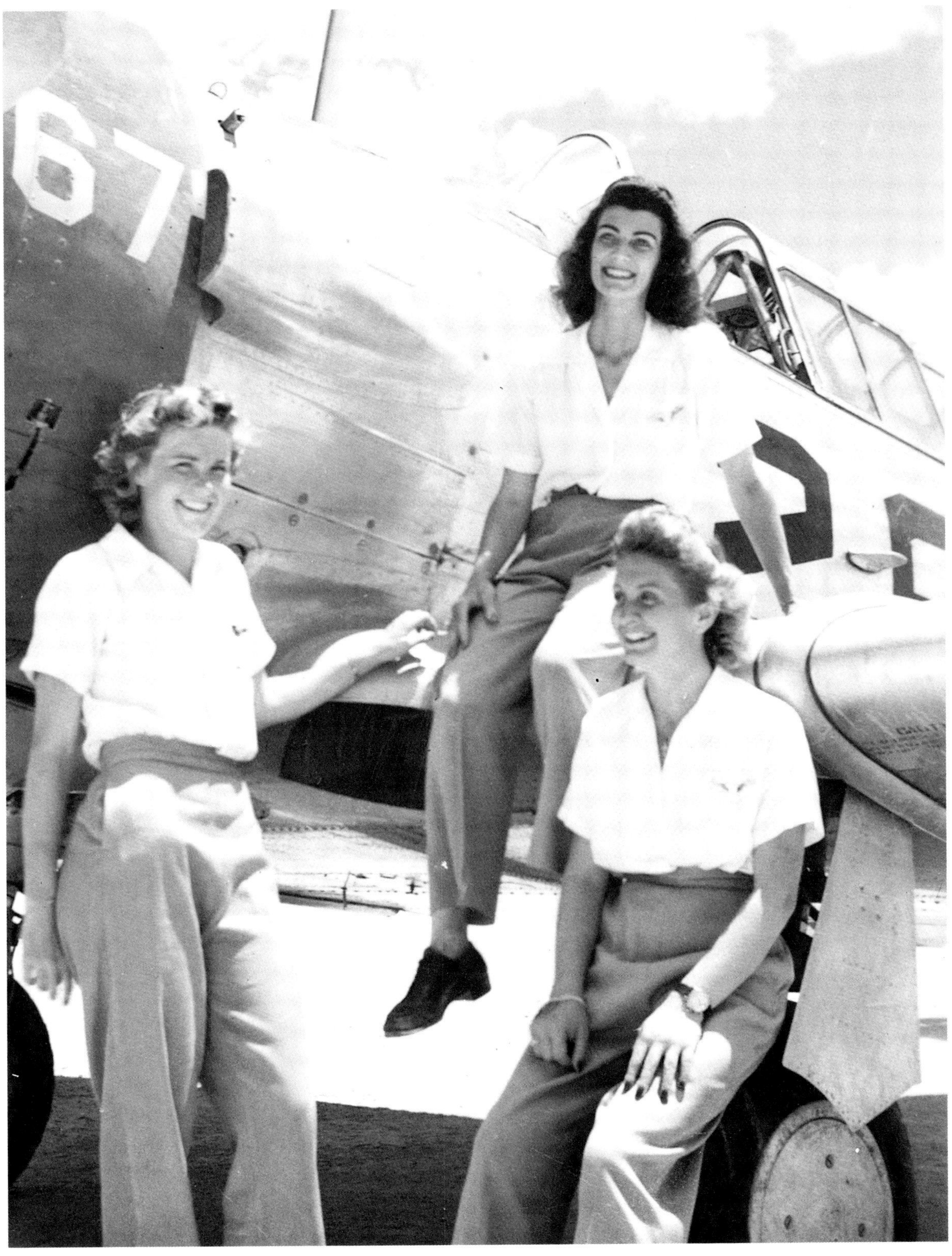

Left to right: Jeanne (Bennett) Robertson, Eolyne Nichols, and Rosalie Grohman of Class 43-W-4. They were happy to be at Avenger Field and happy for the opportunity to fly.
Jeanne Robertson

"We didn't care what they paid us. I would have paid them if they had just let me keep flying."

—Gene (Shaffer) FitzPatrick, Class 44-W-1

Florence (Emig) Wheeler, Class 44-W-10, with her mother and father, after receiving a telegram from Jackie Cochran to report for WASP training. Florence's father was very keen on flying, and he encouraged her to learn.
Florence Wheeler

nemucca School as a secretary and a guard of the small hangar and planes. In order to do this I became a deputy sheriff of the State of Nevada and had to wear a gun when left alone at the hangar. Of course I didn't know how to shoot."

"Dot" (Swain) Lewis: "I was a camp counselor, I taught riding, and went by an airport on my way home on Saturdays. I saved up my money and took some lessons with this great, huge fat man. When he sat up in front, I couldn't even see out, and he didn't know how to instruct. At the end of almost four hours I was still holding the stick in both hands, he was doing the throttle, and I realized 'Heck! I'm not really flying.' He didn't let me land, he didn't think women wanted to land. He took my money and taught me nothing.

"So I went over to Hendersonville and went up with Oscar Meyer, and he was so excited to have a girl student. He thought that was the cutest thing in the world. So he taught me and next thing I knew, there I was flying. By that time, I had eight hours and was ready to solo, but storms kept me grounded for three weeks.

"As soon as the weather was clear on my day off, I drove to the airfield. Nobody was there except a little boy; he was the guard and he opened up. I said, 'I'm supposed to solo. I've got eight hours.' So I soloed myself, a four-minute flight.

"I went up, and part of the field was still under water, but I managed to take off around the water. I went around the pattern and made a perfect landing. I was so happy I raced back as soon as I could and bounced all over everywhere, and from then on every time I would get a nickel or so I was flying.

"I went to work for Piper after the war started. Piper let me fly planes, inexpensively, after work to build up air time. I flew an average of an hour a day. I was there 200 days, I got 200 hours. There were about thirteen of us WASPs that came from Piper. For fifty-six cents we could fly for half an hour (we made something like twelve dollars a week, thirty-five cents an hour in the factory). That's where I met Nancy Baker, Anna Flynn, Anne Shields—a whole bunch of them. I didn't go through the CPT program, I paid right through the nose for everything."

"Maggie" Gee: "I went to Nevada in order to learn to fly. While there, I constantly encountered prejudice and discrimination, but not because I was female or because I was Asian. I was always being taken for an Indian, so people said I couldn't go here and couldn't go there.

"I didn't come across any discrimination in the WASP for being a woman or an Asian. Asian people always want me to say that I experienced discrimination. And I say, 'No, no, not at all.' It might have been there and I wasn't aware of it.

"As you know, Jacqueline Cochran wouldn't accept any black pilots in her program, although there were several who tried to join. I think that she realized that times being what they were, she was facing enough resistance to women flying, that she didn't want to tackle the concept of black women flying. That's the way our society was. We've changed though. It's remarkable how it's changed, particularly for Asians but not for Blacks.

"But discrimination to women themselves? When I stop and think about it and put it in today's time, you were there and you were young and the instructors said what they wanted to say. They would say, 'You ought to be home. What are you doing flying? You should be raising a family.' And all those things. It was just ignored, it was that time. So what? You didn't take it as you would today. Today you would attack them.

"I do think there was discrimination that we experienced as a group. I mean just the disbanding of the WASPs. There were only 1,074 of us spread throughout the United States. Jacqueline Cochran wanted us to be part of the regular service and they said no, and we were disbanded even though the war was not over."

Once the ladies learned to fly and became aware of the WASP program, they were dying to get in. One of the requirements was a physical.

"Cappy" Morrison: "We were in a group that had to take the regular entrance exam as well as a physical, and I almost didn't get in because the doctor who did the pelvic exam was an Air Force flight surgeon who didn't know an ovary from . . . . He might have thought that he remembered feeling one when he was in Med school, and he told me 'I don't know whether that's a little cyst formed from ovulation or not.' I don't know what it was but he put it down. I got a report back that I had failed my physical because I had a cyst on my ovary. Well, I went roaring off to my family doctor and he said, 'That's ridiculous. The Air Force doctor is an idiot.' I wired Cochran, and they finally agreed that I could go back for another examination. I got another doctor who says, 'Are you sure that your family doctor said you're all right? Because I don't think I'd know a cyst if I felt it.' I said don't worry about it, and he passed me. These doctors didn't know anything about females—they were flight surgeons for men."

Gene (Shaffer) FitzPatrick: "We had to go up to Hamilton Field and get a medical. And my problem then, which I don't have now, was I was too thin. I was five-foot-seven and think I weighed 111. My mother said, 'You're not going up to Hamilton Field by yourself.' So she came over and drove up with me. But before we did,

After passing the physical and the interview, it was thrilling to be accepted for the program. Florence (Emig) Wheeler beamed when the acceptance telegram from Jackie Cochran arrived. Then, the real work began. Wheeler was a very experienced pilot even before she entered the WASP program. In fact she instructed many women who were trying to get their thirty-five hours to qualify for WASP training. Florence got such great reports from these women that she finally decided to give it a try and graduated with the last class.
Florence Wheeler

"My mother . . . . came over and drove up with me. But before we did, we went down to Fisherman's Wharf. We had one of those seven course luncheons, you know. Then I got a bottle of milk and bananas and ate all the way up. . . . And I think the temporary weight got me up to 120. . . . The doctor said, 'Well, you just barely get under the wire.' And I said, 'I've been dieting.'"

—Gene (Shaffer) Fitzpatrick
Class 44-W-1

we went down to Fisherman's Wharf. We had one of those seven course luncheons, you know. Then I got a bottle of milk and bananas and ate all the way up. Fortunately, the first thing they did was weigh us. And I think the temporary weight got me up to 120. I just made it by the hair on my chinny-chin-chin. The doctor said, 'Well, you just barely get under the wire.' And I said, 'I've been dieting.'

The program lasted for two years, from November 1942 to December 1944. For some of these women it would not only be the greatest time of their life, it would be the last great time of their life. Thirty-eight women were killed while on "active duty." And others were killed by the deactivation—some turned to suicide and others turned into alcoholics.

Winifred "Winnie" Wood, Class 43-W-7, wrote a book after the war entitled *We Were WASPs*. "Dot" (Swain) Lewis did the illustrations. It was mostly about Winnie's experiences as a WASP. She tells this story:

"About five or six years ago we got a letter from a young woman. She wrote, 'My mother was in the WASP. I have read your book, but I can't get a copy of it. I want to know more about her and the WASPs.' She mentioned her mother's name, and so I wrote to her. I said, 'I remember your mother. Well, she was not one of my best friends in the WASP, but I do remember that she was my classmate.' Well, the woman was so excited that she and her husband came up, and she told us her mother's story.

"Her mother had died as an alcoholic. Her father (a B-29 pilot) buried her mother with her wings. The woman said she always thought her mother felt that after the WASPs there was nothing to live for. She just loved to fly. The woman never really knew her mother very well. I talked to her, and she came to one of our meetings. I introduced her to members of 43-W-7 who knew her mother. She met 'Micky' Axton who was stationed with her mother and knew her well, and W-7 adopted her. She comes to all the reunions now, and she's a part of our class."

"Dot" (Swain) Lewis adds: "She's a flyer now, and she's gotten her instrument rating."

It was devastating for some of the WASPs when it was over, but for most of them it was a wonderful two years that gave them a confidence they would not have otherwise had. They went on to many fulfilling careers.

Alyce (Stevens) Rohrer: "Some girls just simply couldn't take the stiff requirements and the austere barracks and the emptiness with constant nose-to-the-grindstone work, and so it's not surprising the washout rate was high. But those that got through have been very successful women, and I'm truly proud of belonging to the group. Every single one of them that I know has made a tremendous success of their lives, becoming doctors, lawyers, teachers, writers; very individualistic, very determined. They're all leaders—not a single follower. It's a nice group to belong to."

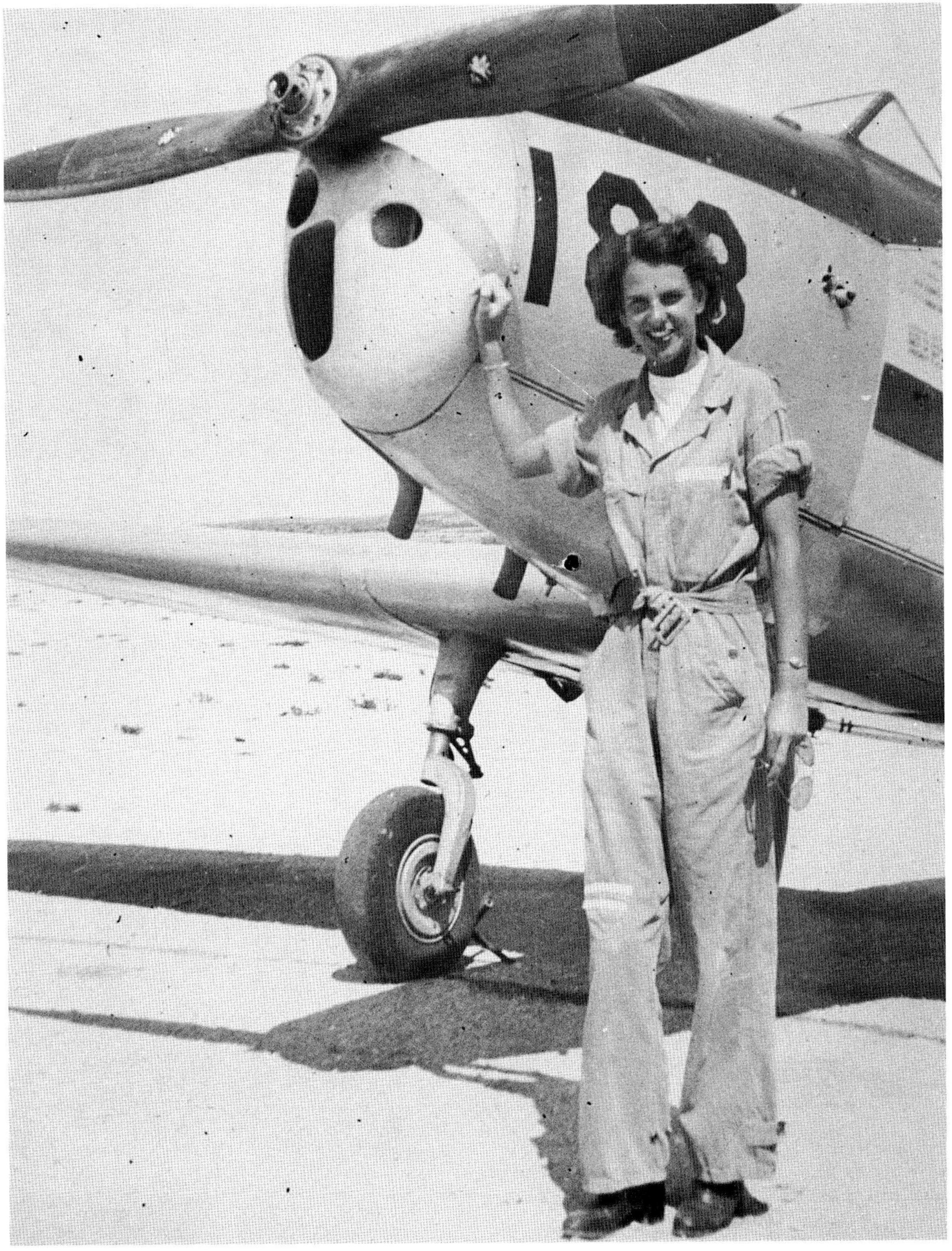

Gene (Shaffer) FitzPatrick loved being a WASP trainee but hated having to wear these oversized flight suits, called "Zoot Suits." *Gene FitzPatrick.* Previous page, WASP trainees pose with one of their Army Air Forces instructors. The WASP program was probably the greatest adventure available to American women of their era, and competition to get into the program was fierce. They had to be highly qualified to get in and highly motivated to withstand the rigors of the WASP training program. For those who passed, earning their wings ranks among the greatest achievements of their lives. *Jeanne Robertson*

Chapter 2

"We Were Only Only Fooling"

Two Visionaries: Jackie Cochran and Nancy Love

Jacqueline Cochran should be the remembered as the most famous woman flyer of all, but it is Amelia Earhart that most people have heard of.

Earhart accomplished many things, but she wasn't the first female pilot, she didn't fly the fastest plane, she didn't win the most trophies. Earhart got credit for being the first woman to fly across the Atlantic, but she was a passenger on the aircraft. She was the first person to fly from Hawaii to California, and the first person to fly alone from Los Angeles to Mexico City. She was a feminist who believed that parents needed to stop saying *shouldn't* and *can't* to their daughters. She became a role model for women at that time.

I believe that Earhart's popularity and fame stem not from her accomplishments but from her style of living and style of death. She was charismatic and graceful. She gave interviews readily. She was intelligent and articulate and she sort of looked like Charles Lindbergh. Her lifestyle was a poised mingling of appropriate womanly behavior of the time with daring-do. And her death at such a young age sparked the imagination of the world. Amelia Earhart is famous because she disappeared without a trace.

She wanted to be the first woman to circle the globe and the first person to fly around the world at its widest point. She had made it almost all the way before her plane disappeared somewhere in the Pacific Ocean, and her body was never found. She went down in history as the most famous female aviator of our time.

"Dot" (Swain) Lewis: "Amelia became famous because she got lost. She made a big foolish mistake, and the biggest search in aviation history was for her. And because she sort of looked like Charles Lindbergh. She wasn't nearly the pilot Cochran was."

"Winnie" Wood: "A person can't be perfect at everything, but I don't think Earhart knew radio the way she should have. They lost their trailing antenna, which decreased their radio's range."

Amelia Earhart's plane was supposed to have been equipped with a 250-foot-long trailing antenna. This antenna was crucial in that it was supposed to home in on a Coast

Jacqueline "Jackie" Cochran in the cockpit of a P-40 Warhawk fighter plane. Before starting the WASP, Cochran was a famous aviatrix during the 1930s. She earned her pilot's license in the early 1930s and competed in her first major race in 1934. In 1937, she was the only woman to compete in the Bendix race. That year, she also set a new woman's national speed record. By 1938, she was considered the best female pilot in the United States. She had won the Bendix and set a new transcontinental speed record as well as altitude records (by this time she was no longer just breaking woman's records but was setting overall records).
USAF (neg. no. 117391 AC)

We Were Only Only Fooling
(Tune: "Glory, Glory, Hallelujah")
When we go to ground school we're as happy as can be
We work and sweat and slave like mad and never get a D
When we go to ground school we're as happy as can be
Like HELL we are, like HELL!

We were only, only fooling
We were only, only fooling
We were only, only fooling
Like HELL we were, like HELL!

When we leave Avenger, we will all sit down and cry,
When we leave Avenger, we will all sit down and cry,
When we leave Avenger, we will all sit down and cry,
Like HELL we will, like HELL!

(Repeat chorus)

When the war is over, we will all fly Cubs again,
When the war is over, we will all fly Cubs again,
When the war is over, we will all fly Cubs again,
Like HELL we will, like HELL!

(Repeat chorus)

When the war is over, we will be instructor's wives,
When the war is over, we will be instructor's wives,
When the war is over, we will be instructor's wives,
Like HELL we will, like HELL!

(Repeat chorus)

Guard cutter stationed off Howland Island, her refueling point in the Pacific Ocean. All the navigators she spoke with about her trip said that it would be impossible to find Howland Island without this aid. Due to technical difficulties, Earhart could not get the antenna to work with her other antennas and left it off. Without this huge antenna, Earhart was not able to get a radio bearing on the cutter.

One of the WASPs interviewed said that some women who are prominent in aviation today reject having Earhart as a role model because hers was a big mistake.

It is interesting to compare Jackie Cochran's flying records to Amelia Earhart's. Cochran established women's altitude records and women's and *men's* speed records (some of these records still hold). She was the first woman pilot to break the sound barrier (with Chuck Yeager right on her wing), the first woman to fly a jet across the ocean, and the first woman to fly a bomber across the Atlantic. She won fifteen Harmon trophies as the outstanding

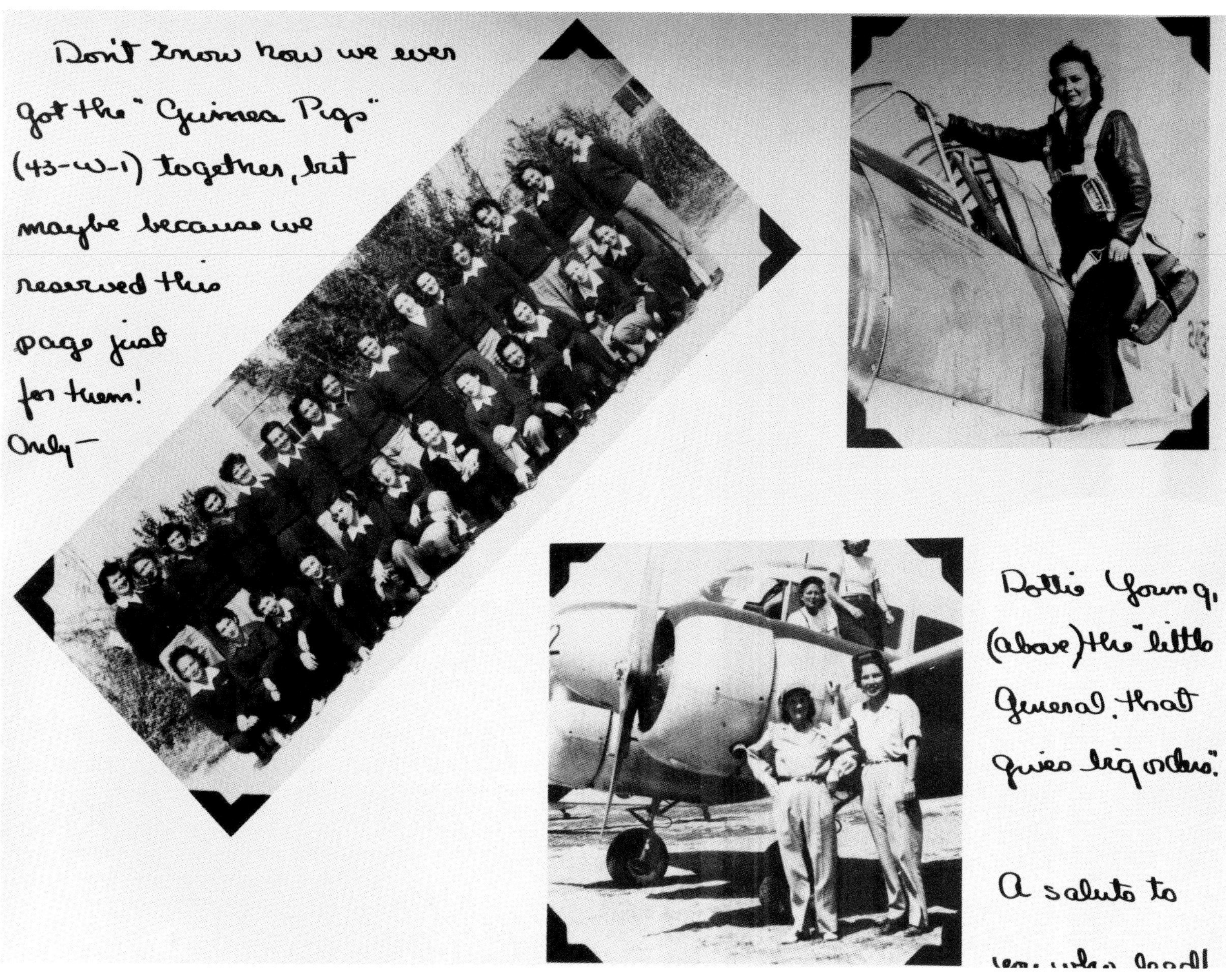

The women were proud to be serving their country, and thrilled to be given the opportunity to fly fighters and bombers. This page is from *The Log Book*, the yearbook of the 319th AAFTD. *Jeanne Robertson*

woman pilot in the world. In aviation history there is no pilot, man or woman, with more speed, distance, or altitude records than Jackie Cochran held at the time of her death. She was sometimes called the "Speed Queen."

Then you go on and look at her other accomplishments. She was the literal rags to riches girl: she wore a burlap sack for a dress as a child and went on to start her own cosmetics company. She learned to fly in less than three weeks, and she advanced to lieutenant colonel in the Air Force Reserve. She was the first woman to be awarded the Distinguished Flying Cross and the Distinguished Service Medal. (In fact, when President Roosevelt was scheduled to present her with the Distinguished Service Medal, the highest honor possible other than the Medal of Honor, she declined unless General "Hap" Arnold would be the one to present it to her (because of her immense respect and fondness for Arnold, she would accept the medal from no one else). She broke down barriers for women. She worked with Amelia Earhart to open the prestigious Bendix Race for women. And she worked at getting NASA to open up the space program for women. They declined, but they did name a small piece of the moon after her!

So why is Cochran not the most famous aviatrix of the twentieth century? Like the song, "We Were Only Only Fooling," Cochran was brazen, arrogant, a little bit of a smart ass, and didn't settle for less than what she really wanted. These traits are not always appreciated in a woman (especially not in the 1940s), and I think that's why Jackie Cochran is not as famous as her accomplishments should have made her. I have come to regard Miss Cochran fondly during the writing of this book. I admire all those characteristics that got her in trouble and wish that I'd had the opportunity to meet this extraordinary woman (she passed away in 1988).

In order to understand Jackie Cochran you have to realize that she was an orphan who grew up in a very poor foster household. She stole chickens for food and slept on the floor with the rats. She also never felt part of the family, and they never fully accepted her. She decided that this

After the earlier classes graduated, they were doing jobs beside ferrying for the Army Air Force. They were towing targets, training male cadets on instruments, and doing engineering test piloting. These pilots are at the Training Command's advanced single-engine pilot school at Foster Field, Victoria, Texas. Shown are, left to right, Pauline S. (Cutler) White, Dorothy Ehrhardt, Jennie M. Hill, Etta Mae (Hollinger) Grasso, Lucille R. Carey, Jane B. Shirley, Dorothy H. (Beard) Burns, and Kathryn L. Boyd. ***USAF (neg. no. K 3616)***

was to her advantage—she wanted better for her life and so she never chose to accept them.

When there was a lottery for a doll in her town, eight-year-old Jackie worked her tiny little fingers raw as a cook, a maid, a baby-sitter, and carrying water in buckets up to the houses to do the laundry. She did this in order to get enough money to buy lottery tickets for that doll. Some of the families she worked for were so poor that they were not always able to pay her, and she had only enough money for two lottery tickets. She won the doll, anyway. When she brought the doll home, her foster mother said that the eight-year-old was too old for dolls and gave the doll to one of the other children. Later on when Cochran had enough funds she offered to help the family financially—if they would return the doll. She was buried with it.

She was driven to have her own money, her own power, and her own standing in society. Through hard work she managed to get a job at the most prestigious hair salon in New York City. She also worked at the "winter" salon in Miami. In these salons she met the wealthy and powerful, and they met her, they liked her, and began to invite her to dinners. While in Miami at one of these dinners she met the very successful Floyd Odlum, another self-starter who made millions by the age of thirty-six. He was captivated by her and her ideas and jokingly said she would need wings in order to accomplish all of her goals. She took him seriously and, after starting a cosmetics supply business, took flying lessons so that she could cover her large territory more efficiently.

She was quoted as saying after she took her first lesson that "a beauty operator ceased to exist and an aviator was born." However, she still managed to establish Jacqueline Cochran Cosmetics, Inc., as a successful business. Floyd Odlum was her business advisor and then became her husband. They had a long, happy marriage.

Cochran didn't always get along with everybody she met. She learned at a very young age that in order to get what you want you have to ask for it and you have to work for it, and she was always capable of both.

Betty (Huyler) Gillies tells the story about when she and fellow WAFS Nancy Love were all set to ferry a B-17 called the *Queen Bee* across the Atlantic to Britain. They had been to B-17 school in Lockburn, had made three B-17 deliveries, and were checked out (the first women to be checked out in the Flying Fortress). They were on Goose Bay, Labrador, ready to head on to Prestwick in Scotland when a jeep came screeching to a halt, and a young man jumped out and handed them a telegram from "Hap" Arnold that said, "Cease and desist, no WAFS will fly outside the contiguous US." They were heartbroken and angry, and they were convinced that Cochran had used her position as someone who had the ear of General Arnold to get him to stop the B-17 flight to England. They felt that she had always been jealous of the veteran flyers, and of Nancy Love in particular, and did not want them to do this feat and take credit.

However, Cochran was ill at the time and probably didn't know about the flight. She did write a memo afterward that asked that "individual achievements should be avoided, graduation into important new assignments should be not by exceptional individuals but by groups."

While Cochran was in England studying the methods and organization of the ATA, she lived a fairly glamorous life. She ate well, wore furs, drove around in a Rolls-Royce, and lived in a suite in the very posh Savoy hotel. All this in wartime England, where everybody was existing on rationed food, gas, and clothing, and having their homes bombed. Her flamboyant behavior raised some eyebrows and caused comment. Later on, when Colonel William Tunner, the commanding officer of the Ferry Division, was deciding on the policies for the use of the WASPs (at this time they were still called WFTDs), he asked for reports on the performance of Cochran and the American girls in the ATA. He was told that the girls performed beautifully, but he was also told about Cochran's behavior. This convinced Tunner that Cochran was not going to be easy to work with, and he decided that he would demand the right not to hire the graduates of her program if he deemed them unsuitable. The arrogance and flamboyance that made Cochran successful could also be off-putting.

While most of the WAFS and the earlier WASP classes had reservations about Cochran, the later classes all thought her a hero.

Barbara Jane (Erickson) London: "Nancy Love was out here in Los Angeles for a meeting with me for some reason, and Cochran was in town, so Nancy and I went up to a luncheon at Jackie's apartment—she maintained a residence in L.A.—and that's when Cochran let us know she was going to be the most famous woman pilot, it didn't really matter how she did it. But that day we had three B-25s to go to Kansas City. Nancy was going to take one, I was going to take one, and we said, 'Jackie, you take the other one!' What a great big free vacation, but she wasn't about to take it. I never saw her fly an airplane. Almost nobody that was in the ATA saw her fly one, because she didn't fly over there either.

"She lived in downtown London in a very swanky hotel, arrived out at the airport with her mink coat and her chauffeur-driven car, and oversaw what was going on, but she never flew anything. But she had terrific connections. She was able to do anything, and there wasn't anybody else in the world that could have set up this [WASPs] program, because nobody had the influence that she had. She was married to practically the richest

Nancy Love, pilot (left), and Betty (Huyler) Gillies, co-pilot, the first women to fly the Boeing B-17 Flying Fortress heavy bomber. The two WAFS were set to ferry a B-17 named *Queen Bee* to England when their flight was canceled by General "Hap" Arnold.
USAF (neg. no. 118306 AC)

"Do you know that Jackie had to buy the wings initially, and her own money was used sometimes to ship the bodies home of those girls who were killed? She had a vision. I just admired her tremendously."

—Betty Jane "B. J." Williams, Class 44-W-6

man in the whole country. She was a protégé of Eleanor Roosevelt and at that point in time that was tantamount to running the NOW organization of its time, and her husband was a heavy contributor to Franklin Roosevelt's campaign, so anything she wanted she got."

"Winnie" Wood: "I never met Nancy Love but I did meet Jackie Cochran. After the WASP, I worked at Palm Springs Airport, and she had her home in Indio. She was very thoughtful and she did a lot of things that were never written about, but to get where she got, she had to have a tremendous drive and a tremendous 'I'm going to better myself' sort of ambition. Anybody that came from a mill town in Florida with no background at all and lived in a sack cloth. . . ."

"Dot" (Swain) Lewis: ". . . and no role models."

"Winnie" Wood: "She had a lot of determination and people thought she was brash. But anybody that had that 'drive, drive, drive' will be criticized and said to be brash. But if she hadn't done what she did, we would never have had the program."

"Dot" (Swain) Lewis: "No sir!"

"Winnie" Wood: "Nancy Love didn't want any more people trained."

"Dot" (Swain) Lewis: "Jackie could seem rude in a way, but with us she was wonderful. But she must have forced her way into a lot of places. We can't complain. A lot of people compared Nancy Love with Jacqueline Cochran, not knowing much about anything. You [addressing Winnie] were one of the Nancy Love lovers."

"Winnie" Wood: "I never knew Nancy Love."

"Dot" (Swain) Lewis: "I know, but you thought she was such a perfect lady and that Jackie was not one. Jackie was right there and she could brush you aside or not. She was determined that the WASP would be successful. A lot of people thought it was for her own ego—and it might have been, somewhat—but Jackie also sent the bodies of some WASPs that had been killed home at her expense and bought our wings and designed them and gave them to us. It was understandable that there were a lot of elegant people like Winnie who would prefer an upper-class lady running things and here was old common Cochran. (She wasn't really common.)Jackie was in doubt of her own speech and could hardly read and write, she felt. She was very shy about that.

"I've always admired Jackie. She was famous for all the things she'd done flying. She broke the sound barrier, for example. People could criticize her very easily, but she had guts. She made her beauty operation work. She loved her husband, Floyd, and he was devoted to her. He helped her find that there were unlimited horizons. She did all this in spite of the fact that she was always ill. All during the WASPs she had stomach operations. She couldn't have children, and she had many miscarriages."

"B. J." Williams: "I think that every one of us owes Jackie a tremendous debt of gratitude. Our lives would be totally different if there had never been a Jackie Cochran. Nancy Love, who started the WAFS, was a wonderful pilot, very qualified, but her concept was different than Jackie's. Nancy wanted to take highly experienced women and have a very elite group, extremely well qualified. Jackie's concept was to train the women to fly the military way and to give them additional duties besides ferrying.

WASP trainees Lyda Dunham, Betty Naffz, and Jane Champlin in their Zoot Suits, helmets, and goggles.
Jeanne Robertson

When there was a problem on the base, she solved it. If there was a need somewhere for pilots, she looked into seeing if the women could meet it.

"You didn't say no to Jackie; if there was an obstacle Jackie knew how to get around it. That kind of gutsiness and aggressiveness in a woman is not always admired; in a man, it's applauded, not so in a woman. I think in due time that will change.

"My heart used to ache for her because she was not educated, she was always nervous when she had to speak publicly. She didn't have command of the language, and it bothered her. Her handwriting was very childlike. But, my God, what a drive! I don't know of any other woman who did what she did. And it's funny, there were a lot of WASPs who didn't like her.

"A lot of the gals don't know how much Jackie put into this program. She was out to prove a point, and every hurdle that could be put up was put up in her path. Do you know that Jackie had to buy the wings initially, and her own money was used sometimes to ship the bodies home of those girls who were killed? She had a vision. I just admired her tremendously."

The WAFS

Roll Out the Airplanes!
(Tune: "Roll out the Barrel")

Roll out the airplanes,
We've got a big job to do,
Roll out the airplanes
Hurry so we can get through!

We'll practice sequence
When we go up every day,
Just so we can ferry airplanes
For the U.S.A.!

Nancy Love was a very different person from Jackie Cochran. She was a major player in the drama of the WASPs, but her style was in contrast to Cochran's.

"It's stupid to call flying daredevilish," she said. "I don't want to fly to the South Pole. I just want to do a job in the air. And I don't need to wear jodhpurs and fancy goggles to do it."

Nancy Love was beautiful, and ended up marrying a wealthy man, but that was where the similarity to Jackie Cochran ends. Love was born to wealth and had a secure position in society. She attended private high school and Vassar College. She envisioned an elite squad of women, each with at least 500 hours of experience flying. They would be college graduates and US citizens, and would work as a team.

The ladies who ended up qualifying for the WAFS had an average of 1,100 hours experience and backgrounds very similar to Love's. The recruits' names had been taken from the survey information that Cochran had gathered. The plan called for twenty-five WAFS to be used in an experimental program. Once the program got underway, they recruited more than twenty-five, and twenty-eight ended up being accepted into the first group squadron. These girls were called the "Originals," and were stationed at New Castle Army Air Base, near Wilmington, Delaware.

The "Originals" came to the WAFS with a lot of flying experience, but they still were required to attend a thirty-day training course that taught them to march and to talk, tell time, and fill out paperwork in the Army way.

Barbara Jane (Erickson) London: "Everybody that was in the program was a WAF until August of 1943. So the first six or seven classes of Jackie's school were WAFS. Most of them in their minds considered themselves always WASPs, but they weren't. See, we didn't really become WASPs and get the blue uniform until August of '43.

"WFTD was the training command. That's where they went to school. That's the Women's Flying Training Detachment. They graduated. Then they were sent someplace for active duty. The first five classes were split between the four Ferry Command bases. Beginning in the sixth or seventh classes, they began to go to Camp Davis, North Carolina; Hobbs, New Mexico; and Bakersfield, California. They went to all these various other places as later classes graduated, but they went as WAFS until the time that Jackie was appointed and changed the name and we began doing lots of other jobs, then the name 'Women's Auxiliary Ferrying Squadron' didn't fit because we weren't all ferrying. So they picked a new name and called us Women's Airforce Service Pilots, which encompassed all the various capacities in which we were flying. Ferrying remained under Nancy, fortunately, and Jackie wasn't really concerned with that very much.

"As long as Nancy was director of ferrying division the 'Originals' were pretty secure. I often think back that it was by the grace of God that we weren't militarized. If we had been, then Jackie could have transferred us any place she wanted to. As civilians, we could quit and go home, but once we were militarized, we couldn't. It is unfortunate that we didn't get militarized for the families and the kids that got killed, however. The original WAFS were not Jackie's favorite people. I mean we are what practically destroyed her in the beginning, so consequently, had we been in the military I don't think I would have stayed in Long Beach, California. "

Betty (Huyler) Gillies was one of the "Originals," as well. Her nickname was the "Mighty Atom" because she was only five feet one and one-half inches tall. She some-

"Nancy Love, who started the WAFS, was a wonderful pilot, very qualified, but her concept was different than Jackie's. Nancy wanted to take highly experienced women and have a very elite group, extremely well qualified. Jackie's concept was to train the women to fly the military way and to give them additional duties besides ferrying."

—Betty Jane "B. J." Williams, Class 44-W-6

times had wooden blocks strapped to her feet so she could reach the rudder pedals and two or three cushions under her bottom so she could see out the window of the airplanes she flew.

Gillies had been asked to come for a couple of months to help with the administration side of things by Nancy Love. She came right away, in September of 1942, and ended up staying for the duration. She took training the "Army way" at New Castle, where she learned navigation, military law, how to identify aircraft, and how to use a .45-caliber Colt pistol so that she could protect the secret equipment that was used on later planes.

She and all the others were allowed to fly only the light planes at first. Their first deliveries were Piper Cubs. She said that these were the hardest planes she had to deliver. They had no radios, it was winter, and there was no heater, it was hard to navigate in the snow, and the low horsepower made them difficult to land safely. It took patience and skill. With 1,400 hours of flying experience (much of this time as an airborne gofer for Grumman Aircraft), Gillies had both.

Barbara Jane (Erickson) London talks about her first days at Wilmington, Delaware, in the WAFS: "Eleanor Dressen [who was not a pilot], and I got in about midnight, into Philadelphia or someplace like that. Then we had to get from there to downtown Wilmington, and then we took a cab out to the air base. This is in the middle of the night. The guard at the gate took us to Bachelor Officer Quarters 14 where we were given a room. It had a window, a closet on the side with a rod where you put your clothes, an iron cot, and it had something black to cover the windows because we were going through blackouts right then.

"I remember that night Eleanor and I were sitting there on the bed practically crying; here we were 3,000 miles away from home, probably didn't have fifty bucks between us, it was the middle of the night, and all of a sudden everything went absolutely black. So there we sat for the rest of the night. I remember that we were pretty calm by the time we got up in the morning. But I do remember that first night because it was so black. I got up the next morning and reported to Nancy, went through checking the logbooks, and in the next few days, I somehow took a physical, took a flight check, and was accepted.

"I think one of my first ferrying trips was with Betty Gillies. We had Cubs that went to Lake Charles, Louisiana, which is pretty close to New Orleans. It's a long trip in a Cub. In Cubs, you're lucky if you can get a hundred miles an hour out of them and they don't have any radios. We had no radios at all, not in any of the airplanes that we flew those first three months at Wilmington. So we had to watch the map, watch the roads, follow the highways, and find our airport.

"After landing, we went over to New Orleans, and Betty, who comes from a wealthy background, had money. (She learned to fly at Roosevelt Field on Long Island and owned her own airplane, a lot different circumstances than I came from; I worked every day of my life since I was sixteen.) She took me out to dinner that night, and we went to Antoine's, which meant little to me, I hadn't even heard the name before. I think I horrified Betty, and to this day she will always hold it against me. She ordered Oysters Rockefeller and here they come and the first thing I did—picture this, it's a beautiful restaurant, lights are low, the maitre d' is falling all over us—I sit there and very calmly scrape all of the Rockefeller off the top. I loved the oysters but I didn't like the Rockefeller. I didn't like the spinach. She never forgave me for that.

"But we traveled a lot together during that period of time. She takes credit for giving me my first drink. I call her mother, and she calls me daughter. She introduced me to Cuba Libra [a drink made of rum and Coca Cola with a lime], and I introduced her to the bowling alley."

As the program became established, the WAFS were stationed at other bases across the country. Barbara Jane (Erickson) London went on to Long Beach, California. She was very happy there:

"The men were doing the same thing we were. We had the same advantages they had. And where I was stationed it was particularly true. We were well liked. We were well accepted. We got the same transition as the men.

"Here I was, at age twenty-two, and one day I would be flying a P-51, and the next day a P-38, and the next day a B-17 or a B-25. They were all marvelous airplanes. I was so lucky. I didn't have any problems ferrying, mechanical or physical, and every airplane was just a glory and a joy to fly. I was soaring around between all the clouds, being up there in a P-38 was probably as exciting as anything. A P-51 was too. The A-26 Invader that Douglas built was probably one of the most exciting because it was one of the fastest for an airplane of its size. We eventually used it as a night attack plane in the Korean War. Some of them I didn't care for as much. I didn't care for the P-39 or the P-63. I didn't fit in them as well. I didn't fly them as much, either.

"The girls in Wilmington didn't get a lot of the airplanes that we got to fly because they were more limited, really, to the P-47s [which were built at Republic Aviation's Long Island, New York, and Evansville, Indiana, factories]. They did a fantastic job. But, see, the differences were Teresa James and Betty Gillies and the others who were stationed back there would probably deliver three or four airplanes a day, each. They could pick one up from Long Island and get to Newark in a matter of minutes. They had a Lockheed Lodestar that would bring

WASP trainee Amie Thyng climbs into the cockpit of her trainer at Avenger Field. ***USAF (neg. no. K 36941)***

"Here I was, at age twenty-two, and one day I would be flying a P-51 and the next day a P-38 and the next day a B-17 or a B-25. They were all marvelous airplanes."
—Barbara Jane (Erickson) London

RANSPORT COMMAND
S. ARMY

them back. So they would fly their pants off and as hard as they could fly, and they probably would accumulate ten hours a week. In a week, I could make four flights across the United States, and I got fifty or sixty hours in five days. They worked a lot harder than I did to deliver four or five airplanes a day, each just a short hop, whereas I could get in one airplane and go ten hours from Long Beach to Newark and get ten times the flying time but only deliver one airplane. So that's what made each girl's experience different.

"There were hundreds and hundreds of girls who never made it in the Ferry Command, and they did a lot of other things. There were at most 300 of us in Ferry Command out of the thousand or so who made it."

There was a difference between the original WAFS and the following WASPs. The WAFS were already skilled pilots who were meant to ferry planes exclusively. The WASPs were women with basic flying skills who could be trained to fly military aircraft. The first couple of WASP classes, 43-W-1 through 43-W-6, were required to have 200 hours of flying time, but by the time the program was deactivated, the requirement was for only thirty-five hours of flying time. The Ferry Command's requirements were too high for these later class women to qualify, so they went into other areas like tow-target and engineering test flying.

The WASPs were a varied group, interested in flying but ready to learn new techniques and perhaps ready to have a career in the military. The WAFS in general were from a different economic group from the WASPs, as well. Having money was the most efficient way to accumulate the number of flying hours needed to qualify for Nancy Love's WAFS. The women of the WAFS probably intimidated the women who graduated to become WASPs; the WAFS were a justafiably proud and confident group.

So that gives you an idea of who Jacqueline Cochran, Nancy Love, and the WAFS were. Now let's go on with the story of the other more than 1700 ladies: the WASPs.

A group of WASPs based at Long Beach, California. Long Beach was near most of the major aircraft factories, so these women ferried everything from P–51 Mustang fighters to C–47 transports. Back row, from left: Nadine Ramsey (Class 43-W-5), Betty Tackaberry (Class 43-W-1), Katherine Loft (Class 43-W-4), Evelyn Trammell (Class 43-W-6), Thelma Farris (Class 43-W-7), Deborah Truax (Class 43-W-6), Virginia Hill (Class 43-W-4), Carol Fillmore (Class 43-W-2), Barbara Jane (Erickson) London (WAFs). Front row, from left: Rena Wilkes (Class 43-W-4), Lauretta Beatty (Class 43-W-4), Iris Cummings (Class 43-W-2), Lewise Coleman (Class 43-W-2), Dorothy Webb (Class 43-W-6), Jean Landis (Class 43-W-4), Dorothy Kocher (Class 43-W-4), Ruth Thompson (Class 43-W-2), Helen Richards (WAFs). ***Jeanne Robertson***

AVENGER FIELD
AVIATION ENTERPRISES LTD.

Chapter 3

"Gee, Mom, I Want to Go Home"

Daily Life of the WASP Trainees

What most WASPs think of, when they think about WASP training, is Avenger Field, Sweetwater, Texas. They think of bays and bay mates, marching to the mess hall for meals and, in fact, marching everywhere singing their little hearts out. But the first class of WFTDs (they called themselves "Woofteddies"), 43-W-1, reported to the 319th Army Air Forces Flying Training Detachment at Howard Hughes Field in Houston, Texas, for training.

Howard Hughes Field was a civilian airport adjacent to Ellington Army Air Forces Base. The training facility at Houston and the 319th Army Air Forces Flying Training Detachment were under the administration of General Barton Yount's Flying Training Command, but they were run by Aviation Enterprises Limited, a civilian contractor.

The girls at Houston did not have to put up with bays—six women to a bay, two bays to a bathroom—as later classes would at Avenger Field. (That's twelve women in a bathroom, and not one of the women was washed out of the training program for tardiness!) The women in Houston were told, "No housing, find your own."

They did not have to put up with mess hall food. They were told, "Find your own food." There was a snack bar at the airport terminal, and food sickness was a common event.

They did not have to march to and from class. They were not living close enough to march; they were told, "No transportation—just be at the field by 7:45 A.M. and leave at 9:00 P.M."

All of them had to share the public restroom at the terminal, which was rarely clean. A portable latrine was built, and one of the society girls got "crabs."

They had no uniforms, no allowance to buy uniforms, and they wore out their shoes every few weeks. They lived where they could in town.

Some ladies had the inclination and the means to take care of themselves in style. They checked into deluxe apartments with maid service and doormen. For example, Marion Florsheim (daughter-in-law of the shoe man) and her ten trunks of clothes and two afghan hounds took up residence quite comfortably. Those who couldn't afford luxury made do with what lodging they could find—tourist motels, boarding houses for working girls, renting a room in a home.

The first class had come to Houston in November 1942. Jeanne (Bennett) Robertson's class, 43-W-4 was there in February 1943. By this time they had set up some off-base housing for the girls: "I don't think I'd put my dog today in the motel we lived in. It

The front gate of Avenger Field, Sweetwater, Texas, in May 1944. The sign shows that the field was run by Aviation Enterprises Limited, a civilian contractor. ***USAF (neg. no. B 36520 AC)***

Gee, Mom, I Want to Go Home

The coffee that they give us they say is very fine
It's good for cuts and bruises, and tastes like iodine,
I don't want no more of Army life,
Gee, Mom, I want to go home.
The doughnuts that they give us they say are very fine,
One fell off the table and killed a pal of mine,
I don't want no more of Army life,
Gee, Mom, I want to go home.
The johnny's like Grand Central, there ain't no privacy.
Your time is spent in waiting for each utility.
I don't want no more of Army life,
Gee, Mom, I want to go home.
The Army cots they give us they say are very fine,
They're not for beauty resting, but straightening of the spine,
I don't want no more of Army life,
Gee, Mom, I want to go home.
The zoot suits that they give us they say are mighty fine,
You keep right on marching, and they move along behind,
I don't want no more of Army life,
Gee, Mom, I want to go home.
The airplanes that they give us they say are mighty fine,
The darn things can't shoot stages, they will not hit the line,
I don't want no more of Army life,
Gee, Mom, I want to go home.
The quizzes that they give us, they say are mighty fine,
We never know the answers, we're mixed up all the time,
I don't want no more of Army life,
Gee, Mom, I want to go home.
Instructors that they give us we think are pretty swell.
We'd like to see more of them but some darn rat would tell.
I don't want no more of Army life,
Gee, Mom, I want to go home.
But Momma, dear, the truth is, we know it's mighty fine,
We love it all, no kidding, we think it is sublime,
We still want some more of Army life,
No Mom, we're not coming home!

An illustration from the book *The Gremlins* by Roald Dahl. Disney made the illustrations for this book and later added wings to the female gremlin to come up with the insignia for the WASPs. *© Disney Enterprises, Inc.; via Special Collections, Texas Woman's University*

Fifinellas lacked the ability to undertake such hazardous Gremlintrix as (1) playing see-saw on the artificial horizon (2) using the compass as a merry-go-round (3) drinking gasoline (4) sliding down the beam and rolling up the runway, thus making planes undershoot.

—The Log Book

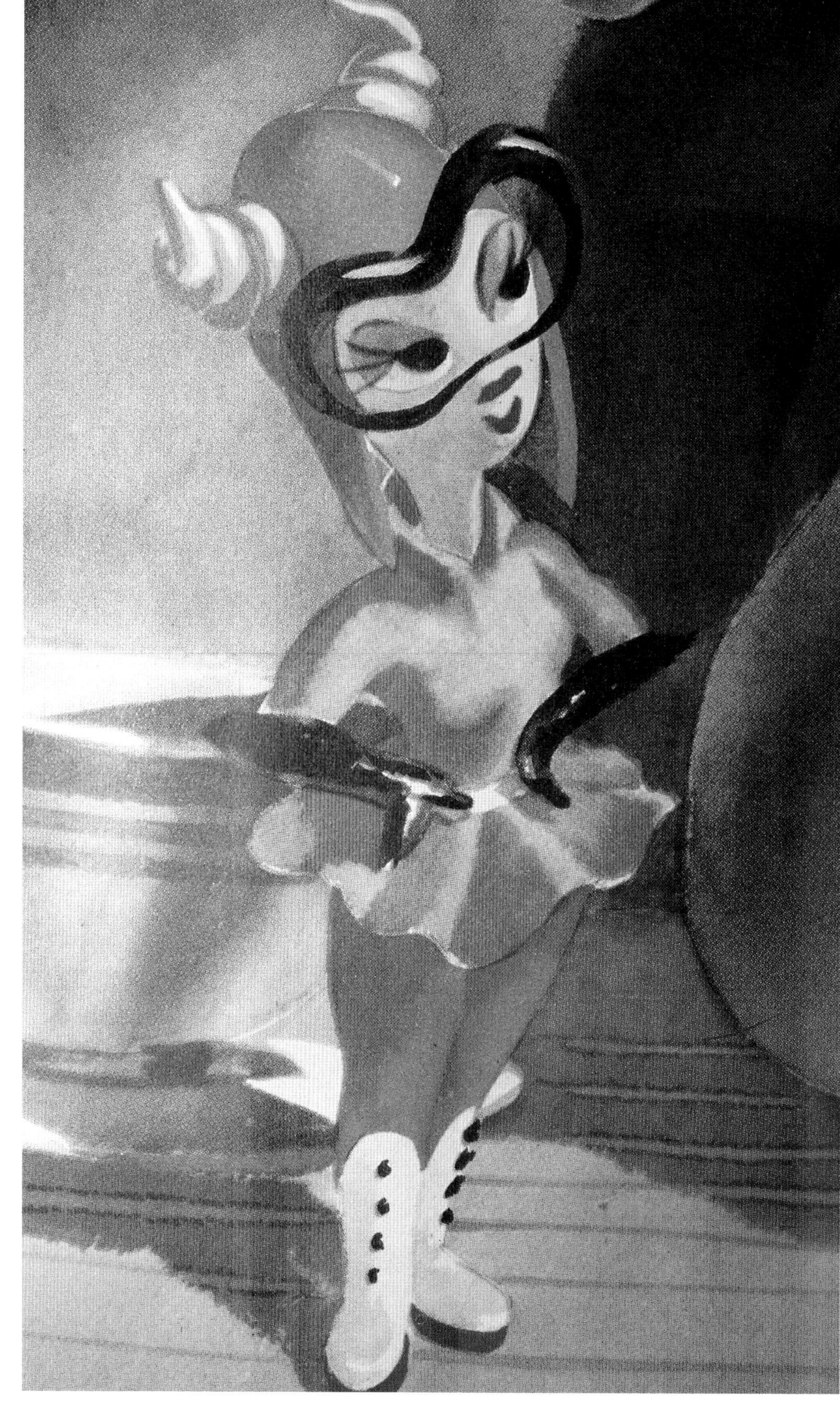

was just cruddy. All the rooms had double beds. We were assigned rooms, and here I was sleeping with some woman I'd never met before. There were rats in the motel. We were, finally, issued uniforms for men, but they were just too big for most of us. And the food was horrible. Still, we were getting to fly; that was the big thing!"

"Kay" (Menges) Brick: "I have to tell you about Houston. I lived on a bayou and when we would go in at night—it was dark—and I would say to my roommate, 'Do you want to grab the phone book or do you hit the light tonight?' And when the light would go on, these cockroaches—a couple of inches big—would be all over the place. We had decided we would try to kill some, so one of us would push the light and the other would get ready and would throw the book.

"I had a lovely robe with beautiful pink flowers on it and green leaves. The roaches ate off all the green leaves, down the back. Judy had a navy blue dress and it had a bunch of frosted purple grapes, and the bugs ate all of them. We were scared to death that at night they would crawl up into bed with us. This was at the Oleander Courts."

No one was quite sure how to train "girls" to fly. The WFTDs were given really worn-out planes and bad equipment. They had no crash trucks, no fire trucks, and one ambulance on loan from Ellington Army Air Forces Base. And every day, it seemed, one more plane was sent to that plane cemetery in the sky.

Jeanne (Bennett) Robertson: "We started out in Houston with the dregs: anything that the military didn't want to fly, they let the women fly. And they weren't very well organized. The rules were made as we went along; it was really kind of helter skelter.

"So there was a lot of resentment among the men instructors—why did they have to teach the women? Some of the instructors who gave us flight checks were very hard on the girls and some of them were understanding. It just depended upon their background. There are chauvinistic males, and we had them in abundance back then. It was the attitude of, 'Well, you think you can fly? All right, show me!'

"A girl I met on the train was going to Houston, and she and I roomed together. We had been in Houston about a month, and she found out she was pregnant. She had to go through this male board to ask for a leave of absence, and she came back laughing. One of the men had said, 'Well, we understand you'd like a leave of absence for health reasons, and that is granted, and when that condition has been eliminated you can return.' And she never returned. Someone else moved into her space."

The morale at Houston was very low, bad equipment, bad food, bad planes, and so on. So the girls came up with the idea of starting a newspaper that would have gossip and tidbits and information. They called it *The Fifinella Gazette.* A Fifinella is a female gremlin. She is responsible for troubles such as fog, missing runways, and maps that fly out of cockpits on cross-country jaunts.

Roald Dahl wrote a book for Britain's Royal Air Force called *The Gremlins.* It was a lovely book about all the mishaps that pilots experience—fog, missing landmarks, sputtering engines. The book was a real morale booster for the men flying during a time of great duress. Walt Disney illustrated the book, with mischievous little gremlins taking the blame (or the credit) for these mishaps.

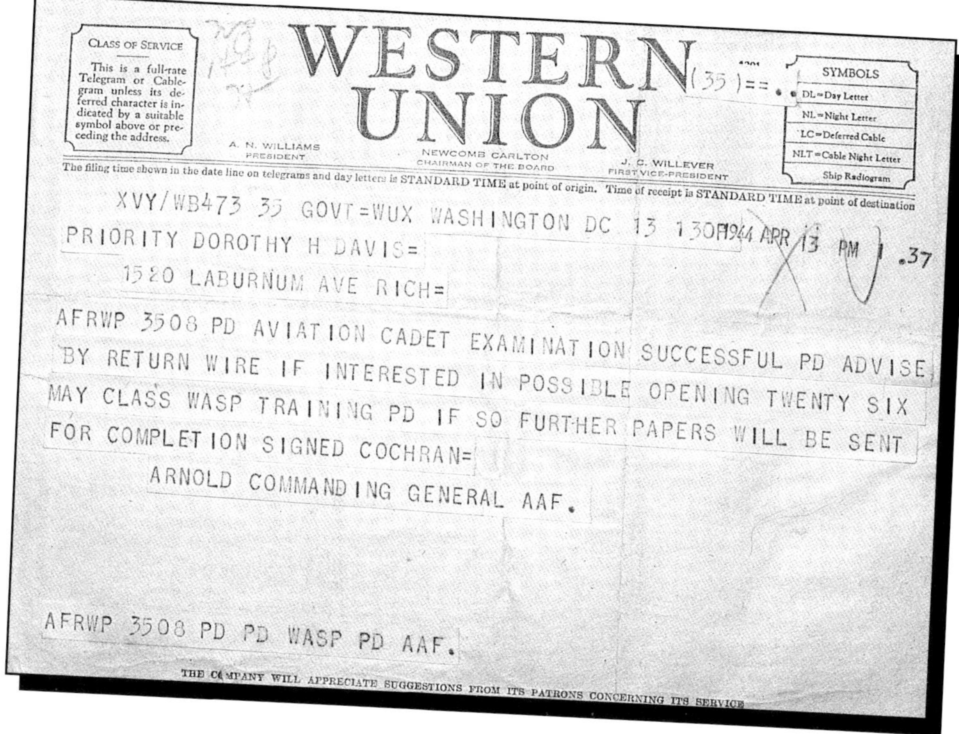

CLASS OF SERVICE
This is a full-rate Telegram or Cablegram unless its deferred character is indicated by a suitable symbol above or preceding the address.

WESTERN UNION

A. N. WILLIAMS, PRESIDENT — NEWCOMB CARLTON, CHAIRMAN OF THE BOARD — J. C. WILLEVER, FIRST VICE-PRESIDENT

SYMBOLS
DL=Day Letter
NL=Night Letter
LC=Deferred Cable
NLT=Cable Night Letter
Ship Radiogram

The filing time shown in the date line on telegrams and day letters is STANDARD TIME at point of origin. Time of receipt is STANDARD TIME at point of destination

XVY/WB473 35 GOVT=WUX WASHINGTON DC 13 130P 1944 APR 13 PM 1 37

PRIORITY DOROTHY H DAVIS=
1520 LABURNUM AVE RICH=

AFRWP 3508 PD AVIATION CADET EXAMINATION SUCCESSFUL PD ADVISE BY RETURN WIRE IF INTERESTED IN POSSIBLE OPENING TWENTY SIX MAY CLASS WASP TRAINING PD IF SO FURTHER PAPERS WILL BE SENT FOR COMPLETION SIGNED COCHRAN=
ARNOLD COMMANDING GENERAL AAF.

AFRWP 3508 PD PD WASP PD AAF.

THE COMPANY WILL APPRECIATE SUGGESTIONS FROM ITS PATRONS CONCERNING ITS SERVICE

Telegram from General "Hap" Arnold instructing "Dottie" Davis to report for WASP training. This was the beginning of a great adventure for Davis. *"Dottie" Davis.* Left, the front of the Oleander Courts in Houston, where many WASP trainees were billeted. The first couple of classes reported for training in Houston, Texas. There were no official housing arrangements and the ladies were sent into town to live where they could. This photo shows a typical room at Oleander Courts, where some of the girls were billeted. They were assigned two (strangers, sometimes) to a room and had to share a double bed. *Jeanne Robertson*

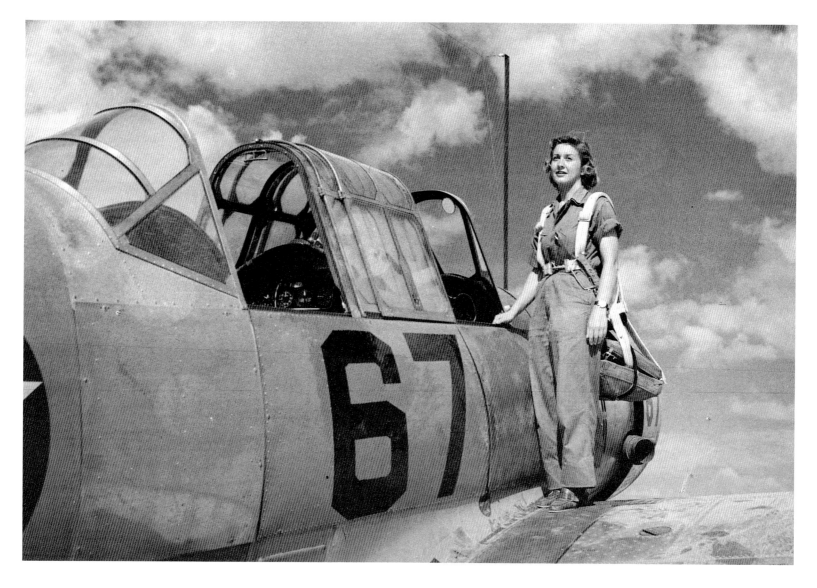

Rosalie Grohman, Class 43-W-4, is about to climb in the cockpit of an AT-6 Texan advanced-trainer aircraft. *Jeanne Robertson.* Right, Transportation to the airfield in Houston. The vehicle was called the "cattle car" by the trainees, who sat on wooden benches on either side of the bus. Despite the windows, the gals couldn't see out because the windows were covered. *Jeanne Robertson*

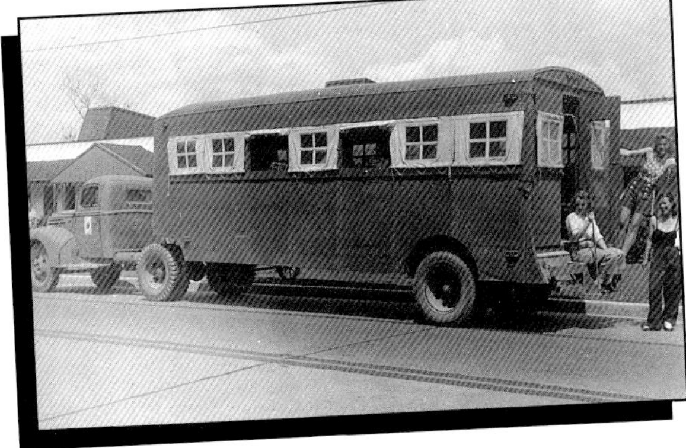

The book refers to a female gremlin, and calls her a Fifinella.

When the WASPs wrote to Disney (who was known for designing insignia for other flying groups) and asked him to design an insignia for the women, Fifinella was a natural choice. Disney added a pair of goggles and some wings to the character from the book, and a perfect WASP mascot was born.

In April, Class 43-W-1 became the first class of WFTDs to graduate and the only class to graduate at Houston. Because they were not rated military pilots of the United States they were not going to get wings, so Jackie Cochran paid for wings from the post exchange and for engraving by a local jeweler.

By the time they graduated from training, the "Woofteddies" averaged well over 500 hours of flying time, and they were checked out on several kinds of primary and basic trainers as well as the AT-6 and the twin engine AT-17. (Many of the "Originals" still hadn't flown an AT-6.) The "Woofteddies" had soloed at night, they had instrument training, Link simulator training, landings, takeoffs, patterns, loops, and slow rolls.

Avenger Field

The WASP program was expanding rapidly, and girls with fewer and fewer flight hours were being accepted for WASP training, so the Fying Training Command began to look for a second facility at which they could train these new recruits. Jackie Cochran looked around and found Avenger Field in Sweetwater, Texas, which seemed perfect for the WASP program because it had housing, dining facilities, classrooms, and planes to fly. (Avenger was then being used to train pilots for the British, but they would soon be vacating the facilities.) Meanwhile, the Flying Training Command wanted to build barracks, hangars, classrooms, and toilets for the 319th AAFTD at Hughes Field, but the Civil Aeronautics Authority refused to lease them the additional land, so it was decided to move the whole WASP training program to Avenger Field.

A new detachment was formed at Avenger Field, the 318th AAFTD, but Aviation Enterprises Limited was given the contract to train these girls, as well.

The move to Avenger was done in stages. In April 1943, Class 43-4 was just starting training, and they flew their primary trainers (Fairchild PT-19s) to Sweetwater from Houston to continue their training. A month later, the half of Class 43-3 that was training in Houston flew the basic trainers (Vultee BT-13s, nicknamed "Vibrators") up to Sweetwater and continued their training. A few weeks later, Class 43-2 flew their advanced trainers (North American AT-6 Texans) up to Sweetwater and graduated the day after.

"Micky" (Tuttle) Axton: "The first WFTD class in the program was successful, and more and more women were applying for the program. And so they moved to Avenger Field. I have to tell you something funny about that. I heard this, first hand, from a young man who was in high school at the time when they were going to ferry one hundred planes from Houston over to Avenger Field. He said that everybody in Sweetwater packed a picnic that day and went out to the airfield along the road, and all the men were making bets on how many of the girls would crash, how many would get lost, and all this. And they said they were just flabbergasted when every one of the girls flying one hundred planes came in and landed, no problem. He also said a lot of the parents wouldn't let the kids play out in the yard for a while. They were afraid that the planes were going to crash and kill 'em. Isn't that funny?"

Jeanne (Bennett) Robertson: "Our class was the largest class [43-W-4] because it was really two classes—half started in Sweetwater, half in Houston. In Houston we didn't know there was a class at Sweetwater, and the Sweetwater girls didn't know we were in Houston.

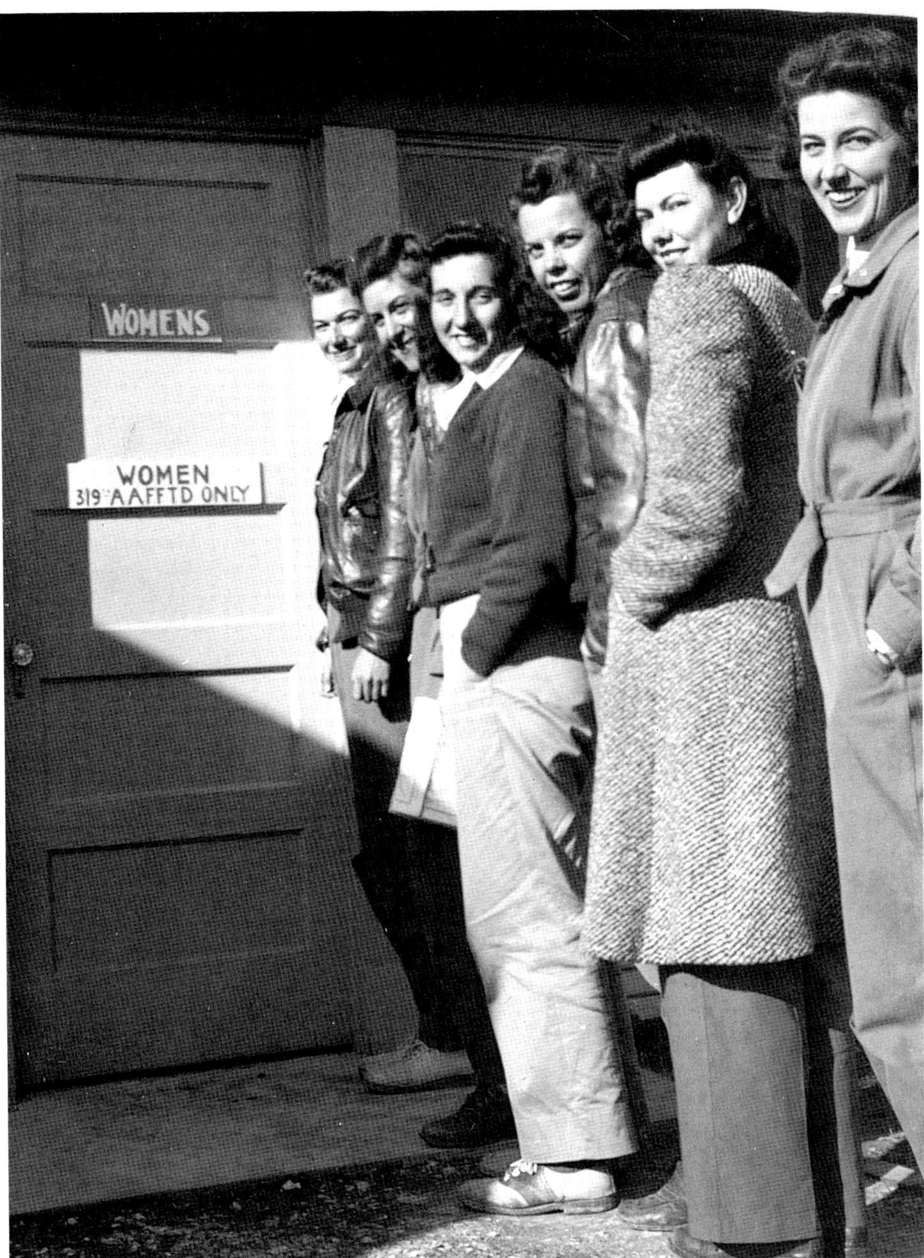

The line for the ladies room at Howard Hughes Field in Houston, Texas, March 1943. The facilities at Houston were completely unprepared for the everyday presence of dozens of young women. ***Jeanne Robertson***

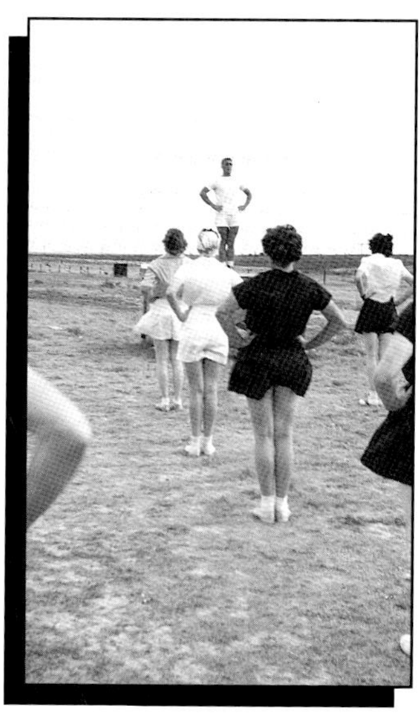

Daily calisthenics being led by Lieutenant LaRue. *Jeanne Robertson.* Below, two WASP trainees in front of their bays at Avenger Field. They slept in these bays, ate in the mess, and lived the military life. *Florence Wheeler*

"We didn't ever really get to know the Sweetwater group until we were almost through the program, and I'm talking about months, living right next to each other in long barracks. We had these barracks which were big rooms with six cots, six little closets just like gym lockers, and a desk down the middle of the room. These were connected to another bay by a bathroom with two johns, two wash basins, and two showers for twelve girls.

"When we first got there, there were no partitions around the johns. This was very hard on some of the women who had never been in any gym classes with other girls or anything. I had gone to camp so it wasn't too hard on me. They finally put in partitions for us.

"What was difficult was that we would have maybe five or ten minutes to clean up if we came off the flight line and then had to go right to class. We'd get four or five of us in a shower. They were big showers with two spouts, and you didn't know sometimes if you were washing your own back or someone else's."

Alyce (Stevens) Rohrer talks about her first night in Sweetwater, before going out to the field. She stayed at the one hotel in town, the Blue Bonnet.

"Everybody was scared to death because we were told that the instructors and the pilots out there didn't want the program. That they hated women and that we had to be better than good to even get through, because everybody could wash out. We were really worried.

"Three of us had decided to share a hotel room because there were so many girls all coming in at the same time. We called the base and they said tomorrow morning at ten o'clock the cattle truck will be in to pick us up. And we thought, My word, I hope that isn't indicative of what they think of us. Of course, we found out later that it had been named the 'cattle truck' by a previous trainee. But it came in at ten o'clock that morning, picked us up, took us out to the base. We got a lecture by Mrs. Deaton [Leoti 'Deedee' Deaton], our establishment officer, about where we'd be placed and that the rooms were called bays and we'd be six to a bay and that we would be assigned not by number but alphabetically."

Cochran's Convent

Cochran wanted the girls to be above scandal, because she knew that any missteps in moral conduct could be more damaging to the WASP program than training mishaps.

The novelty of women flyers had not worn off for most male flyers, so Avenger Field became a very popular spot for "forced" landings. Male cadets would call the tower and state, "Engine running rough," or any number of other hard-to-pinpoint complaints and would come in for a little bit of checking out the engine and checking out the girls. As a result, the base was soon closed to all outside traffic, and a rule was made barring social contact with Army Air Forces staff or civilian instructors. Avenger Field became known as "Cochran's Convent."

Rigdon "Rig" Edwards (an instructor at Avenger): "They were a fine bunch of ladies. Maybe 1 or 2 percent of them were a little on the wild side, but you can expect that of any group. These girls realized that they were guinea pigs, that it was a trial deal. Jackie Cochran impressed on them that it was necessary for them to conduct themselves in a manner that everybody'd be proud of—and they did a good job of it."

But there were inadvertent ways of creating a scandal. Marguerite "Ty" (Hughes) Killen, Class 44-W-8, tells a story about training during the summer months. Many of the trainees were known to enjoy sunning themselves even while flying on cross-country treks. In order to get the most of their tans they would sometimes remove their shirts. Male pilots from other training fields started to catch on to the "cockpit striptease" and enjoyed sneaking up on the girls for a closer look. One time—probably the last—Killen was getting a tan, and one plane came along one side and one on the other. When she grabbed for her shirt it flew out of the cockpit! When she came in for a landing she had to ask her flying partner to run in and get her a blanket to wear.

Songs and Food

A typical day at Avenger Field would start with reveille and then the trainees would march to breakfast.

Fifinellas Adopt 319th

Members of the 43-W-2 will recall that in their early days at Houston a warning was posted that all students must carry used postage stamps to feed and pacify Them Gremlins.* Not long thereafter, female Gremlins, or Fifinellas, were seen shoving ships off the runways into the tenacious Texas mud. However, no male or female Gremlins were seen in the air.

The first student to see a Fifinella on board in flight was Sidney Miller, whose phenomenal, practically on-the-back spin recovery during a check ride was definitely due to three Fifinellas visibly (1) swinging on the throttle (2) holding the stick firmly forward (3) throwing dust into the Lt.'s eyes so he failed to note the goings-on.

Those familiar with Them Gremlins will recognize that something new has been added. Formerly only Gremlins and male children, or Midgets rode the air waves, it being claimed that the diminutive Fifinellas lacked the ability to undertake such hazardous Gremlintrix as (1) playing see-saw on the artificial horizon (2) using the compass as a merry-go-round (3) drinking gasoline (4) sliding down the beam and rolling up the runway, thus making planes undershoot.

Like members of the 318th, Fifinellas needed only training in order to turn in a good job. When the 319th was formed, a squadron of pioneering Fifinellas arrived with the first Gremlins, forcing Them to undertake specialists jobs such as that of the big-stomached Puff Gremlin, who sucks air from under a plane, making it jounce.

At Houston, Gremlins and Fifinellas are breeding at a rate sufficient to supply each cubstuff flier with a Flipperty-Gibbet, or young Fifinella, which reaches Fifinellahood upon the student's graduation to PT's. For the benefit of those students who have not been adopted to date (by the way, Them Gremlins take the name of their pilot, as in Fifinella Richards) we present left, the first Fifinella to arrive at the Houston Municipal. Fifinellas are about a foot high. Whereas Gremlins have stubby horns, those of Them Fifinellas are delicate and curled.

Them Gremlins have come a long way from their original homes of a 1000 years ago in the quiet shadows of river pools, thence to the mountain crags and finally taking to the air. Now Them have taken another step: Them Fifinellas, like the gals of the 319th, are taking the air.

Watch out fellas! They're dillies!

*It is a grave social error to refer to Gremlins as anything but Them.

Reprinted from The Log Book, *the yearbook of the 319th AAFD*

The Disney illustration of Fifinella that appears in *The log Book. Illustration © Disney Enterprises, Inc.; photo by Hans Halberstadt.*

In order to get the most of their tans they would sometimes remove their shirts. Male pilots from other training fields started to catch on to the "cockpit striptease" and enjoyed sneaking up on the girls for a closer look. One time—probably the last—Killen was getting a tan, and one plane came along one side and one on the other. When she grabbed for her shirt it flew out of the cockpit!

Then they would march to class, march to Link training class, march to lunch, march to the field for flight training, march to dinner, march to the field for night flying and then, maybe, march to their bays for sleep. Lots of marching going on, huh?

Talking while marching was not allowed, and that is how the songs got started.

The Mess Hall Song

(Tune: "Long, Long Trail A-Winding")
There's a long long trail a-winding
Up to the mess hall each day.
We tramp, (we tramp) that never ending road
Three times a day.
When the long platoon has halted
That's when we all comprehend,
No matter where we're standing
They peel off from the other end.

There's a long, long line a-waiting
A-waiting patiently to eat
We only stand an hour or so
Upon our weary feet,
When at last we get to dining
We're all so tired, we're just all in.
Then comes the call that drives us crazy,
Everybody fall in!

The food at Avenger Field was really pretty good for the most part; it was plentiful and served by friendly peo-

Jeanne (Bennett) Robertson and her bay mates. They are wearing "general's pants" and white shirts, an unofficial dress uniform. *Jeanne Robertson.* Right, The women were issued these coveralls in one size—large! Most of them had to cinch up and roll up and tape up to get the suits to fit better. "Micky" (Tuttle) Axton (right) and Leonora "Nonnie" (Horton) Anderson, both of Class 43-W-7, model their Zoot Suits in May 1943. *"Micky" Axton*

ple. Sometimes the kitchen staff would prepare special treats for special occasions: birthday cakes and picnic lunches, and thermoses of hot coffee and sandwiches for the night flyers.

Rita (Davoly) Webster: "Let me tell you about the food. I come from an Italian background and we like food. At Avenger they made the best potatoes that I have ever eaten before or since. They were big Idaho-style potatoes, they were peeled, and they were cooked on the outside like fried, and on the inside like baked, potatoes. I have tried and tried to make potatoes like that but I could never duplicate them.

"Then in the morning we were awakened out of a sound, sound sleep. We had a half hour to get dressed and make our beds very tight and put everything away, and do whatever we had to do in this one bathroom with all these others. So by the time we got in line we were still groggy. We went in to breakfast, through the line, and it seems like scrambled eggs were always there. Of course I was always ravenous, and I would get the scrambled eggs.

"One morning I was more awake than usual and I'm forking through these scrambled eggs, and I said to Carol (one of my bay mates), 'There's something in these scrambled eggs that's not eggs.' She says, 'Yes.' I asked, 'What is it?' She said, 'Brains.'

'What!!'

'Of course. Haven't you ever had scrambled eggs and brains before?'

'Well I'm not eating that!'

'You've been eating them ever since you came here!'

Well I had never heard of scrambled eggs and brains but I ate it, and it wasn't bad. No, the food at Sweetwater wasn't bad."

Barbara Jane (Erickson) London: "It got so that I liked Spam. I told somebody I liked Spam, and they almost died. But I couldn't handle the powdered eggs."

"Maggie" Gee: "I had never had catfish, and the one thing I always remember is catfish every Friday. It was good."

Gene (Shaffer) FitzPatrick: "The food was good. It was all cafeteria style. They had these metal plates to eat off. They had signs up. One sign was, 'Take all you want, but eat all you take.' Another one said, 'Butter's critical.' We'd always say, 'We want some critical butter.' I think they had another humorous sign about milk. We had all the milk and stuff like that we wanted.

"And if we didn't want to eat in the mess hall we could eat in the canteen and get hamburgers and hot dogs and all that other stuff. I remember the Cokes were five cents.

"We had macaroni and cheese and a lot of starches, which today are called carbohydrates. They had to put some of the girls on a diet because some really got carried away with that."

The WASPs were young, exuberant, and loved what they were doing, so songs became part of everything they did.

Opal Vivian "Hicksie" (Hicks) Fagan (who, today, prefers to be called Vivian), Class 44-W-7: "We had a lot of songs. There were graduation songs and songs for every occasion and even when the wind blew, there were songs about that. If we had a wind storm, and they seemed to happen quite often, we all had to run out to the runway and hold the wings down on the Stearmans, because there were no hangars."

Rita (Davoly) Webster: "Oh some of the songs were shocking, but I sang them along with everybody else."

The favorite song for many WASPs was "Zoot Suits and Parachutes."

Zoot Suits and Parachutes

(Tune: "Bell Bottom Trousers")
Before I was a member of the AAFTD
I used to be a working girl in Washington, D.C.
My boss he was unkind to me,
He worked me night and day,

I always had the time to work
But never time to play.

Singing zoot suits and parachutes
And wings of silver, too
He'll ferry airplanes like his mama used to do.

Along came a pilot, ferrying a plane,
He asked me to go fly with him down in lover's lane
And I, just like a silly fool, thinking it no harm
Cuddled in the cockpit to keep the pilot warm.

Singing zoot suits and parachutes
And wings of silver, too
He'll ferry airplanes like his mama used to do.

Early in the morning before the break of day
He handed me a shortsnort bill
And I heard him say,
Take this, my darling, for the damage I have done,
For you may have a daughter, or you may have a son;
If you have a daughter, teach her how to fly,
If you have a son, put the (bleep) in the sky.

Singing zoot suits and parachutes
And wings of silver, too
He'll ferry airplanes like his mama used to do.

The moral of this story as you can plainly see
Is never trust a pilot an inch above the knee.
He'll kiss you and caress you, and promise to be true
And have a girl at every field as all the pilots do.

Singing zoot suits and parachutes
And wings of silver, too
He'll ferry airplanes like his mama used to do.

"Zoot Suits"

The trainees were issued huge flight suits in a large men's sizes, and these were nicknamed "Zoot Suits." The name came from the full-legged, narrow-ankled suits that men in Harlem were wearing. Wearing these suits wasn't so bad for the tall women, but it was a nightmare for the short ones. They talk about marching with their suits following along behind.

Some of the trainees who came from outside of Texas were intrigued by cowboy boots. "Winnie" Wood was from Florida so she bought some beautiful black cowboy boots when she arrived in Texas. She was wearing them the day everybody had to get their shots. She fainted and the next thing she remembered, she was lying on a couch in the outer room, a line of girls were going by her on their way in to get shots, and she heard one of them

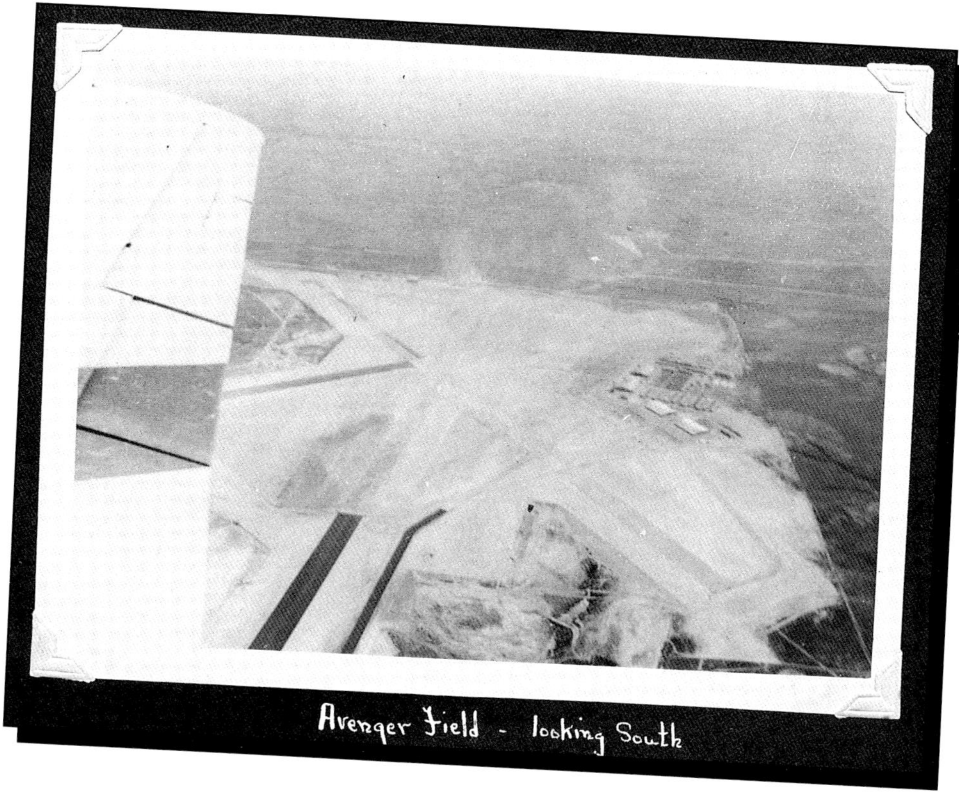

Avenger Field from the air. Although the townspeople eventually adopted the WASPs, at first they were afraid to let their kids play outside because they thought the WASPs would be crashing all over the area. *"Dottie" Davis.* Left, an illustration from *The Avenger,* the newsletter created for the WASPs at Avenger Field in Sweetwater, Texas. Vol. 1, No. 1, May 11, 1943. "You didn't know sometimes if you were washing your own back or someone else's." *Jeanne Robertson*

Formation flying in AT-6s. The AT-6s were everybody's favorite trainer plane. *"Dottie" Davis.* Below, wings of Class 43-W-4. Up until Class 43-W-8 the graduates were given these "unofficial" but beloved wings with a shield. They were usually paid for by Jackie Cochran and were purchased at the local post exchange, where they were also engraved. *Hans Halberstadt*

say, "Poor Winnie, she died with her boots on!"

After graduation, when Class 43-W-1 arrived at the ferrying bases, the new WAFS didn't like their appearance. The WAFS had been wearing gabardine grays and thought the outfits were stylish and useful for ferrying. They had lobbied the Secretary of War to make this the official uniform for the WAFS, but General "Hap" Arnold had his own ideas. He wanted to have a separate Air Force with a unique blue uniform. So he wanted the women to have a blue uniform as well (Santiago blue, in fact). He asked Jackie Cochran to develop one. The WAFS request for their gabardine grays to be official was denied. They blamed Cochran.

Having a uniform for the WASPs was crucial. The WAFS in their smart gabardine grays were taken for stewardesses on commercial flights and reprimanded for their laziness when they refused to bring coffee for the passengers. They were also taken for ferry boat pilots.

The WASPs, who started out wearing Army pinks, were sometimes taken for stewardesses, senior girl scouts, or part of the Mexican army, or were thought to work on planes and allowed to wear wings in an honorary way.

Alyce (Stevens) Rohrer: "There were so few of us—only 1,074 ever got through the training. And whenever we flew somewhere and were coming back on the train or a plane, most people took us for stewardesses. I remember talking to one lady on a train for thirty minutes. I told her what I was doing, and when I got off the train she asked me what airline I was working for. I mean, people never had a clue. There were a few articles in national magazines about us, but the majority of people didn't even believe us when we told them what we were doing. We could talk to them for an hour and then, all of a sudden they would say, 'You mean you actually fly those planes?'"

On one ferrying trip, four WASPs were delivering Cubs to an airport in the south. They RON (remained over night) in Lebanon, Tennessee. There were Army maneuvers going on, and all the hotels in town were booked. Finally the ladies found one room at a very run-down motel in a very run-down area. They were exhausted and needed sleep so much that they didn't mind the surroundings too much. They were spotted by some of the Army men as they were entering their room, and an uproar occurred. The men, not knowing who or what these "ladies" were but figuring they were fair game, proceeded to rattle their doors, call out remarks, and made a general hullabaloo. The MPs were called and they concluded that these ladies were the "of-the-night" variety and hauled them off to jail. Their protestations were ignored at first until finally the commanding officer at their base in Romulus, Michigan, was contacted, and he got them off the hook.

Without uniforms they were getting into trouble.

Turbans

The other problem the trainees, or actually the trainers, were having was with their hair. It was getting in the eyes of the instructors and the trainees were ordered to wear hair nets at first and then turbans. These were their least favorite accessories.

Gene (Shaffer) FitzPatrick: "One girl by the name of Patricia [(Jones) Perry] had beautiful red hair and when they would open the hatch, her hair would go out like in a convertible. Her instructor said, 'We can't have that.' So she was responsible for us having to wear these horrible flight turbans. They kept your head hot. So you're in and out trying to dry it off or shampoo every couple of hours.

"They finally got around to giving us a flight cap when they gave us a uniform. They had one for me, but I didn't like it. So I kept saying it was the wrong size. And I got all the way through without wearing one. I would get called on the carpet sometimes: 'Where's your hat?' I would say, 'Well, the one I have is too big. It just flops around, but another one's on order.' So they let me get away with that. Some people hate hats. I'm one of those. The turban was terrible. We had a big bonfire once we didn't have those things anymore.

"They made us wear the turbans because the instructors couldn't see around the flying hair. We didn't care. Who cares about the instructors? But I guess they had their reasons for it. Then we had to wear the turban to

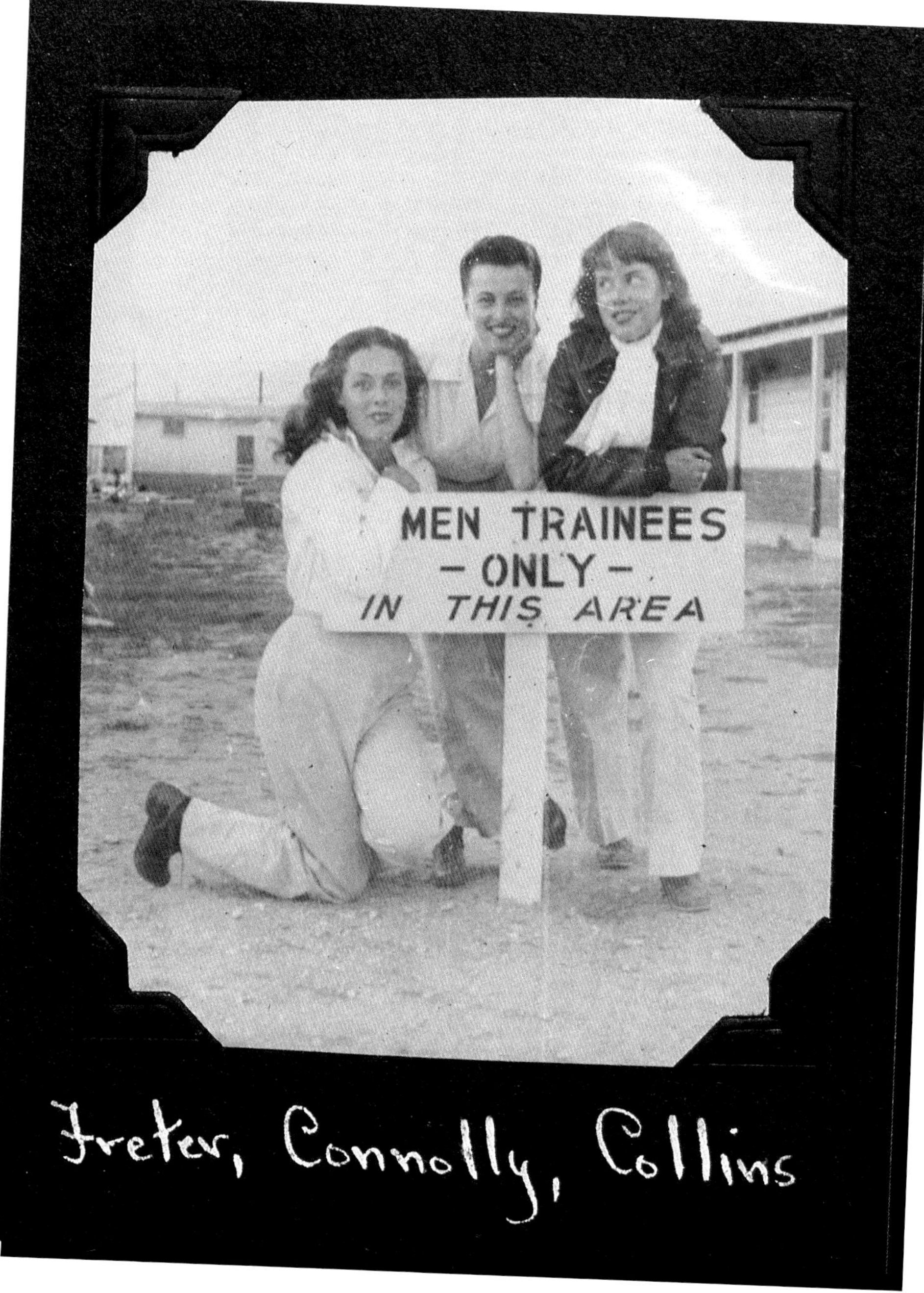

Wishful thinking by the lonely girls of "Cochran's Convent," so called because Jackie Cochran imposed a rule barring social contact with Army Air Forces staff or civilian instructors. ***"Dottie" Davis***

Jeanne (Bennett) Robertson, Class 43-W-4, in front of AT-6. Robertson's class was the largest because it was really two classes, one of which started training in Houston while the other started in Sweetwater. The program was expanding rapidly, so the decision was made to move all WASP training to Sweetwater where the facilities were bigger and better. *Jeanne Robertson.* Next page, a page from "Dottie" Davis' scrapbook shows a montage of Instructors with students. Instructors were mostly loved and respected. *"Dottie" Davis*

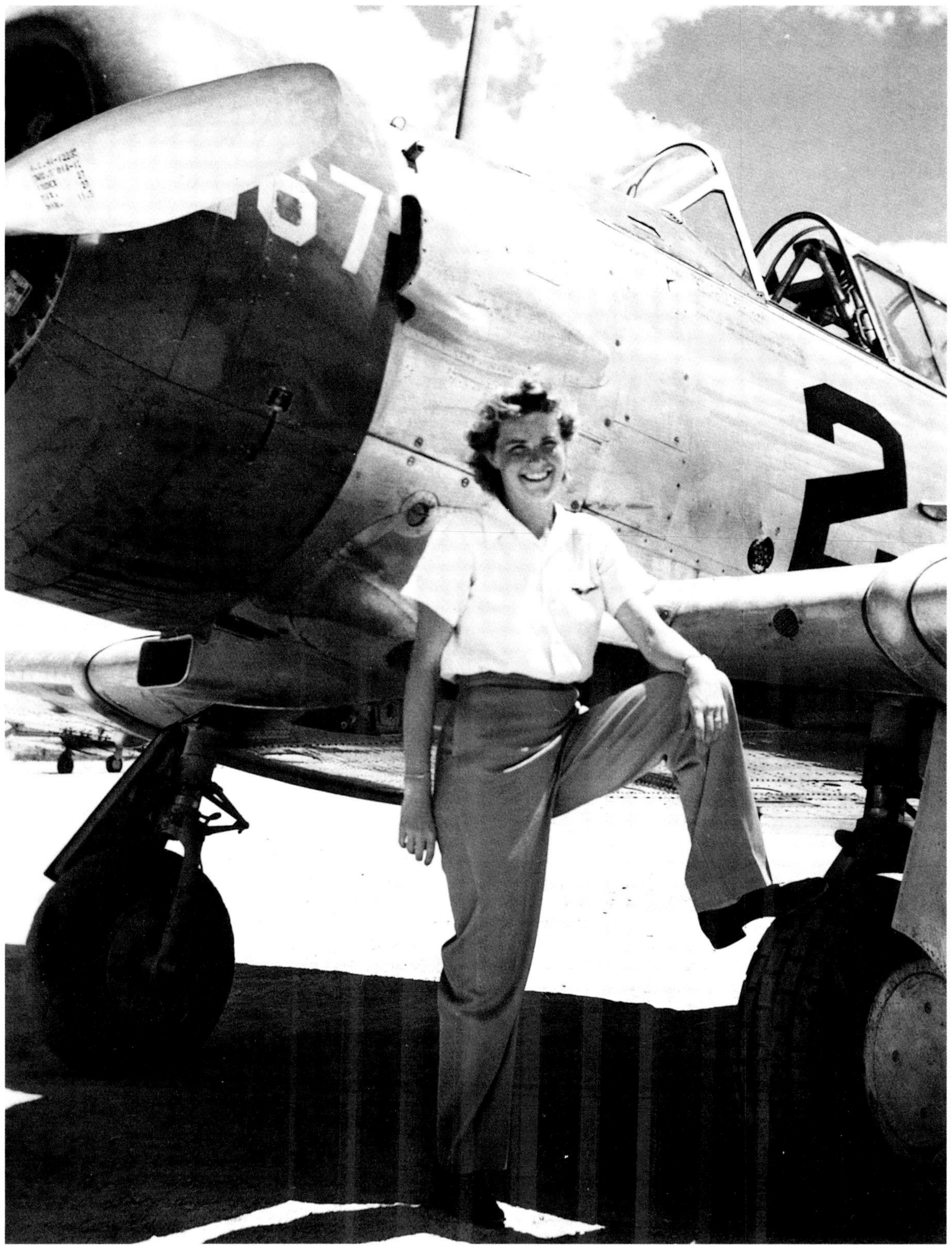

ground school, too, which we couldn't understand. But we wore them. The only reason I know that is that I have pictures of us in ground school with these horrible turbans on. Another reason I hate hats, I guess."

Santiago Blues

Jackie Cochran found a designer who put together a uniform that was gorgeous. She hired a professional model and showed General Arnold and the others in charge her uniform. They approved the design and finally the WASPs had an official uniform and wings.

Vivian (Hicks) Fagan: "The first time we got to wear our uniforms was on our long solo cross-country so we all looked forward to that. They were nice uniforms, a nice blue, tailor-made, well-fitted. We had a variety of pieces, the battle jacket and the dress jacket and the slacks and the skirt, but we all wore Zoot Suits during training, the discarded coveralls, and none of them fit. I was tall, so the Zoot Suit almost fit me, but some of the short girls were rolling up pants legs and arms. Then we wore beige pants and white shirts for ground school.

"We had to buy our own uniforms. We paid our own way out and our way back home afterwards as well. After we graduated and were stationed, we paid room and board out of our paychecks, but at least we were getting something. Remember we were Civil Service then."

WASP trainee Mary Shaw was injured in November of 1944. She was acting as a safety pilot for a student who was learning to fly on instruments. They crashed on take-off and both the women were seriously injured. Mary's leg was so badly damaged that she would walk with a limp for a very long time after her accident. Her brother saw that she was having a hard time in town. He thought that part of her problem was that she had no uniform to help signify that she had been injured in the service of her country. He felt that although she hadn't graduated and won her uniform, being permitted to wear one would help her keep her head up and speed her recovery, so he wrote to Jackie Cochran. She sent a Santiago blue WASP uniform to the hospital for Shaw.

Wings

The other thing every pilot needs on his or her uniform is wings. Jackie Cochran had to pay for regular engraved wings for the first seven classes. The eighth class was supposed to get wings from the Army, but they didn't arrive and once again, Cochran purchased them. This time instead of the shield being engraved, it was cut away and a diamond or lozenge was added. The rest of the classes received the official WASP wings. The diamond-shaped shield on the wings was chosen because it represents the shield carried by Athena, goddess of war and protector of the brave and valorous.

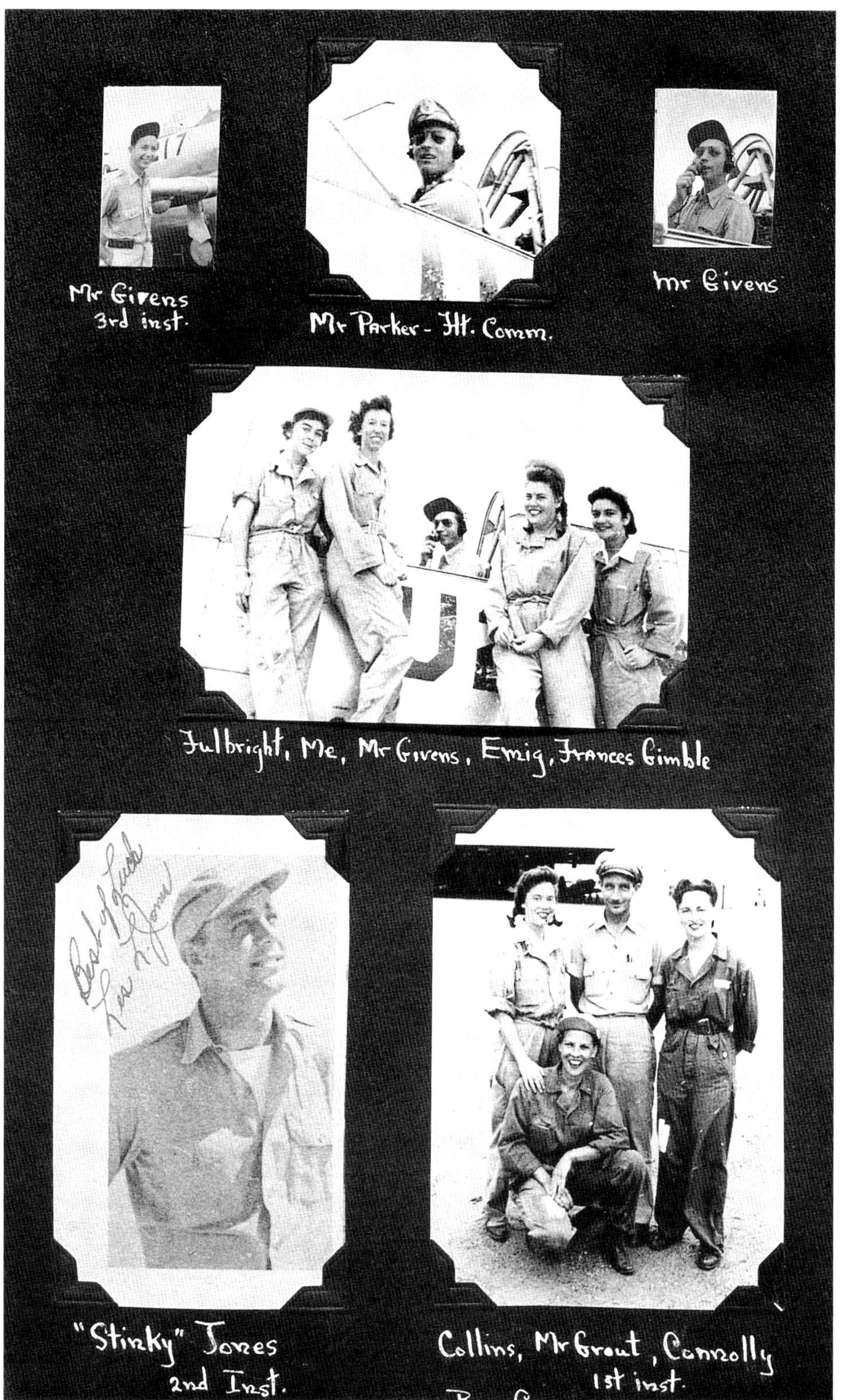

Though they were technically civilians, the WASPs had to march and endure inspections just like the male cadets. *Jeanne Robertson; Vivian Fagan.* Right, lunch in the WASP trainees' mess hall. Left side of table, from left: WASP Madelyn (Sullivan) O'Donnell, General "Hap" Arnold, Jackie Cochran, and Lieutenant General Barton K. Yount. WASP Susan Clarke peers into the camera from the right side of the table. *Special Collections, Texas Woman's University*

Jackie Cochran was a whiz at getting things done. She was also a master at organization. She had to be—her worries for the program were many. She worried about the wings and about designing a proper uniform but also about the moral image of the WASPs. She worried about trying to get the salary situation straightened out, acquiring insurance, death benefits, rank, veteran's benefits, and adequate medical and dental care. She needed to figure out the best way to discipline and discharge misbehaving WASPs. Then, once the women had successfully completed their training phase, she had to figure out which bases they would be sent to, how they would be treated there, where they would be housed, and how she could get all the bases to conform to standard Army Air Forces regulations and not just arbitrarily ground the WASPs, as was happening at Love Field in Dallas. She was also working on the issue of militarization for the WASPs. While she was working on all of these issues and a hundred other ones, her health was deteriorating; she had an intestinal obstruction that was causing her pain.

The "Relief" Tube

The one problem that Cochran was not working on, however, was the problem of waste management. Where were the ladies to tinkle when they were up in those planes on long missions?

Rita (Davoly) Webster found out how the gentlemen took care of business: "They had a relief tube. At least one person in each bay questioned what this tube was in the cockpit. The instructor was always too embarrassed to tell her. When she would find out she would come back and say, 'Now, whatever you do, don't ask what that thing is, on the side, because this is what it is.'

"If we're sitting there piloting, how were we going to get our pants down? So it wouldn't work for us at all. I think nature really played a dirty trick on women."

Most of the women learned to not drink anything before a long flight, especially not coffee or tea. The ground crews at various fields learned that when a WASP was bringing in an airplane, they had to let her make a beeline for the nearest facility.

Jeanne (Bennett) Robertson said she tried to use the relief tube once. She snaked the tube up her pants leg but it proved too short. So she scrunched down in her seat to try to get closer. It still didn't work. She said she was just glad that nobody was flying around her to see her plane going all over the sky.

Opal Vivian "Hicksie" (Hicks) Fagan, Class 44-W-7, in front of a Stearman trainer. "Having a nice day."
Vivian Fagan

The following memo was dated October 8, 1943. It was on North American Aviation letterhead and was addressed to the Commanding General of the Army Air Forces Materiel Command:

It's really beyond the Contractor's belief
That nothing's been done for the female relief;
A pot or privy or bedpan or such
Would not make a C.G. differential of much,
And it's really a most ungracious demand
On the unrelieved women of the Ferrying Command.

The Contractor proposes a circular basin
In accord with the pertinent specification.
The suggested design provides comfort and ease
And can quickly be stowed wherever you please.
Since privacy counts when the "unrelieved" goes,
The Station shouldn't be in the Plexiglas nose.

The Contractor foresees that considerable abuse
Could be made of this item right after its use.
So in addition to heating, the Contractor provides
An A-2 release to dump its insides.
When the bomb bay is open and P.D.I. lit,

The Bombardier switches a switch and that's it.

The circuit is made, the bomb latches displace,
And the basin and all sail out into space,
If the bombardier's sharp, down, down, it caroms,
With results more "offensive" than 1000lb bombs.
So, from this point of view 'tis the Contractor's belief
That this unit's designed for much more than relief.

The reply is dated October 12, 1943:

Materiel Command has received the suggestion
Eliminating female pilots' congestion.
The design is approved and so is the heating
But requests further study to provide for the seating
Of pilots who are a bit broad in the beam
That is to say, not as small as they seem.

Perchance an adjustment or two can be made
To give satisfaction, also first aid,
Consider this deal in the class of red hot
And enable the pilots to get on the pot.

Please finish the thing so as to make it attractive,
If possible make the affair retroactive,
At least let us know when the change point is found
So the gals get relief when not on the ground.

As for pitching the works out the bomb bay,
This would really be hard on the poor USA,
Since the gals fly all over the country, Good Grief!
Would you like to get hit with someone's relief?

Thank NAA for setting the pace
The Ferrying Gals get relief now with grace,
The change order'll follow as soon as we've seen
Your cost quotation on the flying latrine.

Needless to say, no one at Army Air Forces Materiel Command took this memo seriously, and nothing was done to relieve the situation, or the girls.

Learning to Fly

The following are stories about training experiences.

Jeanne (Bennett) Robertson: "The training was very thorough. We went into a primary trainer, a PT-19A, which was an open cockpit. Then a BT-13 Vultee Vibrator and then the AT-6, which was used by both the Army and the Navy. It was a honey, it was built by North American Aviation, and it was just a nice flying airplane. Then we flew the AT-17. That was a Cessna twin engine, more like a large Piper Cub."

"Micky" (Tuttle) Axton: "When I was sitting on the flight line waiting to fly at night, two girls came in and stalled and crashed, and the plane exploded and burned. We were so upset at the time. And yet our instructors made all of us fly that night. And it was really hard. But it was the right thing to do."

Alyce (Stevens) Rohrer: "I loved night flying. It's very beautiful up there at night when the moon and the stars are out. You can see all the lights twinkling on the ground; it's gorgeous. And the exhaust streaming out of the ship, just flying in lazy circles. I heard music. Orchestra, full orchestra: drums, cymbals, and wind instruments, even my long-neglected piano. Nobody believes me, but it was for real."

Jeanne (Bennett) Robertson: "One of the things I liked the least was when we had to do night flying and we

WASP trainees wearing their Zoot Suits and turbans. ***Vivian Fagan and Jeanne Robertson.*** **Previous page, WASPs Mary (Koth) McCabe and Harriet Kenyon stand in line for chow in the mess hall at Avenger Field. Brains and eggs for breakfast? Spam for lunch and dinner. Um, um, good!** ***USAF (neg. no. 36487 AC)***

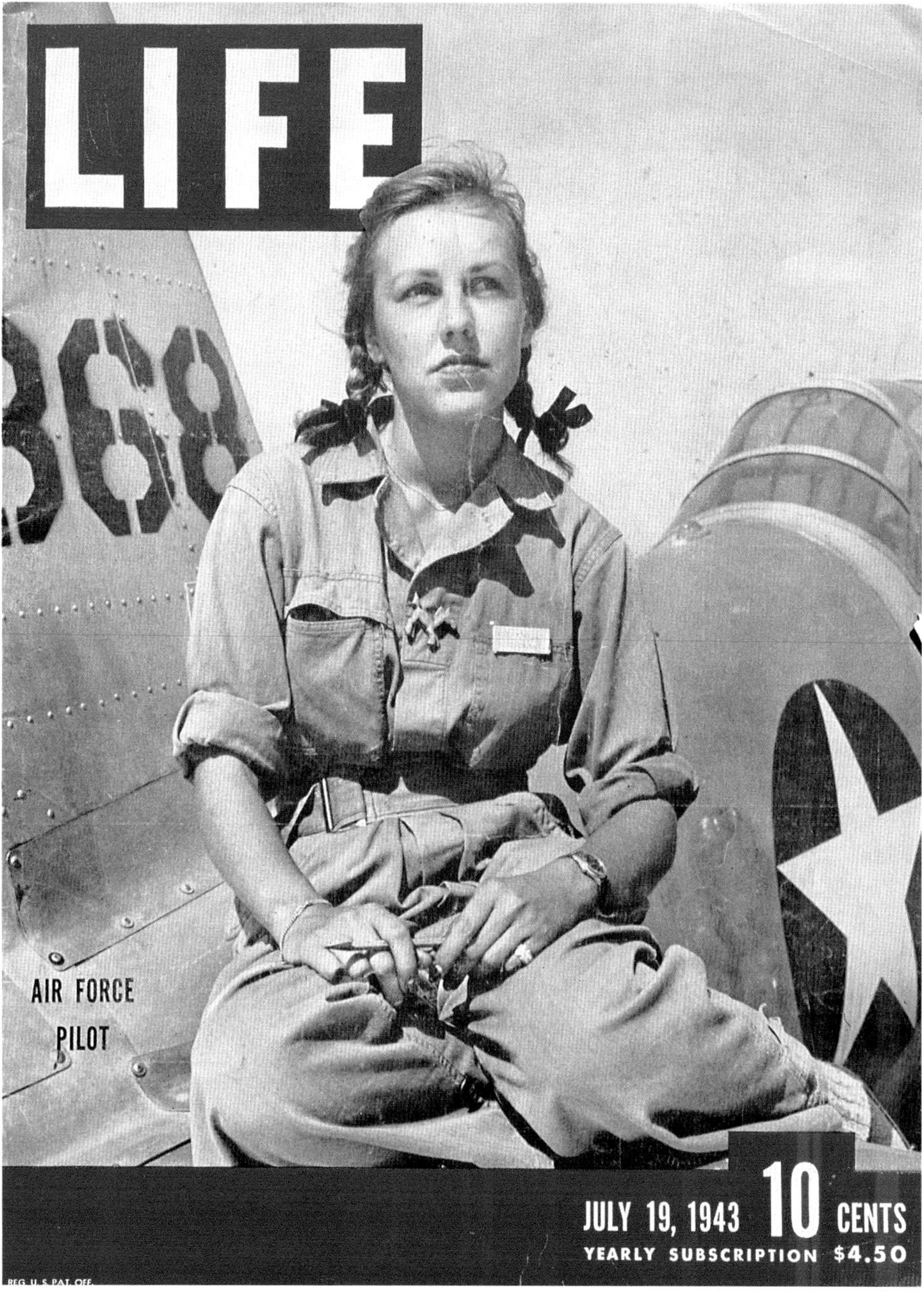

Shirley Slade on the cover of *Life* magazine. *Life Magazine, July 19, 1943*

were stacked up over the airport. They had divided the airport into four quadrants, and they would assign us a quadrant and an elevation so there would be airplanes at 5,000, 6,000, and 7,000 feet in this one quadrant. We just circled in that quadrant. Then we would have to go in and make a landing; a touchdown and takeoff, and go back to our place and keep continuously circling.

"That was kind of hairy because night flying is a tricky thing to begin with. We weren't on instruments, we had Link Trainer time, but none of us were qualified for instrument flying. You lose your horizon line very easily, and you distrust what your instruments are telling you.

"One of the girls flew in one night with her instructor, and they crashed. There were a few girls killed in training."

Florence (Emig) Wheeler: "I had had night flying experience, as I recall. And I loved it. My cross-country night flight was out to Midland, Texas, and at that time they burned the gas off the oil wells, and I was up five or six thousand feet and could read my map by the light of those oil wells. I never have forgotten that. Night flying is fun and beautiful."

"Cappy" Morrison: "I went up night flying, illegally, for the first time with a friend. I was scheduled way down on the list, and it seemed everybody had gone up except me, and so when one of my bay mates went up, she offered to let me sneak in with her. I went out with her to check the plane, and I never came back, I just crawled in. When she took off and landed I had to duck down. I couldn't let anybody see there was another body in the back. But that was sort of fun.

"They did not have an altitude chamber for us at Sweetwater, and so we flew down to San Antonio. We flew down in Stearmans, and that's one of the few times we got to fly with one of our contemporaries. Normally we flew with an instructor or by ourselves. So anyway we were flying down together and showing off for each other. They had told us that the first field where we were to land and get gas was a basic training [the intermediate level of flight training] school. We saw all these other little Stearmans out, so we thought, Good, let's play for a while! So we bounced those Stearmans and scattered them all over the sky. When we landed, we found out that it was a primary [beginners] school, and the Stearmans had been flown by novice male cadet students out there with their instructors. So we were kind of in trouble."

Rita (Davoly) Webster: "I don't know whether I had a mental block or whether my night vision wasn't really all that good. We shot I don't how many landings, and then my instructor said, 'Bring the plane to the line.' I came in, and he said, 'You take it up by yourself.' I said, 'Who, me? Oh, I'm not ready for that.' He said, 'Yes, you are.' I said, 'Oh, no. I think you better go around the circle a few more times.' 'Oh, no, you're fine,' he said.

"In the meantime, he was getting out. I said, 'Why don't you go around with me one more time?' 'No,' he said, and I just panicked. I said, 'You know, if something happens to me, my blood is going to be on your head.' But he kept on going.

"I just didn't think I could do it. So I sat there and tried to figure out what I was going to do next. Then the tower came in. She called my number and said, 'Are you parked or are you going to take her up again?' I said, 'Well, maybe I *can* do it.' I think I had to shoot three landings.

"And so I took off and went around and did my landing, and everything was fine. I came around again, and as I came in for the second landing—I hadn't touched down yet—the plane taking off ahead of me hit the high-tension lines at the end of the runway. There was this flash and every single light on that field went out. It was just like there was nothing there. It was an overcast sky. There was no moon. It just wasn't there. And of course the radio went out. Everything went out.

"I thought, My God, what am I going to do now? And then, Well, I just gotta keep my head in gear. So I did what I was supposed to do. When you take off, you keep looking back to make sure you're nice and straight. Well, there was no way to check that. So I thought, Well, I'll just keep going as straight as I can. And when I thought I was supposed to, I made the turn and I was coming around and there was really no way to guide myself. I was just floating in that air. There were many other airplanes in the air with me. It seemed like I saw navigation lights everywhere, and I was just so scared.

"Eventually a voice came on the radio. One of the instructors, of course, was up there, and he switched the radio to broadcast. He said, 'Anybody that's in the air, just keep flying the flight pattern and be careful of running into everybody else. Keep your height.' Well, I don't know how many times we went around before they began putting smudge pots up and down the runway.

"Finally the tower came on; I guess they had a generator or something. Then they put us all in a holding pattern. I swear, I was in the fourth quadrant, the very highest level, and I was up there circling forever. I was still scared to death. Then I thought, I'm going to run out of gas. And believe it or not, this thought crossed my mind: You know you could put an end to all this. You're going to spin in sooner or later, so why don't you just push the nose down and get it over with? But I didn't. I swore that if I ever got on the ground again, I would never go near an airplane. Finally, I just pulled in, landed, parked the plane, and got out.

"I began thinking of the gal that hit the high-tension line. I walked into the ready room, and there's my instructor sitting on the table, smoking a cigarette, acting nonchalant. So I said, 'Who hit the high-tension line?' 'Oh,' he said, 'were you up there?' I said, 'Of course I was up there. Who hit the high-tension line?' He said, 'Nobody.' I said, 'Of course they did. I was right behind her, and I could see that.' He said, 'Nobody hit the high-tension line.' He said, 'Everybody's accounted for.' I said, 'That's impossible.'

Official wings for the WASPs. The diamond or lozenge in the middle was to represent the shield of Athena, goddess of war and wisdom. *Hans Halberstadt.* Left, an officer's shield. WASPs wore this shield on their Berets. *Hans Halberstadt.* Below, the wishing well at Avenger Field was a center for many traditions. One tradition was to toss in a coin at graduation, for a check flight, or just to make a wish. *"Dottie" Davis*

"I went trudging home and decided I was not going to go on any more. I decided that I'd go back to the bay. This was about two or three o'clock in the morning. I decided that I would pack in the morning and leave. Everybody was sound asleep, so I slept. The next morning I woke up and the sky was blue, and the planes were all in a

"Micky" (Tuttle) Axton, May 1943. *"Micky" Axton*

"When I was sitting on the flight line waiting to fly at night, two girls came in and stalled and crashed, and the plane exploded and burned. We were so upset at the time. And yet our instructors made all of us fly that night. And it was really hard. But it was the right thing to do."

—"Micky" (Tuttle) Axton, Class 43-W-7

line. They were so beautiful. So I thought, What the heck; if that ever happens again, I won't be nearly as frightened.

"It turned out that it wasn't until bed check that they found out that this gal, I think her name was Margaret Lowell-Wallace (she was a concert violinist from New York), was missing. So they sent out a search party to look for her. It turned out that she had landed right across the highway. She didn't know where she was, so she just sat there all night 'til the next morning. And she didn't have a scratch. Even her Ray Ban sunglasses, were unbroken in her pocket. From then on she was nicknamed 'Lucky.'

"I'm glad I had that experience because I did have to fly at night after that. One evening I had to fly this young officer somewhere. Fortunately the moon was so bright that the ground was just like daylight. We got in, and I was very circumspect, with 'Yes, sir' and 'No, sir' and all that.

"I was flying along, you know, and here he changes the frequency on the radio and this wonderful dance music came on. And so he said, 'Isn't that nice music?' And I said, 'It's just wonderful.' He said, 'It's a beautiful night, isn't it?' And I said, 'Yes.' And this went back and forth, you know. And he said, 'It's too bad that this is a tandem airplane.' And I said, 'No comment.' That really was a very nice flight, you know. I don't remember his name, and I never even saw him again. It was really a beautiful night. And I thought at the time, What a difference in night flying experiences."

A little Different from the Norm

The kind of women who learned to fly in the 1930s and 1940s had to be a little different from the norm.

Rita (Davoly) Webster: "You meet people and they say, 'Ooh! You were a pilot!' and to themselves they're thinking, I bet she was pretty fast. Back when I first started working, people were not accustomed to women working, and so nurses were considered fast because they knew everything, and hairdressers were considered fast. And waitresses, well you knew waitresses! When I had my first job as a secretary I remember my mother saying, 'I hope you're not going to be like those secretaries who sit on the boss' lap.' We had some whose morals were a little loose, and we had some lesbians there—we didn't even know the term then—but mostly I think the gals were very shy and retiring. I'm not so sure about my bay mate, Carol Webb. She had been married before and that makes a difference. But most of us were probably virgins—not all but most.

"We were a cross section of the population of that time and the percentage of fast girls was very low. In my class there were two of what we used to call 'tomboys' that graduated—they probably didn't even know they were homosexuals.

"There were many girls that didn't strike you as being the type to learn to fly. Physically, there were a couple that were really small. Maurine [(Brunsvold) Wilson] was a very small person and she had to carry four cushions beside her parachute when she flew. She would walk out to her plane with her instructor, and Carol would say, 'Wouldn't you think he would pick up a couple of those pillows and carry them for her?' But he never did. She was a good pilot. She entered several powder puff derbies after the WASPs."

The Instructors

The instructors were a diverse group. Some had respect and affection for the women, some didn't.

"Rig" Edwards was one of the Avenger instructors: "In my opinion we had the cream of the crop of the women because there were over 25,000 who applied and there were only 1,830 that were accepted. They really screened them out.

"A lot of the women who came here at first had a lot of flying hours. A lot of them could outfly their instructors. They had so many hours and were so good at flying."

After instructing the women for a while, Edwards came to the conclusion that they reacted to the excitement of flying just the same way men do—some were unnerved by unexpected events and some used them as learning experiences.

For example, Florence (Emig) Wheeler had about 1,500 hours when she entered the WASP training program. Although she had many more hours of experience than her instructor, she had total confidence in him. He asked her to do an outside loop in a Stearman. Although she had never done one and had no idea whether the airplane would hang together, she had confidence that if her instructor told her that both she and the airplane were up to it, she could complete the move. She admits if she thought about it today, she would have said, "No way!"

Marjory (Foster) Munn, Class 44-W-5: "My night-flying instructor was the kind who flew by the seat of his pants. He was kind of wiry and rough around the edges, but he was respectful. Looking back on how they ran the school, it must have been very difficult for them because here we were as civilians under the direction of other civilians, and then the Army was there with its control. It was an interesting experience, an experiment. I don't think they'd do it again."

Muriel (Rath) Reynolds, Class 44-W-7: "At the end of training I had to test a PT-17, a Stearman, and do short-field landings. So I got in the airplane and here was this 'Robert Taylor' type. He was a lieutenant, with his goggles and his helmet and his scarf, six foot two inches, mustache, and very handsome. We get in and get up in the air and he wants to know where we're supposed to go. I said, 'I didn't know.' I thought he would know, since he was a military man and had taught the other check pilots.

"Meanwhile, there were great big black clouds coming down. We fly and we fly, and it's only a little tiny field that we're trying to find. Finally, we see the rest of our group on the field, all looking skyward, fifty people looking up. They are all waiting because they can't leave until we get in.

"He takes over because, of course, he's going to land this airplane—never mind that there is a stick in the back and I'm supposed to be learning. He's already embarrassed because everybody was wondering where we had been, so he strides out, stands on the wing, and does the unforgivable: He takes off his parachute and throws it on the ground, symbolically blaming me for getting lost. That was that; he went home with somebody else."

"Another day I was not feeling well, but they said, 'Hey you, get up, get up. They are waiting for you on the flight line.' There was this decorated captain, a war hero, waiting to check my crosswind landings. I wasn't feeling well and forgot my seat cushions. These were a big help

Graduation portrait of Vivian (Hicks) Fagan in her Santiago Blues. In February 1944, the WASPs were finally issued Santiago Blue uniforms. The uniform consisted of two jacket styles (one an "Eisenhower" style), a skirt and trousers, a beret, silver wings, and a trench coat. The girls were required to purchase shirts (white and blue cotton and blue flannel), some black neckties, gloves, shoes, and a handbag. *Vivian Fagan.* Below, the WASPs were really loaded down, especially in winter. They had to carry heavy parachutes, some had to carry cushions (as many as four) to get themselves high enough in the seat to see out. Some also carried blocks for their feet so that they could reach the pedals. Scrambling up into those cockpits was reason enough for the girls to do their calisthenics. *Jeanne Robertson*

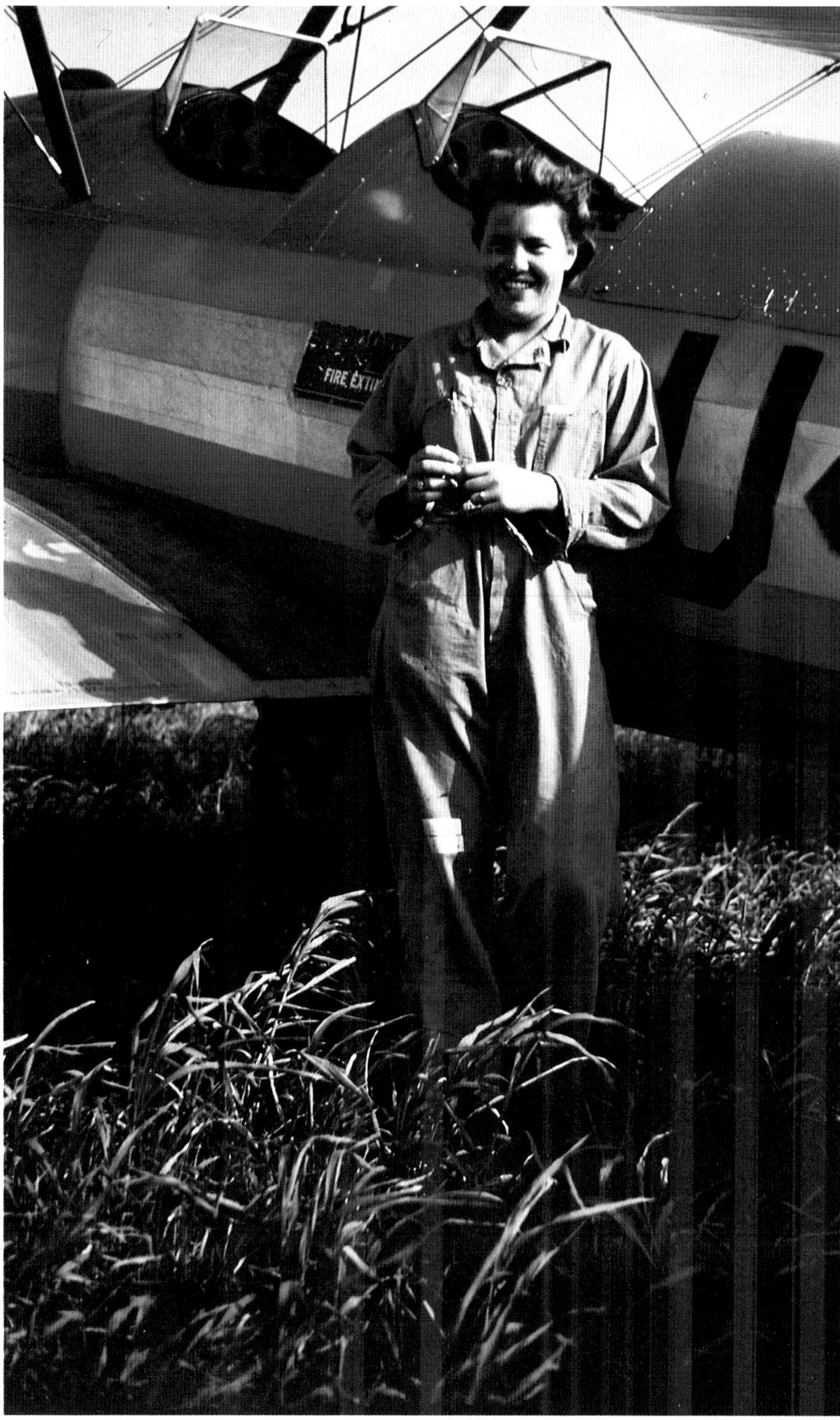

because my legs were too short. So I got in, and of course I groundlooped the plane.

"On the way in, in a very nice way, forgetting that all these other people had been watching this mistake, he says, 'Show me what was happening. You were on the controls as fast as I was.' He was such a gentleman. He didn't criticize me for groundlooping, he was concerned about correcting the situation, not saving himself embarrassment."

"Cappy" Morrison: "Different instructors had different personalities. I had for about an hour, oddly enough, an instructor I had had as a civilian. He was an old barnstorming type guy, and he hated goggles. We flew in an open cockpit, and he could hardly see. He got mad because they told him he had to have those goggles on in military flying. He would chuck 'em up on top of his head as soon as he got off the ground.

"Then I had this marvelous man whose named was F-U-C-H-S. Everybody looked at him when he came in, and he said [deep, serious voice], 'It's pronounced *Fox*.' He was just a very wonderful man. He thought women could fly, and he knew he could teach 'em. Not all of the instructors thought that way.

"There was one instructor of some of my bay mates who was particularly cruel. When he didn't like what they did, he'd take the stick and bash it back and forth. They couldn't very well get their legs out of the way in the cramped confines of the cockpit, so they would come back to the bay with their knees black and blue.

"One of the girls in our class was washed out at the last minute by a little old guy who was shorter than I am. He looked at her and said, 'I think you're too short to fly that airplane. Come with me.' And right out of the blue, he took her up for a check ride. Of course she was petrified, and she flunked it. They washed her out with two weeks until graduation."

"Rig" Edwards: "I nearly lost a girl one time. This was our last flight, and we went up to do acrobatics. While we were up, I asked her to do a slow roll, and she did a snap roll. I said, 'No, I want you to do a slow roll.' She indicated to me that she wanted me to show her a slow roll. So I went into the slow roll. When we were inverted, I felt the stick pop. I looked back, and she was hanging out of the airplane. She was holding on to the wind screen and her feet were straight out (this was an open cockpit plane). She wore long braided pigtails, and those pigtails were flying in the air. That scared the hell out of me, but I just let the airplane keep rolling until she was settled down in her seat. I thought she had forgotten to buckle her seat belt, but she held up her seat belt and showed me that the catch was done up. The mechanics had failed to secure the belt to the seat. Anyway, that's an experience she remembered and I remember!"

The instructors also put the WASP trainees through their paces in the Link Trainer, a forerunner of today's flight simulators. The student sat in a little, dark, hot box with no visual aids and only instruments and a radio connection to an instructor. The instructor would have the student practice maneuvers and the box would move around a little to simulate the moves the student would make.

Mary Jane (Lind) Sellers, Class 44-W-10: "I got into great conversations with my Link instructor who was a tall, dark, and handsome airman by name of Andy. Through our radio connection, he asked me for a date, and from then on until graduation we dated every weekend in Sweetwater. Since we students were forbidden to date any instructors and could be washed out for doing so, I spent many a Saturday and Sunday night squeaking by the twelve o'clock curfew."

After Link training, the women had to move on to flying an airplane "under the hood" to simulate flying on instruments only, during bad weather or at night. The trainee sat in the front seat with an accordion-shaped hood pulled over her, so she wouldn't be able to see out. The person in the back was there to take control of the plane in case of an emergency.

Alyce (Stevens) Rohrer: "I think I was flying with Doris Tanner, and I remember we were coming in for a landing. She shook the stick and took over, zooming out of the pattern. That was disturbing because I had all my instruments lined up. It was scary, but then when I peeked out and saw what was happening, I was glad to get out of there. There were five other ships, one on the ground, three lined up behind us, and another one coming in from the side. That was what the 'shotgun gal' was supposed to do, watch out for things."

No matter how good the training or the pilot, accidents did happen. Mary Hausen was killed while landing after a cross-country flight. Hausen was coming in to land when another girl, on one of her first solos, was coming in for a landing at the same angle. The two aircraft collided, and Hausen was killed. The other pilot was inexperienced, and so was not blamed.

These things happened more often on the male cadet bases than they did on the WASP bases. The difference was that because the women were Civil Service employees, there was no money allocated for life insurance, or for a coffin. Often the women would take up a collection and would pay to have the body shipped back to the family with one of them as escort.

The Wishing Well

There were a lot of traditions to help the girls get through the hard times. The wishing well played a role in two of these. When a trainee was going up for a check ride she would throw a coin into the well for luck. When a trainee soloed for the first time, she was thrown in and could retrieve her coin if she so desired.

"Maggie" Gee: "I said thank God when I got tossed in the wishing well. If I hadn't gotten tossed in the wishing well, that would mean I was washed out, sent home. Oh, yeah, it was so exciting—just toss me in again. I think we all had pictures of ourselves coming out, with our hair all wet."

Sweetwater Snakes and other Critters

One of the appropriate hardships that WASPs had to put up with were critters. Four-legged, six-legged, eight-legged, and especially no-legged.

Sweetwater is the rattlesnake capitol of the world. To this day they have the annual rattlesnake round-up where they collect hundreds of snakes. Some of the girls were pretty terrified by snakes.

One trainee was up with her instructor. He got her attention and told her to look out at her wing. She saw a two-foot-long snake crawling around on the wing, and then the wind caught the snake and whisked it off. Maybe he was trying to become a member of the Caterpillar Club. In order join this club you had to have the dubious distinction of having jumped out of a plane, lived to tell the tale, and showed everyone your D-Ring from pulling the rip cord.

Another trainee ended up joining the Caterpillar

Alex B. Lowery was "Dottie" Davis' first instructor. His photo is saved in her scrapbook. *"Dottie" Davis.* Previous page, WASP trainee Florence (Emig) Wheeler, one of the few WASPs who loved night flying. *Florence Wheeler*

"My cross-country night flight was out to Midland, Texas, and at that time they burned the gas off the oil wells, and I was up five or six thousand feet and could read my map by the light of those oil wells. I never have forgotten that. Night flying is fun and beautiful."

—Florence (Emig) Wheeler, Class 44-W-6

203

Club while on an instruction flight. Her instructor noticed that the plane was on fire and ordered her to bail out. She successfully completed her jump from the plane but was terrified of the snakes. She landed in a field pretty close to Avenger. She sat down with her chute spread out around her and would not budge. She figured somebody would come get her, and she wasn't going to walk across that field with those snakes.

Vivian (Hicks) Fagan: "I never saw any snakes but I was stung by a scorpion once. One morning, during ground school, I was putting on my beige pants. One had gotten inside the pants leg and stung me on the lower hip. It's a very sharp sting, and I threw off the pants, and the scorpion tried to get away. We'd heard that it could be fatal, so we went over to the hospital. The nurse said not to worry because they were not fatal at that time of year. That gave me a lot of encouragement, but the sting did swell. When I came back to the bay, one of my bay mates had a little sign outside that said, 'Ten cents to see the scorpion that stung Hixie.' In the bay she had a little jar with the scorpion inside. She commercialized on my hard luck!

"Then, the locust infestation was terrible. I had never seen them before, but when they started coming it was like a black cloud on the horizon. They invaded the entire base for about two days. We couldn't sleep. We were picking them out of our hair. We'd cover up, but they'd be down under the covers with us. They were so thick on the flight line that you would actually skid on them. It was a mess. That was a terrible experience."

"Dot" (Swain) Lewis: "I found a little dog out in the cornfield one night and we called him 'Little Off Course,' because we were studying off-course problems. We bathed him and had a good time with this nice little dog. A couple of weeks later he was found dead on the porch by our house mother who had him checked for rabies.

"It turns out the little dog had died of rabies and a couple of us had several scratches. So we had to take the rabies shots. They were real painful. We went into town every morning at ten o'clock for fourteen days to get a shot in the stomach. They were big needles, but it wasn't too terrible. I was healthy. But after my seventh one, everyone of those original shots swelled up to the size of a fist. I couldn't even fasten my pants, and I was not very well. Every shot after that was painful, and I had a reaction, so some days I didn't fly.

"I went down for my last shot, my fourteenth, with my house mother. After I had gotten it, she said, 'You're through now; we're going to stop by the Key Club and have a drink.' So we went in there and I had some awful drink, scotch I think. (People had to have their own bottles, and that was her bottle.) So we had this drink, and I was just sure I was dead drunk.

An instructor poses by a Stearman. ***Florence Wheeler.*** **Previous page, Wilda Winfield, Class 44-W-8, on a photographic mission. Someone's not wearing her turban!** ***USAF (neg. no. 121648 AC)***

"We went back to the field, and there was a message to get down to the airport. The inspector was there to give me my flight test. I still couldn't close my pants, I hadn't flown in a while, and I was sure I was drunk, but I had to go. Up we went, and I yawned a little and was totally calm with him in the back seat. I was the only one that passed. That was the best lesson I ever had 'cause I was really relaxed. If you tense up, you can't fly."

Inspections and Demerits

Even though the girls were not officially in the Army Air Forces, military inspections were part of daily life at Avenger Field.

Florence (Emig) Wheeler: "Saturday morning inspection—they'd come around and we'd stand at attention. One time I got a demerit 'cause my shoes were out of line. They'd go along with white gloves to see if there was any dust or water in the sink.

"One girl by the name of Patricia [(Jones) Perry] had beautiful red hair and when they would open the hatch, her hair would go out like in a convertible. Her instructor said, 'We can't have that.' So she was responsible for us having to wear these horrible flight turbans."

—Gene (Shaffer) FitzPatrick Class 44-W-1

AVENGER FIEL
U.S. ARMY-PT-19A
AIR FORCE SERIAL NO 42-3
CREW WEIGHT 400LBS
FIRE EXTINGUISHER

"We had two rows of bays. The inspectors would start down one side and go across and come up the other side. Sometimes, the girls on that end would time it so that they would be ready by the time the inspectors had gotten to their side of the room. Well, one day the inspectors went the other way and caught these gals just as they were coming out of the shower."

"Cappy" Morrison: "We could actually get washed out with too many demerits if our towels were crooked or if we were stuck someplace we weren't supposed to be. Once a week we had to roll our mattresses. I learned to choose a mattress that rolled properly, over one that was comfortable. If I had a real junky mattress, I could roll it up and the ends would stay down. If it was a good mattress, then the ends would pop right out.

"These little bitty captains would stand up on chairs with white gloves; they would look for dust on our open beams."

Freezing and Roasting

Another part of the WASP trainees' daily life was suffering through the extremes of the Texas weather. They froze in winter, and they roasted in the summer. According to the February 10, 1943, *Fifinella Gazette,*

Ida F. Carter and Ruth Craig Jones of Class 44-W-1 get instructions on flying from civilian instructor Frank Seay at Avenger Field, August 1943. *USAF (neg. no. B 36503 AC).* Below, this scrapbook page shows that not all the instructors were male. *"Dottie" Davis*

At the wishing well, WASP trainees throw in a coin at graduation. Left to right: Carol Fillmore, Alma (Jerman) Hinds, Betty (Eames) Joiner, Margaret (Kerr) Boylan, Jacqueline Cochran, Marie (Muccie) Genaro, unnamed officer, Rita (Moynahan) McArdle, Betty (Whitlow) Smith. *Jeanne Robertson.* Next page, WASP Ethel (Lytch) Miller, Class 44-W-10, gets instructions from Sergeant Charles Willard on operation of the Link Trainer at Avenger Field, July 1944. There were few trainees who enjoyed their time in the Link Trainer. *USAF (neg. no. A 36500 AC)*

"Anything can happen. Sleet at breakfast, dust at noon, the hot sweats by supper."

Alyce (Stevens) Rohrer: "I remember in midwinter, the gas mains broke, and our blankets weren't warm enough. We were freezing. We got up and put on all our winter gear that we flew in and then lay down under our blankets to get warm."

Rita (Davoly) Webster: "The barracks were built so that you never got a breeze either through the front door or through the back window. And it was stifling hot. It was so hot that when we were finished with dinner and came back to study, we would all sit around in our bras and panties. Well, we had a very, very sympathetic flight surgeon. Usually, whatever you asked for he would see that you got it. So, a couple of the gals complained about not being able to sleep. They asked permission to sleep outside. And he said yes. We pulled our cots out, but there were tarantulas and scorpions. So we had to get into bed and then tuck everything in so that nothing trailed on the ground."

Alyce (Stevens) Rohrer: "The lack of privacy was difficult. I was accustomed to being home, having my own room. Maybe we had miserable old siblings who intruded on our privacy now and then, but when you live six to a bay and share a bathroom with six on the other side, of course, the lack of privacy is almost complete. For some girls who were more sophisticated than we were, I supposed it didn't matter, but Smith [Flora (Smith) Reece], and Standefer [Frances (Standefer) Acker] and I were the three youngest in the group. We had all, I think, lied about our ages because we were only eighteen. We were supposed to be twenty-one, and we weren't very sophisticated. We didn't know anything. Sometimes when I think back, I wonder, God must take care of kids. We were out of our depth with a lot of the women who were in that program, but they were all kind to us, and we grew up fast.

"We became more sophisticated about the world when we saw the way the other women behaved, not that we took up any bad habits ourselves, but we began to accept them. There were some women who were quite women of the world. They would go out with men on the weekends. But we never did."

Blowing off Steam

Rita (Davoly) Webster: "We would go into town on Saturday night but you had to be back by twelve, and they'd close the gate if you weren't. There were high cyclone fences around the field. They called it 'Cochran's Convent' 'cause you couldn't get in or out.

"Well, anyhow, this one night, Maurine and I were sleeping outside, and Carol's bed was in the middle. It was after midnight, and Carol was not there. So we said, 'Well, what are we going to do?' So Maurine said, 'Let's get our pillows and fix them so that it looks like somebody's there.' So we did and covered it up, and they never could tell.

"And then this gal who was a pill, a real pain, came around with a little search light. I guess it looked funny, so she went up and pulled the blankets back. And she shook me. She said, 'Where's Carol?' I said, 'She's there.' 'She's not there,' she said, so she goes scooting back to get Deedee [Leoti 'Deedee' Deaton, the house mother]. I said, 'Oh my God, this is it.'

"Every once in a while, Carol would get into trouble, but she always managed to squeeze through. So we thought, This is it, she's really going to be washed out. Then, here comes Carol. And I said, 'Where'd you come from?' 'Oh,' she said, 'I had to climb over that fence.' 'How did you get over the fence?' I asked. 'Well,' she said, 'my date boosted me up, and I managed to get over.' And I said, 'Well, you better get in bed as fast as you can because Dee Dee's going to be here.' She started to take her clothes off, and I said, 'You don't have time for that.' So she took her shoes off and jumped right into bed and curled herself up. Seconds later, here they came. And I heard Elsie, 'Well, she wasn't there a little while ago. They had pillows in there.' So Deedee said, 'Well,

Throw in a coin to make a wish, throw in a trainee to celebrate a first solo. While you were in, you could fish out a coin. *"Dottie" Davis*

she's there now.' Carol was lucky she wasn't washed out."

"Maggie" Gee: "Of course, we went to the instructors' houses and partied. We would have to go out and get the booze. I really don't drink, but I remember we went down this road to a house, rang the doorbell. Some black man came to the door, and we told him what we wanted. He let us in and got a bottle—bathtub gin, I guess it was.

"Then we went to the party, and we were living it up a bit. Not really doing much—we weren't lying around naked or anything—just having a good time, that's all. The doorbell rings, and you should have seen everyone scamper out of sight. We got under every bed we could find. And it would turn out to be another trainee. It was hardly worth going to a party to be tossed out of training, but we did it, anyway."

Mary Jane (Lind) Sellers: "I remember late one summer afternoon, a tremendous dust storm blew in with high winds from the south. All student pilots who were practicing in the air were called down, the planes on the flight line were tied securely to their moorings, and we all went inside the hangars to sit it out over Cokes and cigarettes. Before long, a flight of many gliders with the planes towing them arrived at Avenger. They were brought in from the Gulf, where the storm was proving more severe, and the light gliders had to be kept from blowing away. Our base commander decided this was a special exception to the 'No Males Allowed' rule. He invited the visiting pilots to stay, opened the gymnasium for a dance, and fun was had by all."

The people of Sweetwater had started out concerned for the safety of their children, but they ended up having and showing great affection for "their WASPs." I was at a memorial dedication for the WASPs in Sweetwater in May 1993 and interviewed some of the townspeople. One woman I spoke with told me that she had been a waitress in the canteen. She once had to serve food to General "Hap" Arnold and was scared to death. But her real heroes were the trainees. She was sixteen and had really looked up to the women.

A number of political figures were at the memorial, including Janet Reno, attorney general of the United States, and Ann Richards, governor of Texas. The woman I spoke with said the real celebrities at the event were the WASPs. She was thrilled to be seeing some familiar, if a little older, faces and thrilled to have her WASPs back in Sweetwater.

Jeanne (Bennett) Robertson: "They were wonderful. Some of the people would entertain us on the weekend with a barbecue. Sweetwater is not much of a town, it was just a wide place in the road and now the highway goes around it. There was one hotel in town, The Blue Bonnet Hotel, which later burned down. The town consisted of about five stores and a YMCA. We were the one thing that happened to Sweetwater to make it different. They have a museum dedicated to us, and we've had two reunions there and we've had parades."

Gene (Shaffer) FitzPatrick: "One girl who was not even a teenager, she was nine or ten, lived in Sweetwater, and she would see all of us coming to town. We were her ideals because we all had good tans. She couldn't get over the jewelry that we wore. We came from all walks of life. We didn't think anything of the turquoise bracelets and all the good watches as being anything special. We had to have a watch, because we were flying.

"She had had a few setbacks in her life and she said she would think back to those girls who were flying those big airplanes, and how we had been an inspiration to her all along. We didn't even know the poor kid existed. She and her friends, all these ten-year-olds, had seen us around town. They would say, 'She can fly those big airplanes.' Now we're finding out these years later that they were looking up to us."

Getting Wings

After completing training, sometimes to their surprise, the big day would arrive. They would graduate and be awarded their wings.

"Maggie" Gee: "The first day is very exciting, just getting there, on the train and all. But the best day was getting your wings. Getting your wings wasn't easy. All around you, people were washing out and going home constantly. Half of the people you knew went home, and you wondered, Am I going to be next? When I get down to the flight line, am I going to be the one who's going to wash out next? So you really worked hard."

"Winnie" Wood: "I remember when I got my wings. I remember when they called my name, and it was Mrs. Yount, General Yount's wife who pinned my wings on. I remember Class W-8 was standing right below, and a friend of mine said, 'Yeah Winnie!' and that was a very proud day for a lot of us. It was also pretty special to see those ladies in the other classes parading for us."

"Cappy" Morrison: "I was in the last class. We were told that we couldn't have a class book because of wartime shortages. So, under cover, we came up with a class book because we felt that the last class should have one. We paid for everything ourselves. The printers had many of the standard shots that we could use. We had to borrow the upperclassmen's uniforms or at least a shirt and jacket. You'll notice some of us have wings on in our pictures, and some don't. Some people lent you their wings and some people didn't. You just borrowed a jacket and went down to the photographer and had your picture taken because the rest of it wasn't going to show."

Alyce (Stevens) Rohrer: "We studied together, cried together, fought together. By the time we got through, we were wrung out, and we had been through such a unique experience that after fifty years we're still close friends.

"What did we cry about? Our friends who washed out; instructors who swore at us and flew into rages when we made mistakes; the sand and the wind; and in the winter, the cold."

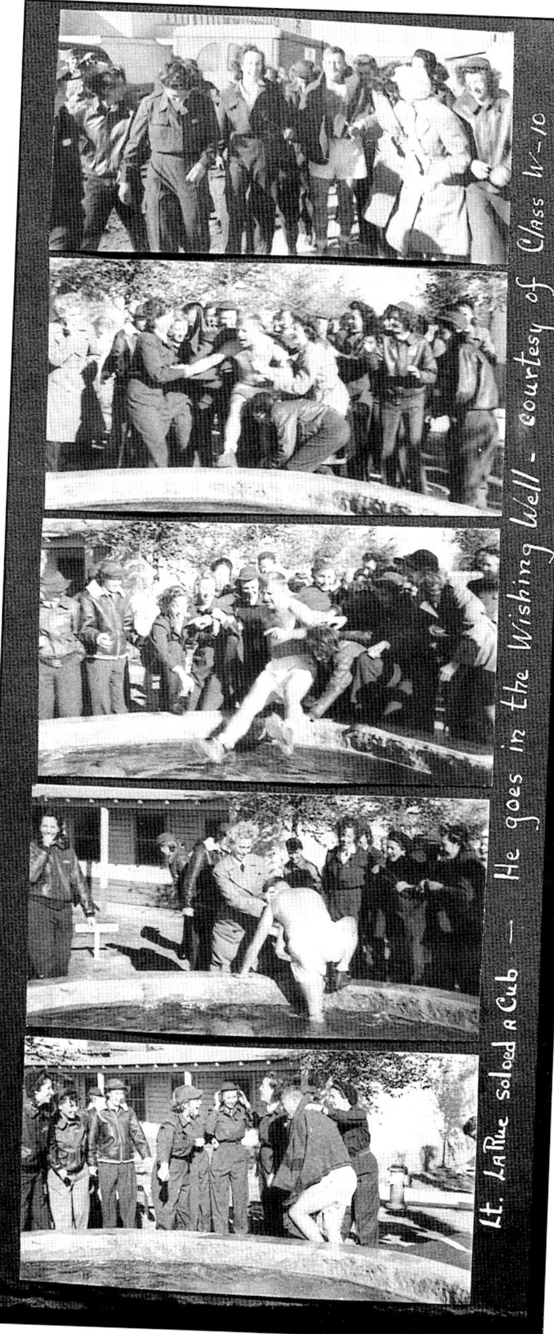
Lt. LaRue soloed a Cub — He goes in the Wishing Well - courtesy of Class W-10

It wasn't just the trainees who got tossed in, either. Here, Lieutenant LaRue, the calisthenics leader, gets tossed in the wishing well by members of Class 44-W-10. ***"Dottie" Davis***

"I said thank God when I got tossed in the wishing well. If I hadn't gotten tossed in the wishing well, that would mean I was washed out, sent home. Oh, yeah, it was so exciting—just toss me in again. I think we all had pictures of ourselves coming out, with our hair all wet."

—Margaret "Maggie" Gee, Class 44-W-9

— PRIMARY TRAINING —
Bay E-5
Dorothy Drobic - Juanita Dreier - Patricia Disston - me
Eleanor Collins - Ailsa Connolly

Sharing a bedroom and a bathroom, baymates became close friends and when one of them was "washed out" of the program, it was a tragedy for them all. *"Dottie" Davis*

"I would say to my roommate, 'Do you want to grab the phone book or do you hit the light tonight?' And when the light would go on, these cockroaches—a couple of inches big—would be all over the place."

—Katherine "Kay" (Menges) Brick, Class 43-W-3

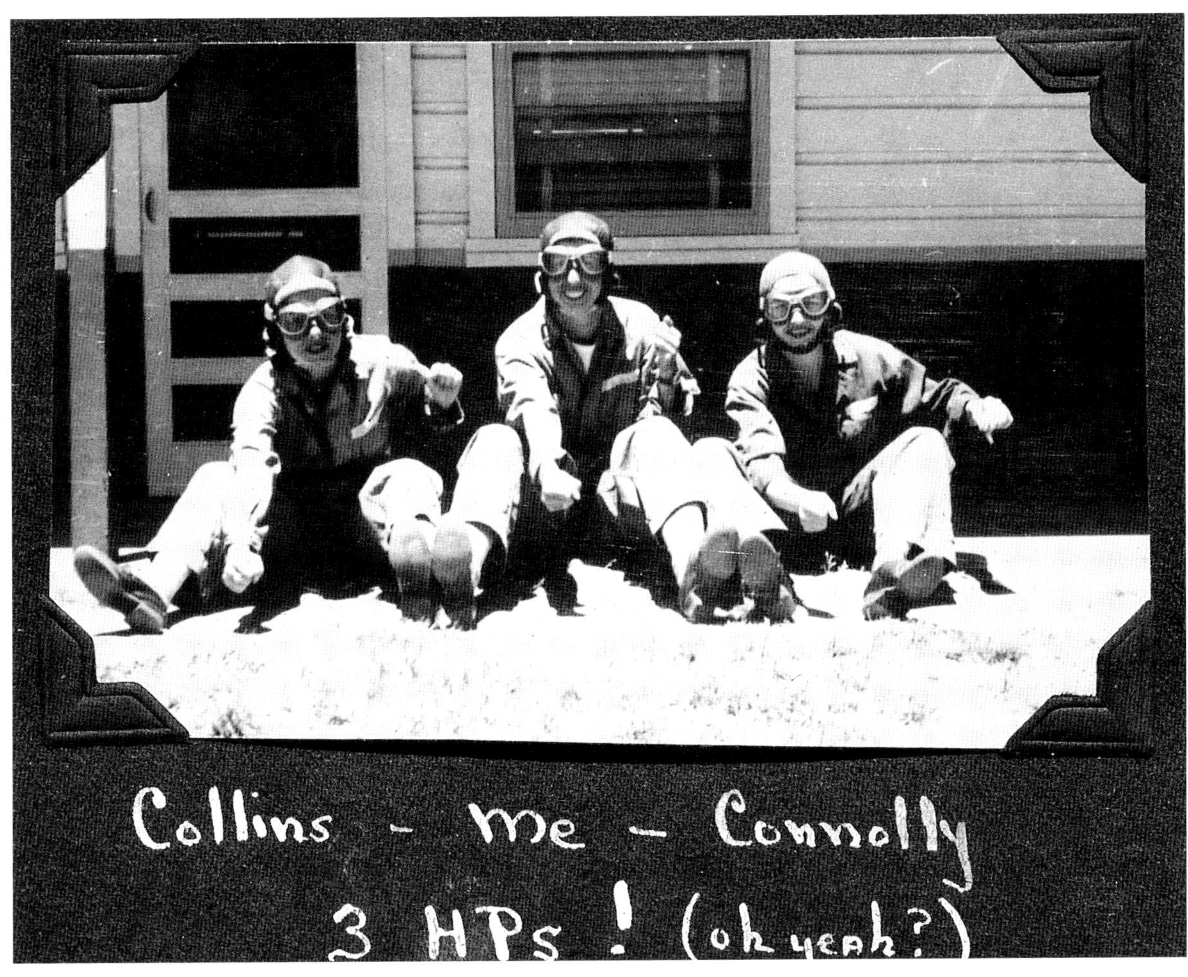

They worked long hours, took tests, did calisthenics, marched, had inspections, and somehow managed to pass check rides. They were young women with little time off, but they managed to enjoy these odd moments. *"Dottie" Davis.* Below, Jeanne (Bennett) Robertson, left, and Betty Naffz of Class 43-W-4 on arrival at Avenger Field, Sweetwater, Texas. They had just flown their PT-19 primary trainer to Avenger from Houston, Texas. Their class had started at Houston and were moved to Avenger after completing their primary training. *Jeanne Robertson*

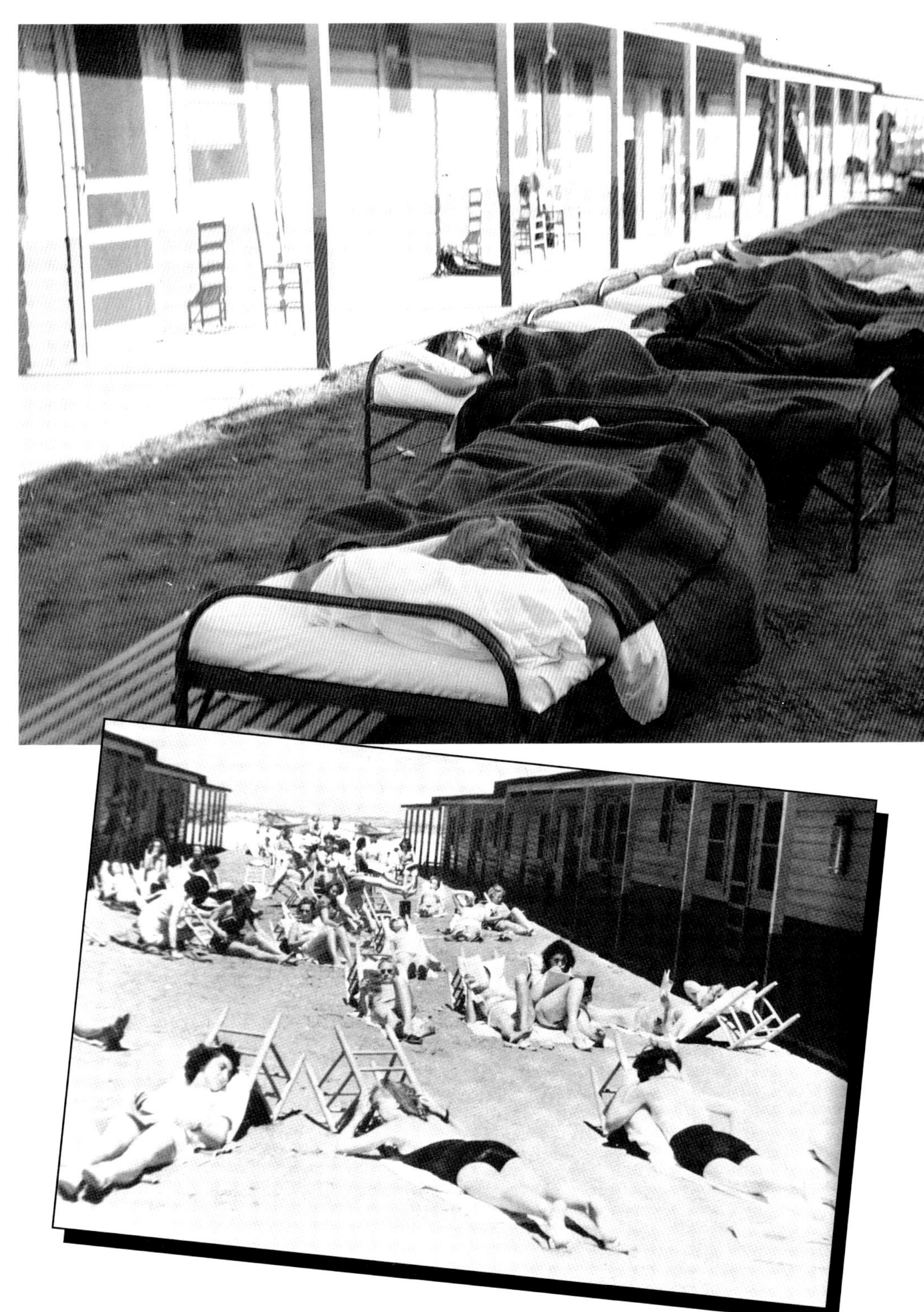

Summers in Texas could be sweltering, so the girls sometimes carried their beds outside into the cooler night air. ***Jeanne Robertson.*** **Below, on sunny days when they were not flying, the WASPs worked on their tans.** ***"Micky" Axton.*** **Previous page, no matter how much fun they seem to be having in the snow, these trainees would rather be flying.** ***Special Collections, Texas Woman's University***

"We pulled our cots out, but there were tarantulas and scorpions. So we had to get into bed and then tuck everything in so that nothing trailed on the ground."

—Rita (Davoly) Webster, Class 43-W-6

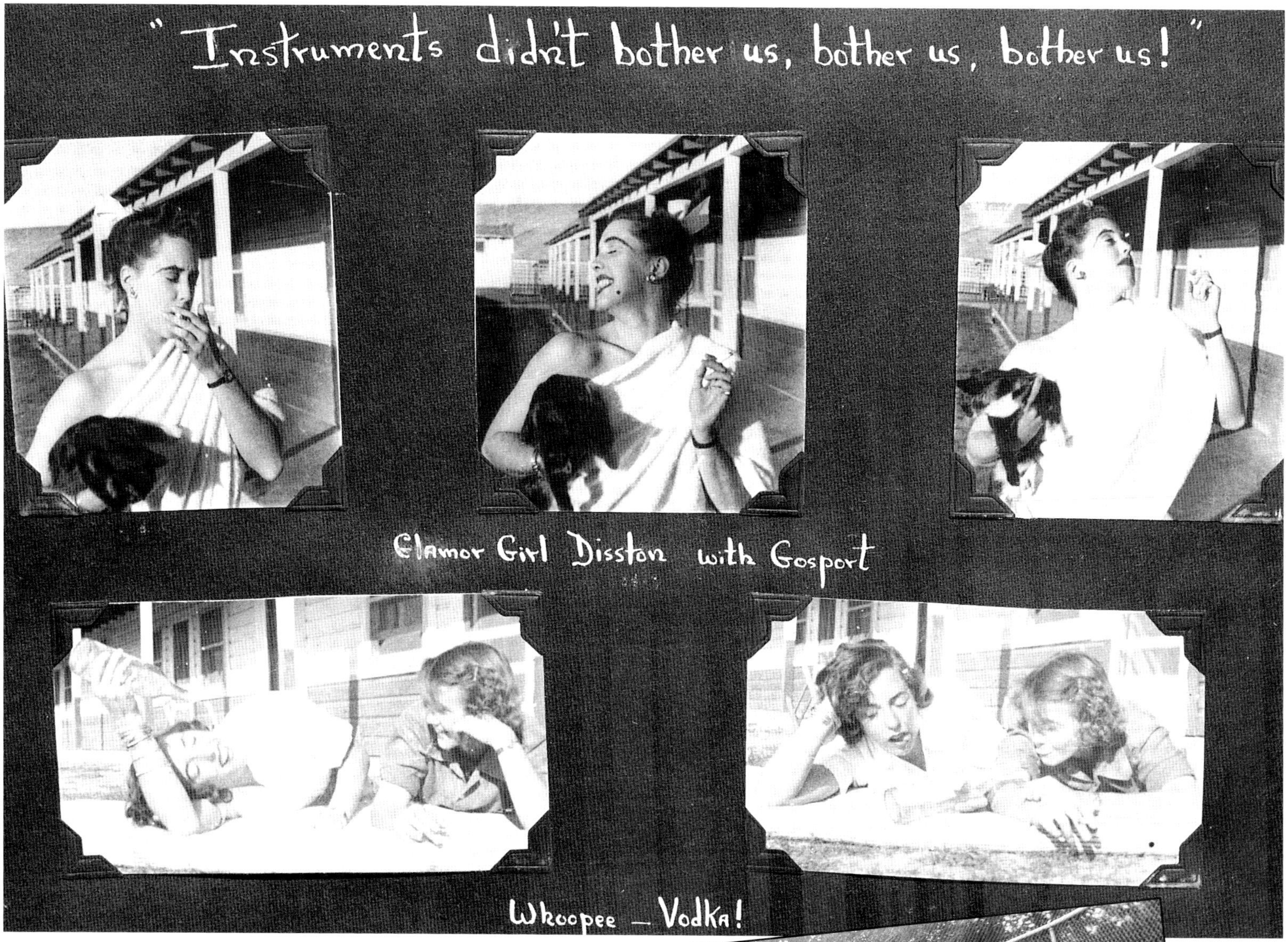

"Instruments didn't bother us, bother us, bother us!"

Glamor Girl Disston with Gosport

Whoopee – Vodka!

Silliness is the best method for dealing with the stress of instrument-flight training. *"Dottie" Davis.* Right, the Sweetwater town pool was a great place to beat the heat. *Florence Wheeler*

There were two flags on the administration building, one red and one green, to designate the dress code for the day—civilian or military. This was the day *both* flags were up. I wonder what they would have done if *no* flags had been up.
Jeanne Robertson

"We would go into town on Saturday night but you had to be back by twelve, and they'd close the gate if you weren't. There were high cyclone fences around the field. They called it 'Cochran's Convent' 'cause you couldn't get in or out."

—Rita (Davoly) Webster, Class 43-W-6

The only class to hold their graduation ceremonies in Houston, Texas, was 43-W-1. The class had twenty-three graduates, and Jackie Cochran was on hand to pin on the graduates' wings. Cochran was on hand for many graduation ceremonies, but this first one must have been as triumphant as the last graduation was bittersweet. The ceremonies were held at Ellington Army Air Forces Base, which was adjacent to Howard Hughes Field, Houston, Texas. This page is from *The Log Book,* the yearbook of the 319th AAFTD. *Jeanne Robertson.* Below, WASP trainees from Class 43-W-7 on the wing root of a UC-78. By the end of training, a WASP had flown single-engine and twin-engine planes, and had flown at night and by instruments. The only differences between her training and that of the male cadets were that the WASPs were not trained in gunnery or formation flying. Standing at left is "Micky" (Tuttle) Axton. *"Micky" Axton.* Next page, ground-school instructor R. J. Patterson is shown teaching WASP trainees Helen Dettweiler, Florence Anageros, and Dale Dailey about radial aircraft engines, May 1943. *USAF (neg. no. A 36527 AC)*

And this is the Big Day--
the graduation of our first class.
Everyone was at Ellington Field
that day - and were we proud!

Another favorite place for recreation, if a trainee had a car, was Lake Sweetwater. *"Dottie" Davis.* Below, here are WASP trainees Eleanor (Thompson) Wortz and Isabel (Steiner) Karkau wearing the dreaded turbans. The WASPs had a bonfire the day they were told to they could stop wearing them. *Jeanne Robertson*

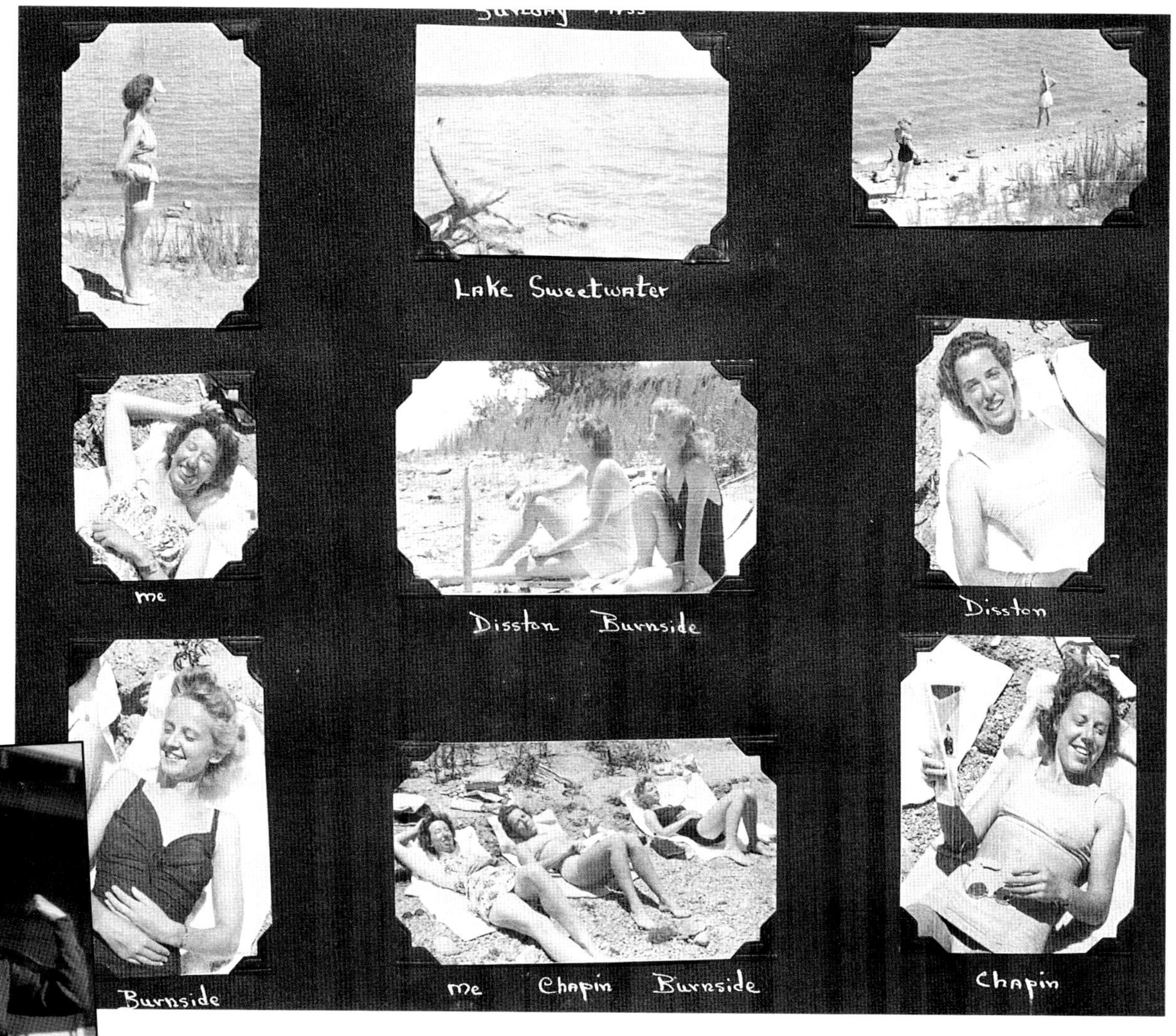

"We studied together, cried together, fought together. By the time we got through, we were wrung out, and we had been through such a unique experience that after fifty years we're still close friends."

—Alyce (Stevens) Rohrer, Class 44-W-4

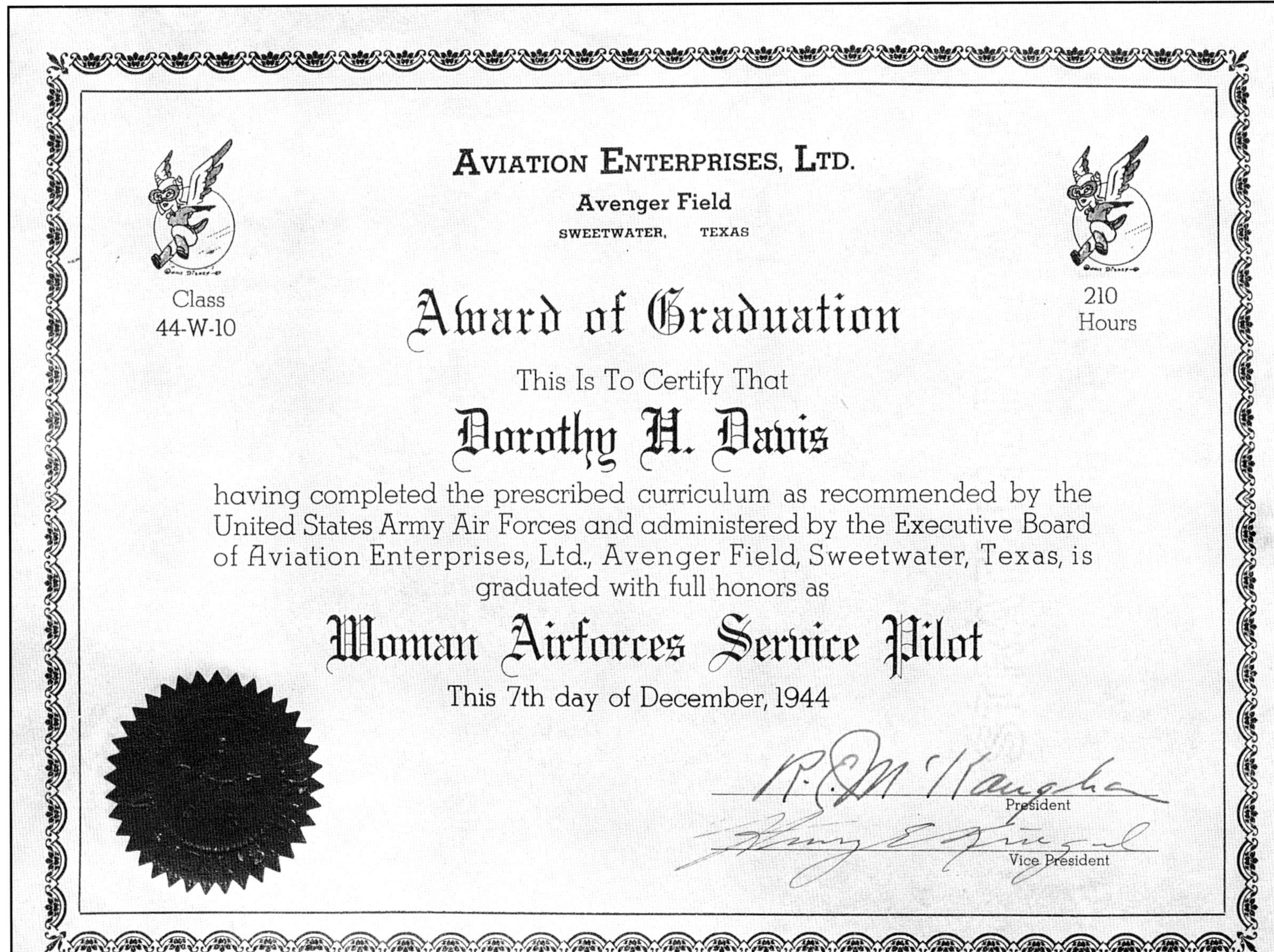

AVIATION ENTERPRISES, LTD.
Avenger Field
SWEETWATER, TEXAS

Class
44-W-10

210
Hours

Award of Graduation

This Is To Certify That

Dorothy H. Davis

having completed the prescribed curriculum as recommended by the United States Army Air Forces and administered by the Executive Board of Aviation Enterprises, Ltd., Avenger Field, Sweetwater, Texas, is graduated with full honors as

Woman Airforces Service Pilot

This 7th day of December, 1944

President

Vice President

Award of Graduation. Eighteen hundred and thirty women were accepted for WASP training, but only 1,074 graduated. They flew important missions for their country during a time of need, and thirty-eight of them gave their lives. *"Dottie" Davis*

Helen (Trigg) Luts' invitation to her WASP graduation ceremony. The proudest day for any WASP was the day she got her wings. She wore her Santiago Blue uniform, and watched the later classes marching and singing for her. She had wings pinned on by various VIPs, sometimes Jackie Cochran or General Arnold. Some of the male VIPs had never pinned wings on a young woman before. With the VIP's wife watching in the audience it made for some tense moments. Once a WASP received her wings she knew she had accomplished a very special thing. *Hans Halberstadt.* Next page, General Barney M. Giles inspecting the guard of honor at Avenger Field on November 1, 1943. Left row, front to back: Dorothy Avery, Emeral Drummond, Dorothy Fowler of Class 43-W-7, and Helen (Trigg) Luts of Class 43-W-8. *USAF (neg. no. A 36488 AC)*

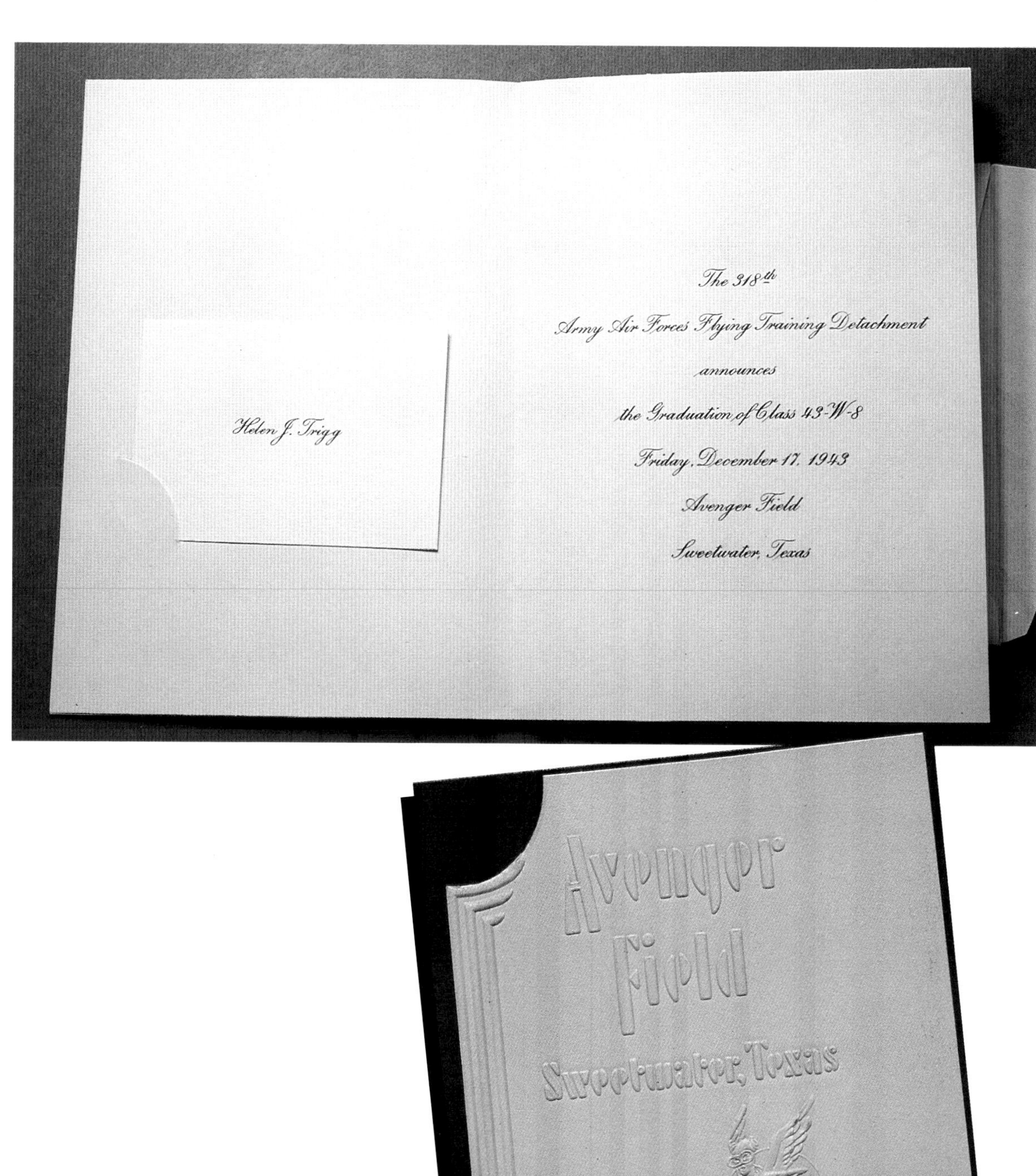

Helen J. Trigg
The 318th
Army Air Forces Flying Training Detachment
announces
the Graduation of Class 43-W-8
Friday, December 17, 1943
Avenger Field
Sweetwater, Texas
Avenger
Field
Sweetwater, Texas

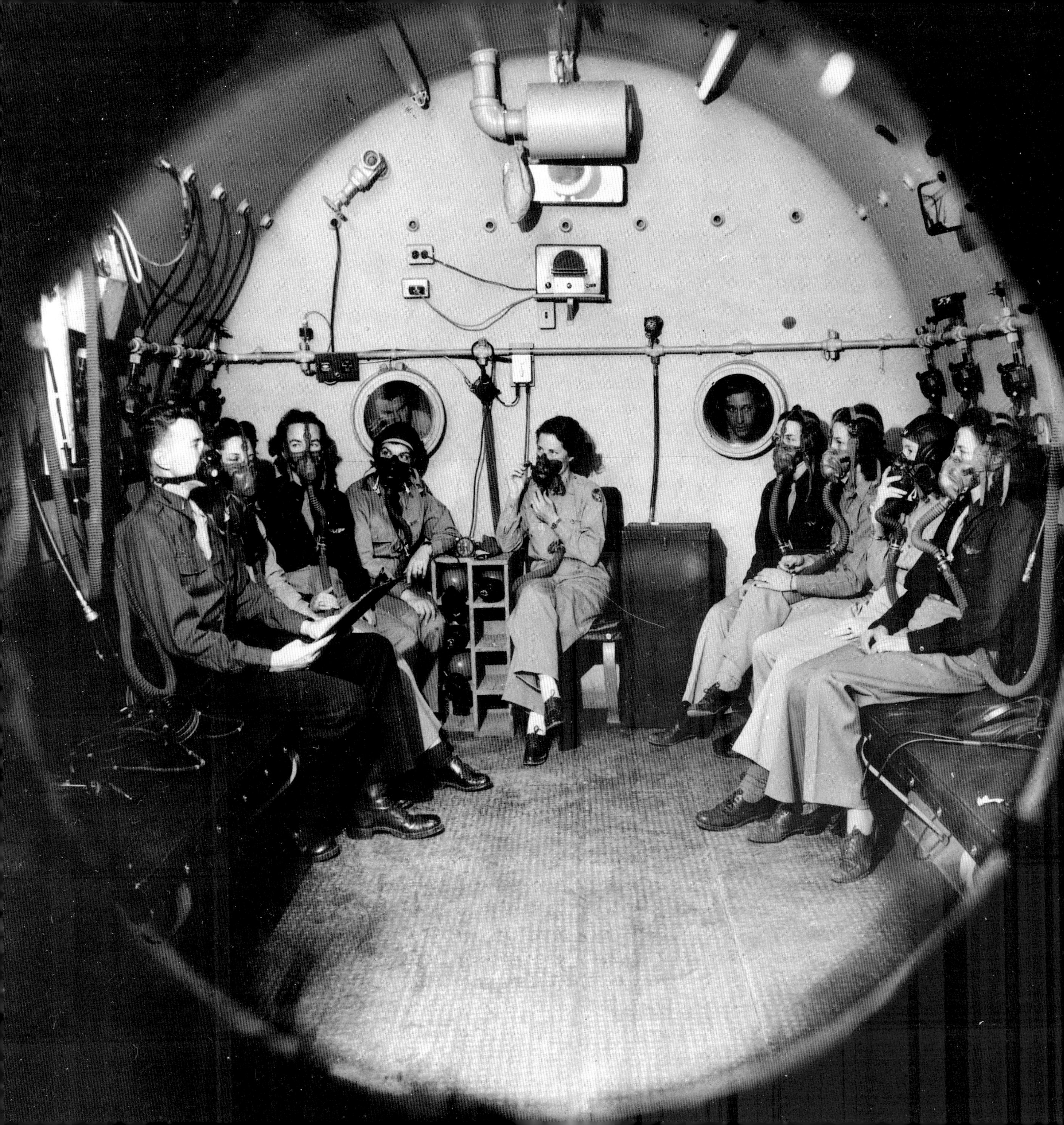

Chapter 4

"I'm a Flying Wreck"

WASPs Get Wings and Fly for Their Country

All the WASPs I spoke with said their best day was graduation day. They had passed their flight checks, been thrown in the wishing well, learned their dots from their dashes, and weren't caught kissing their instructors. They were Army pilots now. But then what?

The "Originals," the first group of WAFS, had been ferrying planes almost from the start. They were happily taking planes from here to there and hitching rides back on whatever transportation they could get—trains or planes or whatever.

They weren't doing it for the glory, but there was glory to be had for some. The first of only three American women in World War II who were given the Air Medal was a very modest one these "Originals," Barbara Jane (Erickson) London, who said, "Anybody could have done what I did had they been in the same spot. I lucked out. The weather was good, I had four good airplanes, I had no mechanical problems, and I made four transcontinental flights in a little over five days."

London flew 8,000 miles in five days, delivering two P-47s, a P-51, and a C-47 from Long Beach, California, to Evansville, Indiana; from Evansville back to San Pedro, California; from Long Beach to Fort Wayne, Indiana; and then finally from Cincinnati, Ohio, back to Long Beach. This was an extraordinary feat for any ferry pilot.

There was also agony to be had.

The first woman to die on active duty for the United States, Cornelia Fort, was also a WAFS. If her name is familiar it's because she was an instructor in Hawaii before the war and happened to be up in a Cub with a student on December 7, 1941, in the morning. She was the first pilot to see the Japanese coming in to attack Pearl Harbor. She quickly grabbed the controls, and, through gun fire, managed to land the plane and get it into a hangar. Her student asked, "What about the rest of my lesson?" and she told him, "Not today dear."

Fort was on a ferrying mission in March 1943 with a number of other pilots, some male. They were taking BT-13s to Love Field in Dallas, Texas. It was a clear day, with great visibility. Fort had over 1,100 hours of flying time, so it should have been a routine delivery mission.

One man in the group insisted on playing games and making a spectacle of himself. I guess he wanted to show the WAFS what a "real pilot" could do. Fort, however, was

The Strato Chamber for high-altitude testing at Randolph Field. One WASP trainee, Vivian (Hicks) Fagan broke a time record for staying conscious without supplemental oxygen at high altitude. Unfortunately, she broke both her eardrums during the descent. ***USAF (neg. no. 28856 AC)***

I'm a Flying Wreck
(Words by Thelma Bryan, Class 43-W-5)
I'm a flying wreck a riskin' my neck
And a helluva pilot too!
A helluva, helluva, helluva,
Helluva, helluva pilot, too!
Like all the jolly good flyers,
The gremlins treat me mean.
I'm a flyin' wreck, a riskin' my neck
For the good ole 318th!

If I had a PT sir, I'd paint it blue and gold,
I'd take it up 5,000 feet and make the damned thing roll!
Oh, if I had a PT, sir, I'd fly it off in the sky,
I'd circle over Germany and spit in the Fuehrer's eye!

If I had a civilian check, I'll tell you what I'd do,
I'd pop the stick and break his neck
And probably get a "U."
If I had an Army ride, I'd take off without my flaps
And show him that an easier job
Would be over fightin' Japs!

When the general comes, sir, To view us in our drill,
We'll do a four winds march, sir, And check out o'er the hill.
And when he calls "ATTENTION," We'll click our heels and yell,
"I'm just a raw civilian, sir, And you can go to HELL."

And when the course is over,
We won't be good at all,
We'll dine and date in every state
And bathe in alcohol.
And when vacation's over,
Of course, we'll all be late.
It'll take six months of LaRue's stuff
To get us back in shape!

Jacqueline Cochran at Ellington Field for Graduation of first Trainees. April 1943.
Jeanne Robertson

minding her own business. She maintained her course because she had too much experience to let this show-off bother her.

Unfortunately, the show-off miscalculated as he was slow-rolling over the top of Fort's BT-13; his landing gear hit her airplane's wing tip and then its cockpit. It must have hit Fort, as well, killing her instantly because she made no move to recover from the deadly spin her plane was in, nor did she try to parachute out. She rode the plane straight into the ground. The stunned "hot-shot" pilot made it to Abilene, where he reported the accident.

The very nature of the ferry pilot's work, flying planes from state to state, exposed them to constantly changing and very dangerous weather patterns that could turn a routine ferrying trip into a wild ride.

Jeanne Robertson: "A group of us were ferrying planes from Los Angeles to Dallas when all of a sudden in the middle of Texas we hit this storm. In Texas the storms are so big you can't see anything else, and you come on them so suddenly. I tried to go over it, but I couldn't. I tried to go under it but I couldn't. So I looked for someplace to land. We were supposed to go back if we couldn't go forward, but I was easily halfway to my destination, so I looked around, saw an airfield, and landed. As I landed, a couple of ground crew came out to grab the wings because it was very windy at that time. Another plane landed right behind me—it happened to be one of my best friends—and the whole group of us were scattered all over Texas that night.

"One fellow tried to continue on in spite of the storm because he was in a hurry to get back. He disappeared. We wondered if he tried to go through the storm and his plane was torn apart, but nobody ever knew. We experienced a lot of close calls because of weather."

"Micky" (Tuttle) Axton: "The WASPs ferried fighters and bombers and everything from the factories to the bases or to the points of embarkation to go overseas. And the girls that ferried bombers with the Norden bomb sight and fighters all carried .45-caliber automatic pistols. If the girls couldn't get to a secure base, like an air base, they had to land at a municipal airport and stay with that plane all night and guard it. So they were taught to use a .45 automatic."

And guarding planes was a good idea. There were a number of instances of sabotage.

WASP Betty Taylor Wood was killed when her engine failed while she was landing. They found sugar in the gas tank. One WASP took her parachute in for inspection, and the parachute riggers found that a tiny vial of acid had been chewing holes in her parachute. She was glad she hadn't tried to become a member of the Caterpillar Club. During inspections, mechanics found fuel lines crossed with coolant lines. On one trip, Byrd Granger, Class 43-W-1, brought her P-51 Mustang in for a landing without hydraulics and with her oil and coolant gauges in the red. The seals had blown, and the engine had seized. She was lucky to be alive, and in this case they found that her lines had been crossed.

Who would sabotage planes and flying gear? Men who didn't approve of women flying, disgruntled employees at airplane factories, even traitors to the United States.

Weather, other pilots, and mechanical problems—either from malice or wear and tear—all contributed to the ferrying experience.

Jeanne (Bennett) Robertson: "We were very proud of what we were doing but sometimes the ferrying of planes was a grind. You'd get a plane delivered and get an order to pick up a plane there or close by to take someplace else, or you'd go back to your base. We had a priority on commercial planes, and we'd bump ambassadors. Often we didn't want to; we would have loved to have gone to a little motel and had a good night's sleep.

"So a lot of it became a grind, but I think it gave us a lot of confidence. It's given me a confidence for the rest of my life that I hadn't had before. This was one small section of my life, but any skill that you can acquire gives you that much confidence for anything else you want to attempt."

Barbara Jane (Erickson) London: "We had the best of all worlds. We had all these beautiful airplanes to fly, all these great people that we were associated with. You know, we lived well, we ate well. Any civilian that would come on our base here and see what we had to eat would be appalled. They had to go and use ration stamps to get a pork chop at their own meat market.

"And we worked hard, because once we came in from a trip, we were put on the list and worked in a rotation. And we never were home more than a day before we would be back up flying. We never took vacations unless we had a family problem and had to go home."

Teaching the Boys to Shoot

Later WASP graduates would be asked to do a variety of jobs. Some of them towed aerial targets. One version involved flying an airplane equipped to reel out a strong mesh sleeve that was similar to the advertising banners sometimes towed by airplanes. The plane was flown up to altitude and an enlisted man in back reeled out the sleeve, usually only a couple of hundred feet behind. Then the pilot flew up and down a prescribed course, and a group of gunners-in-training fired machine guns at the target—or at least they tried to. The machine guns shot color-coded bullets. Once the shooting stopped, the pilot took her plane over a prearranged field, the enlisted man in back cut loose the sleeve, and home they would fly. The sleeve was collected and examined, and if there was a lot of blue paint but no yellow, the blue team got a pat on the back, and the yellow team was told to get more practice.

They would tow targets for guns on the ground or on other aircraft. Mostly this whole process went smoothly. It was a good way for the boys to learn to shoot at a flying target, and the WASPs were good pilots and enjoyed the chance to fly. However, there were dangerous possibilities.

Genevieve (Landman) Rausch: "I was up on one of these missions and the man in back pulled the sleeve in too fast and it wrapped around the tail. I told him I would get up to altitude and he could jump out if he wanted because when that thing hit my tail, it was terrible; it locked up my rudder, limiting my ability to maneuver. I had some play but very little. So the tower said, 'Come down and pass across the field so we can get our binoculars and look at it.' They decided I needed to make an emergency landing, and they closed the field to all other planes but mine. Up above me there were squadron leaders with their planes who were planning to land for lunch, and they didn't like my being in the way. I came in and there was the meat wagon and the ambulance and fire engine all on my wing tips, see. But everything turned out alright."

Now that the WASPs had completed their training they were off to assignments all over the country. ***Jeanne Robertson***

More serious, though, was when the live ammunition hit the planes, which happened to WASP Mabel Rawlinson. Her plane took a direct hit, and although she tried to get back to the field at Camp Davis, she crashed in the woods, and her airplane broke in half. The man in the back managed to get out, but Rawlinson could not get her hatch open, and she burned to death.

In this case, the future of women flying for the Army Air Forces was at stake, and Jackie Cochran decided that in order to protect the program, no publicity would be allowed. The incident was blamed on mechanical failure and was then hushed up.

In addition to target towing, there were other methods for teaching the soldiers to shoot. A fun one for the WASPs was the dog fight simulation. The WASP would be in a pursuit-type aircraft (she would be the bad guy) and the good guys would fly alongside and attempt to shoot her (with a camera). The WASPs flew P-39s, and the gunnery crews flew in B-17s. Las Vegas Army Air Field was one place they did these photographic "shooting" missions.

Another method involved night flying, which some WASPs liked, others did not. But this kind of night flying was especially exciting.

"Kay" (Menges) Brick: "After graduation, we requested that we be posted in El Paso, because of the weather. We got to fly a lot, and we got to fly a lot of night missions. We trained antiaircraft people. They had search lights, and we would do maneuvers at night with-

"I remember taking off in a P-63 the first time. It went so fast, suddenly I was at 300 miles an hour—and I had been accustomed to 140 or 150. When I came back to the airport from flying a couple of hours, I'd make a turn and the airport was gone!"

—Dorothy "Dot" (Swain) Lewis, Class 44-W-5

Women Learning to Be Army Pilots, To Relieve Men in Ferry Command

Hundreds Now in Training in West Texas Would be 'Nastiest Fighters' If That Were the Aim, Says Director

By the Associated Press

SWEETWATER, Texas, April 27—Women fliers by the hundreds are threading the sky of West Texas in the Army's new program to prepare them for war service. There will be thousands of women in the program which the Army is supervising for the first time. From a beginning at Houston, where the first class of twenty-three was graduated Saturday, it has expanded to this neat plant, with its large air field, ample grounds and orderly blue-and-cream buildings.

The Flying Training Command which from its headquarters at Fort Worth administers the schooling of all bombardiers, navigators, and aerial gunners for the Army Air Forces is in charge of the women's training.

The program started almost from scratch. Miss Jacqueline Cochran, its director, surveyed the women pilot potentiality in this country in 1940 and found only four women who had flown planes of 600 horsepower and more. With that to build on, students were recruited and their training begun.

Long, Hard Day of Training

This is the daily program designed to turn out pilots:

6:15 A. M.—First call (bugles and bells).
6:45 A. M.—Breakfast.
7:30 A. M.—Flight line. The women fly from two to two and a half hours a day, more as their training advances.
1:00 P. M.—Luncheon.
2:30 P. M.—Ground school, including mathematics, physics, navigation, meteorology, maintenance.
5:00 P. M.—Drill and calisthenics.
6:30 P. M.—Supper.
8:00 P. M.—Study hall.
10:00 P. M.—Taps.

It's a long, hard day's work, but the course is modified from the regular Army course for aviation cadets and combat flying is deleted. Gunnery is also omitted, as the women are preparing for noncombatant jobs within the United States. Miss Cochran says they learn to fly as readily and as well as men.

During the training period, the women receive $165 a month on civil service status. When they are graduated, they don snappy blue uniforms and go into ferrying work at $250 a month. Their duty will be to ferry planes from factory to field and from field to field, to any point in the country designated by the Army. Men pilots will be thus released for other service.

From thirty States, the girls include former office workers, outdoor girls, small town girls, big city girls and girls who used to live an easy life. Avenger Field is like nothing they have ever known before.

"It's the most miraculous thing that ever happened to me," says Miss Lydia M. Dunham, 22, of Boston, who was graduated from Boston University last June. A stenographer for a brief period after college graduation, she learned flying in the civilian pilot training program and was in the 99s, a women's flying organization.

Apparently there are many others who feel as she does about the work, for girls are now signed up for classes until next Fall, says Miss Cochran.

What is Required of Recruits

To be eligible, a woman must have had at least thirty-five hours of flying time; she must be between the ages of 21 and 34 and must pass a stiff Army physical test. The program has attracted to Avenger Field Helen Dettweiler of Washington, golfer; Nedra Harrison of Tifton, Ga., the "Dragon Lady" on the radio, and Dale Dailey of New York City, a Powers model.

"Gentler treatment" is about the only difference in the instruction of women students, says Major L. E. McConnell, army supervisor at the field.

Could they, if necessary, man fighting and bombing planes on active duty in the war theatre?

"Yes," is Major McConnell's reply.

Miss Cochran is opposed to that idea, presented as a hypothetical question, "but if the time should come, they could do it; when aroused, women make the nastiest fighters."

Reprinted from an April 27, 1943, Associated Press story. Courtesy Associated Press.

General "Hap" Arnold and Barbara Jane (Erickson) London on the reviewing stand at Avenger Field in March 1944. She has just been presented with the Air Medal for completing four transcontinental ferry flights (a total of more than 8,000 miles) in five days. ***Special Collections, Texas Woman's University***

"We had the best of all worlds. We had all these beautiful airplanes to fly, all these great people that we were associated with."

—Barbara Jane (Erickson) London, WAFS

---

out any lights on, and the antiaircraft people would see if their radar could track us. This was rather exciting because we could be blinded by those lights, so we would duck down in the cockpit."

"Winnie" Wood: "We worked a lot with the ground forces to train them. They were learning how to work search lights. The men were on the ground, and we would fly, and they would look for us. If they found us, one moment we would be sitting in total darkness and the next we would be suddenly in this bubble of brilliant light, and we would have to go on instruments. It wasn't scary, but you could get vertigo unless you got on instruments.

"I also did mirror missions. They would look for me in a mirror. Their guns would then be pointed away from me. The mirrors would tell them whether they hit me. So I did search light missions, mirror missions, and I did tracking missions."

Tracking missions were just like tow-target missions, except the gunners got a fix on the plane, not the target, and did not use live ammunition.

Ladies Courageous

After the WAFS and WASP programs were started and the public became aware of them, Hollywood began to be intrigued by the "Glamour Girls" or the "Lipstick Pilots," as they were being called in newspaper stories and in magazine articles. A Hollywood studio produced a movie called *Ladies Courageous*, starring Lorretta Young. There was a WASP on the set as a technical consultant, but she must not have been consulted very often. The movie was turgid and melodramatic. WASPs who saw it in the theater would duck down in their seats in embarrassment. They nicknamed it *Ladies Outrageous.*

Barbara Jane (Erickson) London: "I remember when *Ladies Courageous* came out. We snuck into the theater to see it, but we had to get up and sneak back out, it was so awful. We hung our heads, we were almost afraid of being recognized."

The publicity had a negative effect on the program and caused animosity between the women and the men, which would later help lead to the deactivation of the WASPs. All the attention that the women got must have

A WAFS ferry pilot with a Lockheed F-5 (the photographic-reconnaissance variant of the P-38 Lightning fighter). ***USAF photo courtesy of "Micky" Axton.*** **Next page, WASPs learning about antiaircraft artillery at Camp Davis, North Carolina. After the lesson they were supposed to go up in the air and tow target sleeves that would be shot at by these same artillery pieces.** ***Special Collections, Texas Woman's University***

A WASP in an A-24 Dauntless tows a target sleeve for gunnery practice. Towing targets was another important job the WASPs performed.
Special Collections, Texas Woman's University

"I was up on one of these missions and the man in back pulled the sleeve in too fast and it wrapped around the tail. I told him I would get up to altitude and he could jump out if he wanted . . ."

—Genevieve (Landman) Rausch, Class 44-W-5

been hard for the men to take after awhile. They were doing the same job for their country *and* were being sent overseas to fight and die in combat.

Cochran was very worried about publicity. Drew Pearson for the Washington *Times-Herald* wrote very unflattering articles about the WASPs. Pearson said that the WASPs were just glamour girls, costing the government too much money and not providing any service that available male pilots could not do. And there were all sorts of rumors about the sexual conduct of the WACs. Some had been accused of behaving immorally, and accusations were made that WACs were merely prostitutes in khaki clothing. Jackie Cochran worried—and with good reason—that the WASPs' reputation could be similarly damaged by one person's behavior.

Barbara Jane (Erickson) London: "We got a little bit of notoriety over the fact that we were doing something different. It wasn't that we were smarter or stronger or better; we were just different, and very fortunate.

"Every time there's a class of twenty boys and one girl, the girl is going to be singled out for extra scrutiny. Even when there were four or five guys on a ferry trip and there's one girl in one airplane, that's the one the newspaper usually picks up, because the girl was the oddity in the group."

"B. J." Williams: "We didn't want to say no to any job because of the reaction we'd get: 'Oh! She didn't want to do it. See that's a woman!' So we did a lot of things that we knew were dangerous, but we did them to keep the program rolling and to keep up our image.

"I always felt like a representative. If one of our gals misbehaved in public, I felt it because I thought, They're going to be judging all of us by her conduct. If she used crude language or she didn't conduct herself in a lady-like manner, it would reflect on all of us. It's like one rotten apple in a bushel and all the apples start to decay. You have to be careful, especially if you're in a unique organization. If there were thousands of us, people would say, 'Oh well.' But since we were such a small group, I felt that I had to conduct myself with extra caution."

Dropping "Tinfoil"

There was another mission where the girls sometimes got to play the bad guys and sometimes the good guys. This was a secret, experimental program in which the WASPs flew radar-calibration flights, during which methods were developed to confuse enemy radars and to counter enemy radar-confusion techniques. The girls would fly and drop aluminum bits of foil (called "window" or "chaff") over the radar area. These bits of foil would change an airplane's distinct radar blip to a confusing mess of "snow" on the radar screen.

"Kay" (Menges) Brick: "I loved the radar missions where we'd throw out stuff to foul up radar. It looked like tinfoil. We would take up three airplanes or six airplanes. Once we had twelve, and they were all different types that flew at different speeds. The antiaircraft officer would give us a pattern ahead of time. We would drop six boxes (of chaff) every seven seconds, and then we would fly at a certain altitude and in a particular pattern. They would check on the ground to see if their men could track us.

"The methods we helped develop were used when the Americans bombed Hamburg. They dropped chaff on one side of town and then attacked on the other."

The girls managed to find other uses for the tinfoil. "Kay" (Menges) Brick and Lois (Hollingsworth) Ziler, Class 43-W-3, talked about how one Christmas they were stranded at Camp Stuart, near Hinesville, Georgia. They were freezing because they only had cotton outfits and a coal space heater. They could look down through the floorboards and see the ground. But they managed to keep their Christmas spirit. They went out and chopped down a pine tree in the forest. Somebody had bought some paper ornaments, and they strung popcorn and cranberries and used the chaff in place of tinsel to decorate the tree. It turned out to be a very pretty tree. Even though they didn't get to go home, they enjoyed that Christmas at Camp Stuart.

Towing Gliders

Sometimes the WASPs got to tow things other than targets. During World War II "disposable" gliders were sometimes used to get men and equipment in behind the lines. The gliders would be released from a tow plane, and then the glider pilot would fly the glider to the ground with its load of troops and equipment, including guns, radios, and even jeeps.

Form ACA 935

DEPARTMENT OF COMMERCE
CIVIL AERONAUTICS ADMINISTRATION
WASHINGTON

This Is To Identify

HELEN (First name) JANE (Middle name) TRIGG (Last name)

who has been certificated as an airman by the Civil Aeronautics Administration and whose signature appears hereon.

Signature

Signature ... Civil Aeronautics Representative.

Signature ... Fingerprinting Officer.

This certificate is not valid after VALID UNTIL RECALLED

Place of birth Okmulgee, Okla.
Date of birth Feb. 9, 1921
Color eyes Brown hair Brown
Weight 110 lbs. Ht. 5 ft. 4 in.

FINGERPRINTS—RIGHT HAND

RIGHT THUMB

Training for glider pilots took place at various fields. Six WASPs were pilots in the big C-60s used to tow the gliders. The WASPs had to learn to take off with two gliders attached behind their planes. The C-60s were underpowered, so takeoffs were tricky. Sometimes the glider pilots would try to be helpful during takeoffs by lifting the gliders off the runway as soon as they were moving fast enough for the light gliders to fly. Unfortunately, this would usually shove the C-60's nose into the ground. It took a little while, but the WASPs eventually got the hang of towing the cumbersome gliders. Once they were airborne, they had to fly low with the gliders to simulate flying underneath the view of enemy radar. When the WASPs released the gliders, they had to be careful that their plane didn't pitch up.

Drone Pilots

Another interesting assignment for the WASPs was flying as safety pilots in the PQ-8 experimental drone program. The PQ-8s were tiny, radio-controlled craft that were the precursors for today's guided missiles. During the 1940s, they were developed to be used as flying targets.

The drone was controlled by a pilot (the "beep pilot") in another airplane (the "mother ship," usually a C-45 or C-78) using signals from a radio control box (the "beep box"). To prevent high losses of drones while beep pilots were being trained, a safety pilot flew in the drone to take over in case of emergency.

This was a top secret project, and there was no technical manual. A number of WASPs got to ferry the

The WASP insignia, which was worn on the lapel of the uniform. ***Hans Halberstadt.*** **Top, Helen (Trigg) Luts' identification as an airman. She graduated in Class 43-W-8.** ***Special Collections, Texas Woman's University***

Class 44-19, Flight B, at pursuit school in Brownsville, Texas. This class included WASPs Jill McCormick (left) and Louise Bowden. Pursuit school is where the pilots were trained to fly high-performance fighters such as the P-47 Thunderbolt and P-51 Mustang. This was where the "Miss H.P.s" wanted to be. ***Special Collections, Texas Woman's University***

planes, but only four pilots were qualified to fly on board the little red PQ-8s for missions, and two of them were WASPs. These WASPs talked about how nerve-wracking it was to sit in this little thing—not touching the controls unless an emergency developed—as it barreled down the runway. The safety pilot was not in control and had no idea if the drone would take off or just continue out into the field or fence at the end of the runway. It might be that this was the beep pilot's first time at the controls, or he might have a lot of experience using the beep box. The WASP's job was to stay away from her controls unless a crash was imminent.

In order to have the confidence to just sit there, she needed to be a very skilled pilot, indeed. She needed a keen knowledge of the abilities of her craft in order to second-guess reactions and moves. Lois (Hollingsworth) Ziler's background in engineering and aeronautics [Ziler had a degree before becoming a WASP] made her a perfect pilot for the PQ-8s. She was the first pilot to train in the PQ-8, and she helped develop the program.

Lois (Hollingsworth) Ziler: "We started with the PQ-8, which was a Culver Cadet with a nose wheel. Then we had a C-78 mother ship that would carry the beep pilot. The beep pilot would sit on the copilot's side of the C-78 with a little box to control the drone. The mother ship's pilot would sit on the other side.

"I was a safety pilot for the drone; somebody had to ride in the little radio-controlled airplane while the person in the mother ship learned to beep and make the drone do what it's supposed to do. Safety pilots were just supposed to sit there and hope the beep pilot wasn't going to crash the drone, and if the signal between the mother ship and the drone got interfered with, the drone just went crazy. Then, unless something was mechanically wrong with the controls, the safety pilot could take over and fly it as if it was a regular airplane. We were supposed to delay taking over until the very last minute, otherwise the beep pilots would never know how good they were."

The worst part about being a drone pilot was the unhappy habit of the drone to arbitrarily break away from the radio signal and fly out of control, especially in the midst of a landing. So in addition to a keen mind, quick reflexes were also a must.

Byrd Granger was on a ferrying mission in a PQ-8 and thought she would be cute. She tried to take a shortcut across the grass at the field. She had been told the grass was muddy. Since all the other planes at the field were big four-engine planes, she figured her little "pipsqueak" could scurry across without problem, but she got stuck. A couple of guys in a jeep came along, picked up the plane (with Granger in it!), and placed them back on the runway. How embarrassing!

They Wanted to Fly Them All

One of the goals that many WASPs had was to get checked out in as many different planes as possible. By graduation every WASP had flown the PT-17 or PT-19 primary trainer, the BT-13 basic trainer, and the AT-6 advanced trainer, but they were hungry for more. They continued this alphabet soup, and some went on to fly as many pursuit planes as possible. Some of the planes they flew were the equivalent of the F-16 jet fighter of today. Hot, man!

Barbara Jane (Erickson) London: "I was in the best spot of any WASP there was because not only was I in the Ferry Command, but I was head of the group, and I was in Long Beach, which was the best spot to be. Every one of the major factories with the exception of Republic and Martin were sitting here in the LA basin. So we had access to every airplane. As Betty Gillies will probably tell you, if she wanted to get checked out or something, she had to get to Long Beach to do it. If she delivered an airplane out here they would give her a P-51 or a P-47 or a P-63 to check out in. So we were sitting in the ideal spot. I wouldn't have changed a thing."

"Dot" (Swain) Lewis: "I remember taking off in a P-63 the first time. It went so fast, suddenly I was at 300 miles an hour—and I had been accustomed to 140 or 150. When I came back to the airport from flying a couple of hours, I'd make a turn and the airport was gone! I was afraid I was going to run out of gas before I was slowed down enough to land.

"It was also an idiots delight, with push buttons and all these little gadgets. When I got in it, I hadn't had any instruction, and they didn't have a book so I learned by trying. I found that this gadget lowered the gear, and this gadget was water injection or whatever. And I'd get in it and, wheeew, off I'd go. It was wonderful. I'd get up above the cumulous clouds and go in and out of them. It was fun, and I was doing time on it to break in a new engine. I was supposed to write down anything that was wrong. I enjoyed it.

"On the way back I would try to slow down enough to land, but it was so slick and so narrow that there was no friction, and I would be past the airfield before I knew it. I preferred single engine, and that's the difference between a bomber pilot and a pursuit pilot. I like a Cub and a sporty car."

B-25 School

Some flyers did not have the sports-car temperament. They were more the Cadillac or Mercedes-Benz type. These ladies preferred the big bombers, or multi-engine planes. "Winnie" Wood was one of those who liked to have a lot of metal around her. She also had extensive training in flying on instruments and liked a lot of gauges, knobs, and dials in a plane.

She told about going off to B-25 school at Mather Army Air Base, near Sacramento, California. The school was doing an experiment to see who were the best pilots. The students were divided up into three groups: women, white males, and black males.

"Winnie" Wood: "This was the first B-25 school, and they only took twenty WASPs and sent us out to Mather Field in Sacramento. One squadron of girls, one squadron of black male pilots, and two squadrons of white men. I'm not sure, but I think they were experimenting with us because at the end of our training they gave us all the same tests. The girls came through on instruments, ahead of the others.

"We had to check out on the B-25 at night. I was one of the first ones to check out at night. We got to the end of the runway, and this B-24 that was in front of us took off and crashed. There was this great explosion, and everything burned up. After he saw this, the check pilot got cold feet and said we had to go in, so he taxied back to the line. I said, 'We've got to take off.' He said, 'No, the automatic pilot isn't working.' I knew it was, so I called our captain of operations, and I told him what happened. He ordered us off the ground, and we took off. I always thought, That yellow-bellied son of a gun. I was

Gene (Shaffer) FitzPatrick in sheepskin winter flying gear. ***Gene FitzPatrick***

"Some cadet would come in and park too close and ding a wing. Since we were expendable, we had to take the plane up to see if the wing would stay on."

—Gene (Shaffer) Fitzpatrick, Class 44-W-1

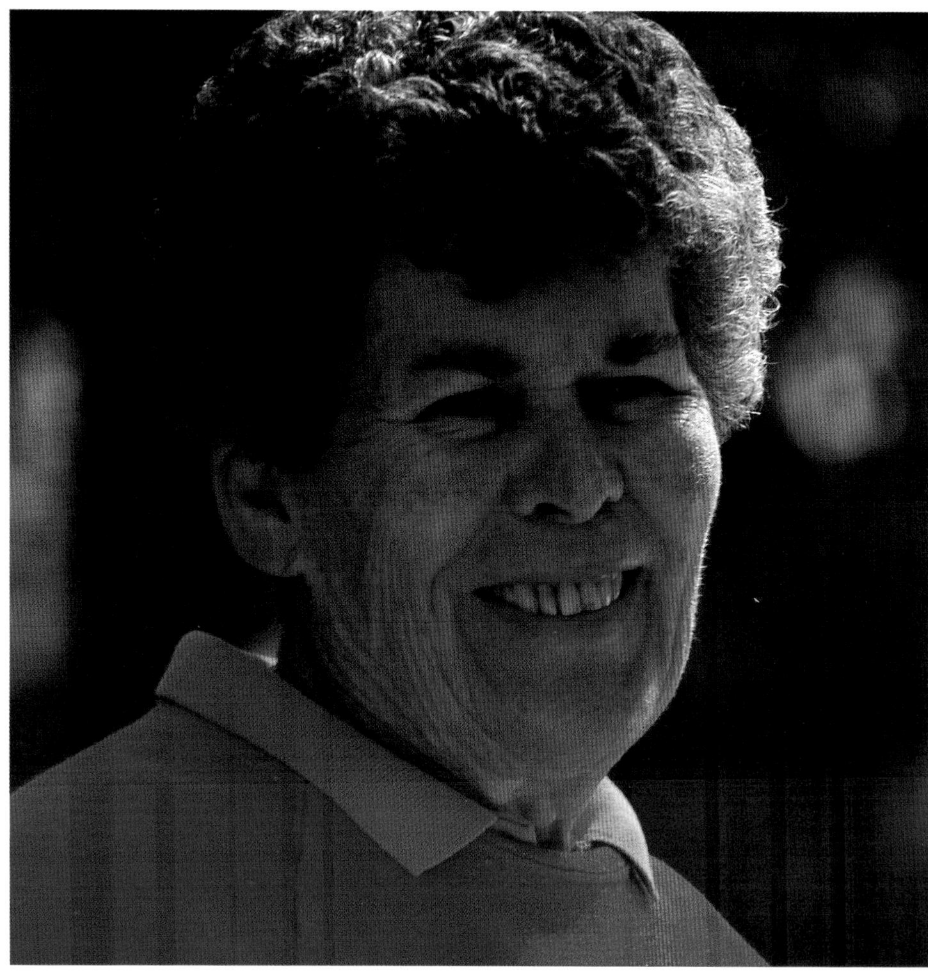

Winifred "Winnie" Wood at her home in California in September 1992. She graduated with class 43-W-7 and attended the special officer's course at Orlando, Florida, and the B-25 school at Mather Army Air Base in Sacramento, California. Next page, this clipboard was buckled onto the pilots leg and allowed the pilot to take notes while flying. They could record time of take-off, time of landing, conditions, and notes about aircraft. *Hans Halberstadt*

scared enough but he was more scared. He should have known we were supposed to go up."

"Dot" (Swain) Lewis: "The men were just as scared as the women but they didn't dare show it. A lot of them were drafted, they didn't come for the love of flying."

Test Flying

WASPs also tested aircraft. They tested new aircraft, tested repaired aircraft, and tested some aircraft that still needed repair.

Gene (Shaffer) FitzPatrick: "I was testing school planes. Some cadet would come in and park too close and ding a wing. Since we were expendable, we had to take the plane up to see if the wing would stay on. I took one up and remember seeing all the rivets popping off.

"Another time, there was this fellow who came back from England with fifty missions to his name and an 'I'm a pilot, I've been to war!' attitude. Well, they put him with me to go up for a test hop. Usually we did that by ourselves, but I took him with me. I think we went up about 15,000 feet to see how the plane felt. Today, you don't go above 12,000 feet without oxygen, but we were young and had good lungs.

"So, anyway, we went up there and did a spin. You do a three-turn spin and then pull out and check all the wings and controls. He wanted to do it because he was a hot pilot. We got into the spin, and it wouldn't come out. He shook the stick to get my attention—not that I wasn't watching—and he said, 'It's not coming out. You take it.' So I did all the normal things you do; I tried everything, but it wouldn't come out.

"You pick up all this information along the way, and you file it thinking someday you might need it. One of these pieces of information was, if you can't get it out of a spin, try giving power. So I put the power in and wiggled the stick every which way, and it finally caught. And I remember when I pulled it out, nice and easy, we started up. I think we were down below 2,000 feet, and I thought, Whooh!

"We landed, and the fellow never said a thing. But I found out that he went in and said, 'They don't pay me that kind of money to be in the testing department.' So he quit, and we kept on doing it."

Legal Buzzing

The WASPs also laid down chemical and smoke screens to train the men to respond to such things.

"Winnie" Wood: "I remember 'Kaddy' [Katherine (Landry) Steele] came back one day saying she'd released a smoke screen on the wrong group. We also did strafe missions. The troops would be out bivouacked in the desert, and our job was to go out and pretend that we were the enemy and strafe them. They were supposed to pretend to shoot us and get out of the way. We had A-24s [Douglas Dauntless], mostly, for this. We'd dive bomb them—this was legal buzzing—and the girls used to just love it."

Instrument Training

At eight bases—from Shaw Army Air Base in Sumpter, South Carolina to Peterson Army Air Base in Colorado Springs, Colorado—over one hundred WASPs were stationed at bases involved in instrument training of male cadets.

Rita (Davoly) Webster: "My job was to give the pilots their last instrument check. They took off under the hood, but then I flew until I got them disoriented. Then they were supposed to find their way back by radio. Most of them did well, except one.

"We were right outside of Victoria, Texas. There was a military field and a commercial field near each other.

He started to land at the commercial field. Well, there is no way you can do that if you're following signals.

"When we came back, he said, 'Did I pass?' I said, 'Of course, you didn't pass.' He asked, 'Why not?' And I replied, 'Because you were trying to land at the wrong field.' 'Well,' he said, 'I got vertigo.' I said, 'You got no such thing. You were peeking there in the back, and you saw the field. Absolutely not—you're not going to pass.'"

And they sometimes instructed by demonstration.

Gene (Shaffer) FitzPatrick: "The biggest thing was night flying at Randolph Field, Texas. We were becoming instructors, basic instructors. We'd had night flying before but this time they said, 'The field will be blacked out.'

"Randolph is a huge base. And at night, it's black, and all of Texas was dark. It wasn't built up then. But you could see the base's four corners with the red lights that marked the field. Takeoff was a snap because we had all had instrument training. But coming in, it was black, no lights.

"We had lights on the plane, but we couldn't turn them on. The instructor said, 'Now, when you get down there, you're going feel this cushion of air.' When I got down there and couldn't hold it any more, I just pulled back, kept the stick all the way back, got it straight, and then let it sink down. The airplane touched down, and oooh, that felt good.

"We went around with our instructor, two or three times. Then he got out and we had to fly by ourselves. I thought, This is not for me, but I went ahead and took off. I thought, I'll go around once and show 'em I can do it, and then I'll go park outside. I took off, got up there, and made my turns in the traffic pattern.

"What I hadn't considered, though, was that the airplane would climb at a much faster rate and 'float' longer on landing because it was 150, 160 pounds lighter without the instructor in the back. Normally I would instinctively compensate for this, but at night everything's different. And Texas was so dark. There could have been little towns around there, but I just remember everything being black, black, black. And no freeways. They had roads of course, but no freeways like they do now.

"When I turned downwind, I thought, Oh, that's the black hole down there. But I set it up and went down and thought, When I land, I'm going to stay down. So I came up and I held the stick back and held it back. I probably leveled off a little high, but it was low enough, so I finally touched down. Then the control said, '243 go around.' So I went around a second time.

"I came in a second time, and it was better because I got down lower, and I could feel the cushion of air. I thought, Ooh, there it is. So they told me go around again. I had to do it three times. The third time wasn't

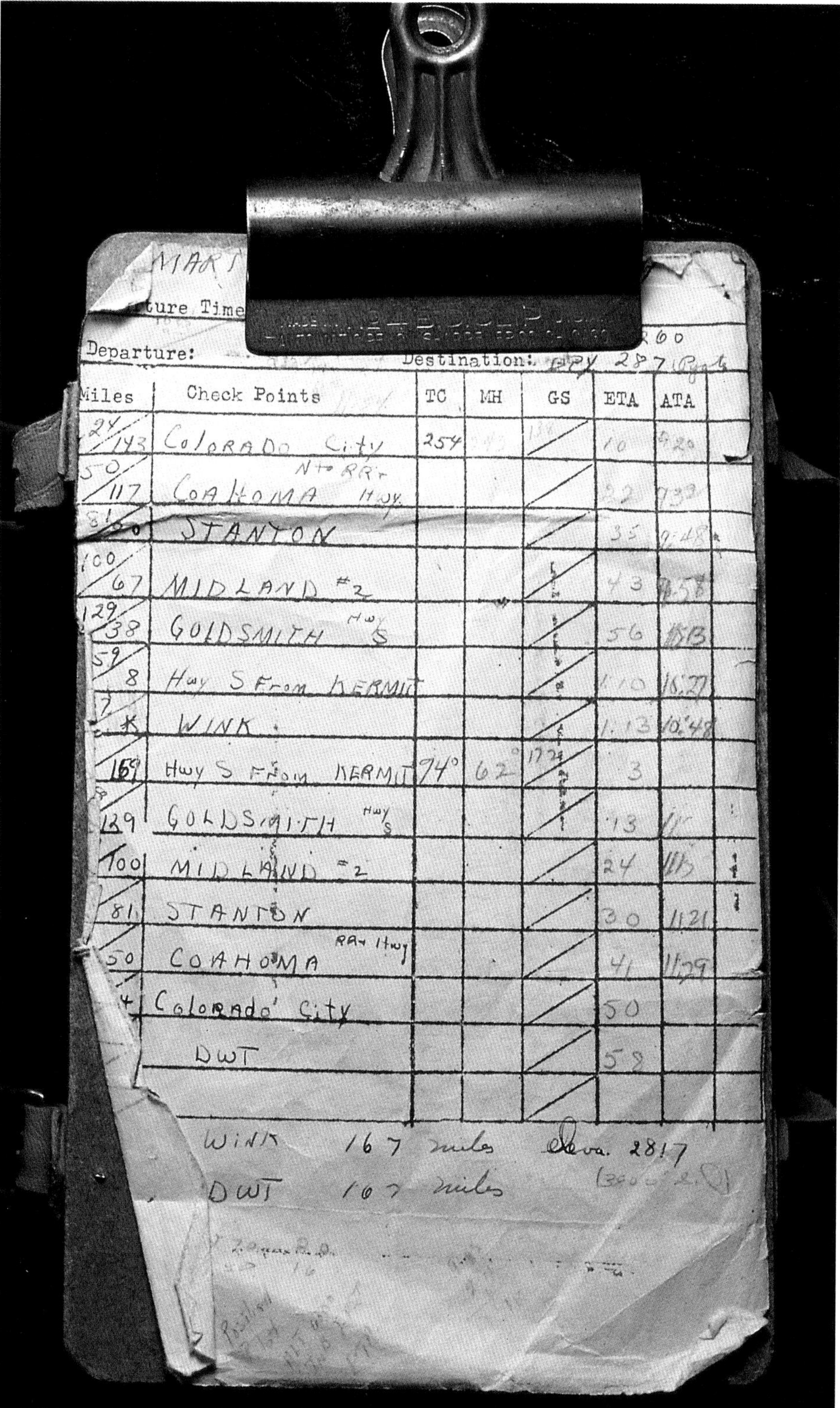

Departure: Destination:

Miles	Check Points	TC	MH	GS	ETA	ATA
24 / 143	Colorado City	254			10	[illegible]
50 / 117	Coahoma (N to RR, Hwy)				22	[illegible]
[illegible]	Stanton				35	[illegible]
100 / 67	Midland #2				43	[illegible]
129 / 38	Goldsmith Hwy S				56	[illegible]
59 / 8	Hwy S From Kermit				1:10	[illegible]
[illegible]	Wink				1:13	10:48
169	Hwy S From Kermit	74°	62°	172	3	
139	Goldsmith Hwy S				13	[illegible]
100	Midland #2				24	[illegible]
81	Stanton				30	11:21
50	Coahoma RR & Hwy				41	11:29
4	Colorado City				50	
	DWT				58	

Wink 167 miles Elev. 2817

DWT 167 miles

WASPs Gertrude "Tommy" (Tompkins) Silver (back), "Micky" (Tuttle) Axton (center), and Audrey Tardy (front) flew as engineering test pilots at Pecos Army Air Force Base. The ladies tested planes that were new, that had been repaired, or that were still in need of repair. Silver was killed in November 1944 in the crash of a P-51 Mustang. *"Micky" Axton.* Next page, these WASPs at Romulus Army Air Field, Romulus, Michigan, were part of the 3rd Ferrying Group of the Air Transport Command. They ferried PTs, ATs, and C-47s. The WASPs also flew as B-24 copilots. Shown are WASPs Barbara Ward, Helen Barrick, Marianne Beard, Joanne Trebotske, Virginia Wilson, and Corinne Nunstedt. *USAF (neg. no. A 29644 AC)*

too bad 'cause by then the stark fear had left. I landed, taxied in, and that was it.

"It turned out the instructors were using a little psychology. They had the girls go first, with all the male cadets standing there watching us. They were just as scared as we were, but they saw us do it so they thought, If those girls can do it, we can do it! We got to go home, but the fellows had to stay there until midnight doing those landings."

WASP Airlines

WASPs were also "chauffeurs." They flew nonflying officers all over the place. Some of these men had never flown with a female pilot before and were anxious. "Maggie" Gee told them to either get in or don't get in. Once they flew with a WASP, they were convinced.

Alyce (Stevens) Rohrer: "I remember I was stationed at Perrin Field, Texas, and I didn't want the assignment at first because it was only a training base. Ever since I had heard of the P-51 Mustang, I had wanted to fly one, and I knew that in a training base I stood a very small chance of getting that opportunity. But, of course, I went where I was assigned, and one of my jobs, aside from instrument instruction and test-hopping, was flying the VIPs all around the country when they came into the base and needed to go somewhere.

"I was an air-going chauffeur. And one time I had a nonflying colonel to take out to St. Louis. The weather office gave me a clear for the trip, so I signed out an AT-6.

"By the time I got up beyond Oklahoma, the weather had closed in around me like a blanket. Well, an AT-6 doesn't have oxygen in it, and you can't go higher than 13,000 or 14,000 feet without oxygen because you immediately begin suffering deprivation and you can lose consciousness without even knowing it's coming. Well, the thunderheads were way above 13,000 feet, and I couldn't get above them. The only option was to go below them because I was beyond the point of no return for coming back.

"So we're flying along under these low clouds with lightning flashing all around us, and this colonel lifted up the phone—he's a little nervous—and said, 'Aren't those lightning bolts coming pretty close?' I said, 'Oh, not to worry. Lightning never hits an airplane in the air because there is nowhere for the lightning to ground.' Well, of course, it was an abysmal lie because lightning does hit airplanes. He believed it, though, and he relaxed and stopped worrying.

"After another half an hour, I knew I was lost completely. I couldn't follow my original course, so I followed a little river until I saw, lo and behold, a little airport down below me. I buzzed around it and landed to find out where I was.

"The colonel had to be in St. Louis for a meeting—joint chiefs of staff or something—so there was no way that we could stay on the ground until the storm stopped. So, once I knew where I was, I plotted a new course, and we started out again through those clouds and easily made it to St. Louis. And that's about the scariest experienced I ever had."

Some were sent down to the Gulf to pick up lobsters for dinner. They delivered the mail. They flew for the weather wing. They logged sixty million miles, and thirty-eight of them were killed.

Killed in the Line of Duty

Hazel Ah Ying Lee (who her WASP friends all knew as "Ah Ying") was coming in for a landing November 1944 at Great Falls, Montana, at the same time as another plane. The tower shouted, "Pull up, pull up!" And did not say to whom they were yelling. Lee pulled up into the plane above her. Her plane crashed and she eventually died of burns. It was a slow and painful death. And it took nearly a year to locate her family and return the body.

WASP Mary Webster was killed while she was a passenger in a UC-78. The pilot and the other passenger were buried with full military honors, and their families received $10,000 in insurance. Mary's body was placed in a pine box, and the other WASPs and officers at her base

SPECIAL EDITION

Some WASP's A-2 leather flight jackets had a Fifinella patch. Testing planes was dangerous work; the pilot would take the plane up to 10,000 feet, put it in a spin, and hope she could get it out. Hopefully, Fifinella was watching over them. ***© Disney Enterprises, Inc.; photo by Hans Halberstadt.*** **Right, a pilots flight log is a diary of experiences, it has a safety purpose but it can also be a wonderful way to remembeer exciting times and reminisce about different planes.** ***Hans Halberstadt***

chipped in to pay to have her body shipped back to her family with an escort. Months later the family received less than $200 to help pay for the funeral.

Proving Themselves in Every Mission

In most cases it was not pilot error that killed the WASPs. They had an extraordinary record of safety.

"Dot" (Swain) Lewis: "Our record stood up. They found that little old ladies could fly. They didn't make mistakes, and they didn't crash the planes, and they didn't jump out."

"Winnie" Wood: "And the girls wanted to fly every mission they were given. Sometimes the men would come back from combat, and they were tired and they didn't want to fly so we'd take the missions."

"B. J." Williams: "When we were first sent to Randolph Field, the major who was head of emergency engineering wouldn't let us fly. We'd sit outside and read tech manuals. One day we were sitting with our backs up against the building, the windows were open and his office was there. I heard him bellow out, 'Who in the Hell is flying that airplane?'

"Well, what had happened was, there were some guys that had been on overseas duty, maybe flying bombers, and they came back and were put on flying duty. They were flying an AT-6. This was a much smaller airplane than a bomber. This guy was trying to land the airplane, and he was bouncing all over the runway. The major bellowed out, 'You get that guy out of there. He's going to kill himself and crash the ship!' Then he said 'What are we going to do? We got all these airplanes stacked up that we got to fly.'

"So the captain said, 'Why don't you let the WASPs fly?' The major said, 'Do you think they know how to fly?' The captain said, 'Well, there's only one way to find out.' So I nudged Petey [E. Marie Pedersen, Class 44-W-6] and said, 'Here's our turn.' The captain comes out and says, 'Hey girls. How would you like to go flying?' We said, 'Oh, yes sir!'

"It hadn't been that long since we'd had seventy hours in an AT-6, and so Petey took one, and I took one. Boy, we came in to land, and we just painted it on. The old captain was just standing there like a proud daddy, and he said to the major, 'I told you, I told you!'

"We had no problem after that. I think in each case where the gals were challenged and questioned, the same story could be told. Once we were allowed to fly we proved ourselves capable. We flew seventy-eight different types of aircraft, in every type of mission except combat."

They also flew some unauthorized missions.

Rita (Davoly) Webster: "A few times, we'd get a plane and just play around up there to release some tension. A couple of times we would play what they called tag. We'd get in line, and whatever the front airplane did, the others did. If the front airplane rolled, everyone rolled. If they looped, everyone looped. You just followed them all through.

"One afternoon, this instructor had a plane, and he said, 'Why don't you hop in with me. We're going to play follow the leader.' 'Okay,' I said. So we were up there going through some clouds when I looked up and saw the wing tip of another plane in the mist—and it was very close! I took the stick, and got us away. I was scared. I don't know whether he saw it or not, but we didn't go in the clouds anymore."

Buzzing

Another no-no was "buzzing." Cows were favorite victims. It was a lot of fun to see them run. Cotton pickers were also fair game; it was fun to see them lay flat. The pilots soon learned not to buzz the sheep, though, because those poor wretches didn't run or lay flat, they would pile on top of each other in a pyramid, getting hurt in the process. That wasn't part of a WASP's fun.

Shrugging off Harassment

A lot about being a WASP was fun. They worked with good people, did exciting jobs, and either shrugged off any harassment they received or managed to take care of themselves in dignified ways.

Rita (Davoly) Webster: "The general in charge of Randolph was violently opposed to the whole WASP program, so it wasn't surprising that others in his command would have problems with us, too. The director of flying, a major, caused problems for us, or at least for me.

"If you had a date on Saturday night, you went to the officers' club and drank and danced or you went to the movies on the base. Several times when I had a date, this major would come in and ace out my date. He would sit on my other side in the movies and would cut in on us when my date and I were dancing and other things. I really didn't care for him at all. When I would ask my date, 'Why did you let him do that?' He would say, 'He's the major and I'm a lieutenant.'

Well, this one night—I really can't tell you how it happened—but this major had a car and I took a ride

"I preferred single engine, and that's the difference between a bomber pilot and a pursuit pilot. I like a Cub and a sporty car."
—Dorothy "Dot" (Swain) Lewis, Class 44-W-5

A pilot's watch is not just a piece of jewelry, it is a critical tool for navigation and safety.
Hans Halberstadt

WASP

with him. He probably pressured me. Anyhow, he drove out, way out, and he was so vulgar. I mean I had to wrestle him. Finally, I got out of the car and started to walk back.

"Well, I had no idea where I was. This was Saturday night, and there were all these big Texans around. I thought, I don't know which is worse, to be in that car or to be walking out here. I had no idea of how to get back. He turned the car around, and he came back and said, 'Get in and I'll drive you back. I promise I won't pull anything.' And so I got in and he drove me back. But I was furious.

"Carol Webb [Carol (Webb) Cook] was sort of the WASP supervisor, so I told her the whole story. She went to the commandant, and in about two days this major's wife and child were on the base, and they stayed there. After that, he wouldn't so much as look at me."

"Go with the Flow"

Another sticky problem for the women was the issue of menstruation. The men were always trying to prove that this was a reason to ground women. At first, they did try to ground the WAFS for the duration of their period—and for a certain number of days before and after. Nancy Love strenuously objected to this. Of course, enforcing this rule proved to be too complicated, so the unwritten rule was to "go with the flow."

Lois (Hailey) Brooks, Class 43-W-3: "The medical doctors would say, 'We want you to be grounded during your period.' Well, nobody would go report to him when their period was, so, of course, he couldn't ground us. If we were off on a ferry trip and we had to deliver the airplane by a specified date, we couldn't allow ourselves to be grounded until we got the job done."

Rita (Davoly) Webster: "It seems to me we had to mark down on some sheet of paper when we had our menstrual period. They also checked our reactions to things other than periods and to see whether we differed in general physiology from the men. We went in the high-altitude chamber to see what the reaction was. I think up until the very end, they were waiting for us to fall on our face."

A group of WASP "guinea pigs" were put in the altitude, and the pressure in the chamber was reduced to simulate the pressure at 28,000 feet. The girls were then instructed to take off their oxygen masks and do some tests like recite the alphabet backwards. All of the girls except Vivian (Hicks) Fagan quickly passed out. Eventually, Fagan began to turn "black," so she was asked to put on her mask. She had remained conscious for a record amount of time without supplemental oxygen—indicating a high resistance to anoxia—but her ear drums burst as the pressure in the chamber was returned to normal.

The doctors who conducted these studies finally concluded that a woman's menstrual period did not adversely affect her ability to fly an airplane. Whew! According to the WASPs, the plane didn't care whether or not the person at the controls had a uterus or not.

It was a fun, dangerous, frustrating, beloved job for the 1,074 women.

"Micky" (Tuttle) Axton: "We were just so eager. We were tickled to do whatever job they wanted us to do."

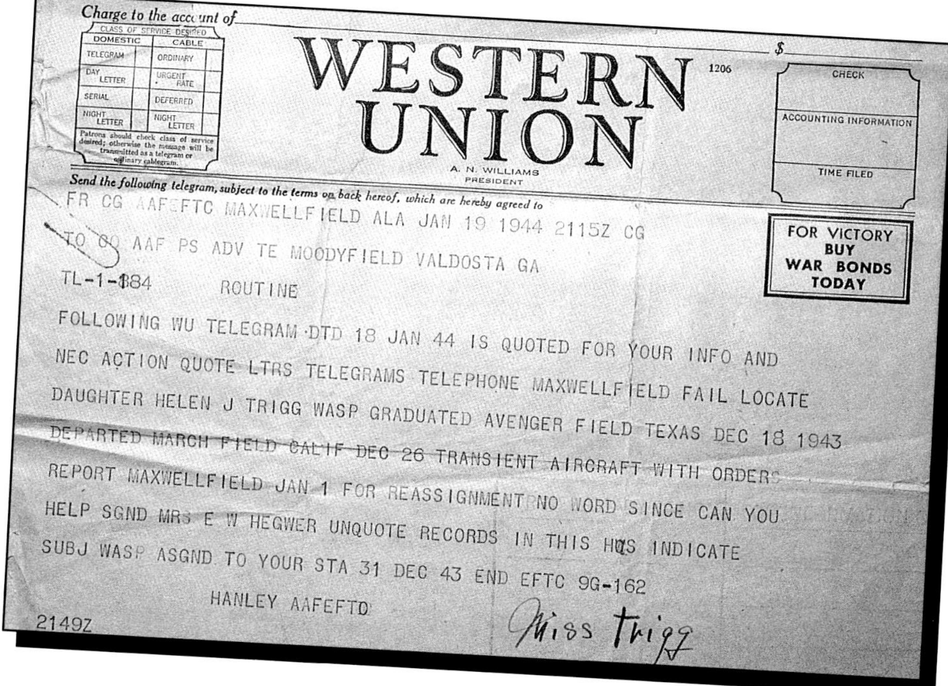

Charge to the account of

CLASS OF SERVICE DESIRED — DOMESTIC: TELEGRAM, DAY LETTER, SERIAL, NIGHT LETTER — CABLE: ORDINARY, URGENT RATE, DEFERRED, NIGHT LETTER

Patrons should check class of service desired; otherwise the message will be transmitted as a telegram or ordinary cablegram.

WESTERN UNION 1206

A. N. WILLIAMS PRESIDENT

$ — CHECK — ACCOUNTING INFORMATION — TIME FILED

Send the following telegram, subject to the terms on back hereof, which are hereby agreed to

FR CG AAF=FTC MAXWELLFIELD ALA JAN 19 1944 2115Z CG

TO CG AAF PS ADV TE MOODYFIELD VALDOSTA GA

FOR VICTORY BUY WAR BONDS TODAY

TL-1-184 ROUTINE

FOLLOWING WU TELEGRAM DTD 18 JAN 44 IS QUOTED FOR YOUR INFO AND NEC ACTION QUOTE LTRS TELEGRAMS TELEPHONE MAXWELLFIELD FAIL LOCATE DAUGHTER HELEN J TRIGG WASP GRADUATED AVENGER FIELD TEXAS DEC 18 1943 DEPARTED MARCH FIELD CALIF DEC 26 TRANSIENT AIRCRAFT WITH ORDERS REPORT MAXWELLFIELD JAN 1 FOR REASSIGNMENT NO WORD SINCE CAN YOU HELP SGND MRS E W HEGWER UNQUOTE RECORDS IN THIS HQS INDICATE SUBJ WASP ASGND TO YOUR STA 31 DEC 43 END EFTC 9G-162

HANLEY AAFEFTD

2149Z

Miss Trigg

Every family's nightmare, a missing loved one. ***Special Collections, Texas Woman's University.*** **Previous page, Nancy E. Batson (WAFS), Gwendolyn E. (Cowart) Hickerson (Class 43-W-4), Betty J. (Hanson) Erenberg (Class 44-W-3), and Shirley Haugan (Class 44-W-3) at New Castle Army Air Base, Wilmington, Delaware. Batson was one of the "Originals."** ***USAF (neg. no. B 29681 AC)***

T.O.NO.13.1.5
C.W

Chapter 5

"Rugged but Right"

The Author's Favorite WASP Stories

When Jackie Cochran heard this particular song, she banned it from Avenger Field. But I think it displays a certain joy of life and living and a little bit of recklessness, which describes the stories in this chapter. This is a montage of stories. Some are joyful, some are sad, and some are heroic. The first one is my all-time favorite WASP story.

Lola Perkins was on a very straightforward ferrying mission and ended up being weathered in. She had not planned ahead and had no change of clothes. It was snowing and windy—and that was *inside* her barracks. So when she rinsed out her undies, she had nowhere to dry them.

When she was finally able to continue her journey, she hopped in the cockpit of the plane she was to fly out and noticed that it was warm and dry. She decided to take advantage of the warmth, hung up her panties to dry, and went off to get some breakfast. When she went back for them, they were gone and a pair of men's pink briefs were in their place. There was a note: "Mine are pink too. Have a nice flight."

There's another one about a trainee that may be apocryphal, but I like it. This trainee was on a cross-country check flight and got lost—in Mexico! She landed in a field, and a flock of sheep came along who thought the fabric on the wings of her plane looked just like supper. She grabbed a stick and was found by a young man, madly trying to protect her plane from these plane-eating sheep. The young man wanted to get her some help, but he spoke no English and she spoke no Spanish, so she wrote a note and he took it sixty miles to the nearest English-speaking person.

Meanwhile, back at Avenger Field they were getting worried. This trainee had been gone quite a while, and they would have to report her missing soon. Just before the report was to be filed they heard from their "lost little lamb." She told them the whole story. When she arrived back at her bay, she was greeted by a resounding chorus of *baaaaaaaaa*ing.

Dorothea (Johnson) Moorman, Class 43-W-4, and Dora (Dougherty) Strother, Class 43-W-3, have the distinction of being the only two women who got to check out in the B-29 Superfortress, the Army Air Force's biggest, most complex bomber. They had been stationed at Eglin Army Air Base in Florida, but Lieutenant Colonel Paul W. Tibbets, Jr., (the pilot who later dropped the first atomic bomb on Japan) took them over to Anniston, Alabama, and trained them on the big plane.

The first time they came in for a landing and Moorman called the tower, the tower

Velma Saunders, Class 43-W-6, pauses before the plexiglass nose of the a Martin B-26 on the flying line at Harlingen Army Air Field, Texas, before climbing into the cockpit.
USAF (neg. no. 28829 AC)

Rugged but Right

I just called up to tell you that I'm rugged but right
A rambling woman, a gambling woman, drunk every night.
I order porterhouse steak three times a day for my board
And that is more than any decent gal in town can afford!

I've got a big electric fan to keep me cool while I eat,
A tall and handsome man to keep me warm while I sleep,
I'm just a rambling woman, a gambling woman,
And boy am I tight.

I just called up to tell you
That I'm rugged but right!
HO-HO-HO, rugged but right!

We may be brown-skinned lassies but what do we care,
We've got those well-built chassis
And that take it or leave it air

We've got the hips that sank the ships
In England, France, and Peru,
And if you're like Napoleon, then it's your Waterloo.

I'll take a fifteen minute intermission in your V-8,
I'd like to make it longer, but I've got a late date,
My motto has always been "Gone with the Wind,"
So let's breeze it tonight.

I just called up to tell you
That I'm rugged but right!
HO-HO-HO, rugged but right!

could be heard to ask the B-29 without a radio to report in. Once it was discovered that the women were flying, a crowd gathered on the field to watch them land. Colonel Tibbets was pleased with their abilities and planned a cross-country trip to show them off. He nicknamed the plane *Ladybird*.

A WASP also got to fly America's first jet airplane type. Ann (Baumgartner) Carl, Class 43-W-5, was the first and only WASP to fly the experimental, twin-engine YP-59. She would be the only lucky lady to fly an American military jet for almost ten years. She was also the only WASP stationed at Wright Field and got to fly a Japanese Zero and a German Bf-109.

"Rig" Edwards: "One day I was instructing a student in a Stearman biwing, and we had just cleared the airport when an oil seal broke and sprayed oil back over the windshield. I made the mistake of looking outside first and got my goggles all covered. I threw those off, and I told my student, 'Down to your right, there's a fire extinguisher—better get it out. You're going to need it.' So while she was digging out the extinguisher—we didn't have radio contact like they have now—I had to wiggle my wings in order to get the tower's attention. We made the turn and had just gotten back down on the ground when that engine just came apart. So it was hairy, but I kept my cool, and she kept her cool too."

Marjory (Foster) Munn: "I had a classmate who was on a cross-country run and her map flew out of her hand and into the back seat. She landed in a grass field, got her map, got back in, and took off again. Of course this was strictly illegal. (Once we landed, we were supposed to stay there and call in to report our landing.) So she came in to her designated field with grass still hanging off of her landing gear. To explain how she picked up the grass, she told them that she must have been flying lower than she thought."

Munn had an experience of her own that wasn't so funny. She was out in a Stearman and was landing when all of a sudden another plane landed right on top of her airplane. The propeller sliced through the fuselage, right behind her head, bounced up, and then sliced right through the wing. Amazingly, she was not hurt at all, but she could hear her instructor yelling, "My God, that's my student!"

She went to look at the plane after it was taken back to the main field, and it looked just shredded. The mechanics couldn't believe there had been anybody in that airplane.

"Then I had a forced landing," said Munn. "I was in a BT practicing my instruments procedures, so I was under the hood and had an observer. All of a sudden we lost power, and she took over. I came out from under the hood to see that the airplane was smoking. We didn't see any fire, but she landed in a cow pasture, anyway. It was a beautiful landing. Soon, we were picked up by an Army Air Forces group and were taken to their field. We had dinner and were treated like celebrities; then they took us back to our base."

Sounds like a pretty nice forced landing.

Muriel (Rath) Reynolds: "I was taxiing once, when I suddenly found myself flying behind a B-17, three feet off the ground.

"I was at Maxwell Field and I was returning from a delivery of some papers. We had been taught not to taxi in back of airplanes, but I didn't see any engines going on the B-17, so I went behind it. Just as I got around the left side, they revved up their engines. My airplane beamed into the slipstream, and my airplane came off the ground three feet.

"There I was trying to keep that AT-6 flying. If I didn't keep the engine going I would be flipped over backwards. I couldn't move forward. I couldn't move backward.

"As if that wasn't scary enough, the tail of the B-17 was between me and the tower so they couldn't see me. And as soon as I beamed into the slipstream, my headset flew off completely, so I had no audio connection with the tower. In order to get the mic, I needed to reach down, but I had the stick in my hand, and my other one was also busy, so I couldn't possibly get the mic. Finally, I had to do something. I put the stick between my legs, and reached down and got the mic. I looked up at the tail of

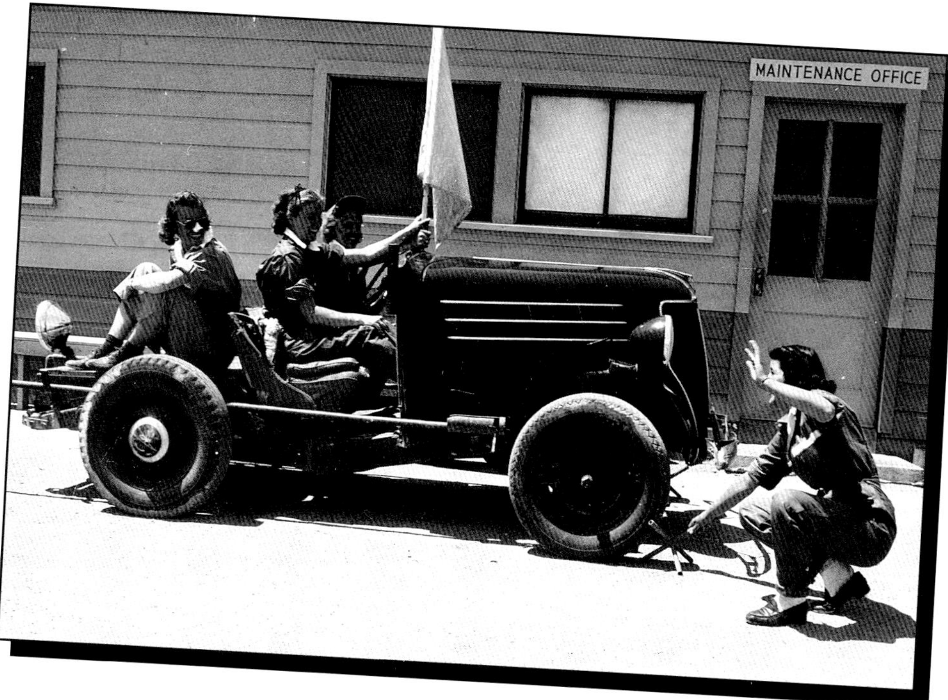

WASP training was tough and demanding, but the girls were always able to find time for a little fun. *Jeanne Robertson.* Previous page, left to right: Dorothea (Moorman) Johnson, (Class 43-W-4), Dora (Dougherty) Strother, (Class 43-W-3), Lieutenant Colonel Paul W. Tibbets (later to pilot the *Enola Gay*, the B-29 to drop the first atomic bomb); and Civil Aeronautics Administration inspector Dean Hudson. This photo was made prior to the WASPs taking a check flight with Mr. Hudson for a type rating on the B-29. *Special Collections, Texas Woman's University*

"We're all good friends. It was such a short part of our lives and we all went our own directions, but I feel very comfortable with them. I feel like I can go to some town and call them up and go to their house. It's a network, and we can count on each other."

—Margaret "Maggie" Gee Class 44-W-9

the plane and got the fifteen-letter designation and called the tower: 'B-17 da da da da da has its engines going. Please, could you tell them to cut their starboard engines?'

"I looked up at the B-17, and there were two little heads, a mile away, looking out of the airplane at the situation behind them. They couldn't believe it, but they quickly cut the engines.

Instrument Commandments

These commandments were written by Patricia Hopkins and printed in the Class 44-W-10 Yearbook. Class 44-W-10 was the "Lost Last Class". They knew that the WASP program was to be deactivated, and that they could hope to see only a few days of active duty. But they were optimistic, hoping for a last-minute reprieve that would keep the WASPs from being disbanded. Courtesy of Special Collections, Texas Woman's University.

Thou shalt control the airspeed with the stick.
Thou shalt control the altitude with the throttle.
Above all else, thou shalt control thyself.
Remember the rate group.
Thy name shall be mud if thou dost not watch the little airplane.
Thou shalt not talk to thyself while flying Pattern B-1.
Thou shalt not peek.
Thou shalt not curse the Abilene radio operator until he has obliterated thy cone three times.
Thou shalt not leave thy directional gyro caged for takeoff.
Thou shalt not hear false cones.
Thou shalt call an "A" an "A" and an "N" an "N".
Thou shalt not turn to the left and claim thou hast turned right.
Thou shalt pretend the nightly ringing in your ears is as of heavenly bells.
As front seat pilot thou shalt automatically take over after thy buddy's first 45° bank on a rate group.
Honor thy Link trainer.
Thou shalt "keep it straight with your little paddies."
Thou shalt not search farther than 100 miles for a fade.
Thou shalt trust thy instruments until they rumba before thine eyes.
Thou shalt not employ a Kelly procedure with a Bryan check pilot.
Thou shalt control the ball with the stick — in Link.
Thou shalt control the ball with the rudder — in the airplane.
Remember that thy landing gear is not retractable.
Thou shalt not covet thy neighbor's beam, especially if his ship is bigger than thine.
Thy gray hairs shalt multiply faster than thou canst subtract 180.
"That's all there is to it, kids. It's easy."

"After my AT-6 settled to the ground, I tried to take off with my head held high. I went back home, and that's all I ever knew about it."

Vivian (Hicks) Fagan: "Everyone's been scared in an airplane at some time because not everything goes smoothly forever. On my first cross-country trip I just happened to get in the clouds. I had never been near a cloud. I didn't even know what they looked like. I thought it was smoke, and that was scary.

"I did what I'd been taught to do. There were no instruments to speak of, only altimeter and airspeed. I just glued my eyes to them and, fortunately, I had a very stable airplane. I don't think I'd be here to tell the story if it hadn't been a stable plane because I ended up flying in clouds for a long time. I don't tell that to very many people. I figure that pilots won't believe it when I say that I flew almost all the way, about forty minutes, in the clouds, in a small plane. I should have spun out, but I didn't. I finally found a hole in the clouds and spiraled down.

"What a blessing! I could see green trees below and knew I was near my destination. I had been heading for Tacoma from Centralia, and when I came out of the clouds I wasn't sure about where I was. I'd been flying blind for so long. I flew for just a few minutes and saw a runway over to my left and water beyond that. I just turned over there and landed, and it was Tacoma Airport. My eyes were so bloodshot I could hardly see. I had been flying about an hour altogether and most of the time was in the clouds."

"B. J." Williams: "I thought my number was up. There was an airplane at Randolph that they were having a lot of trouble with, and none of the male test pilots would fly it. They knew it had been in the repair shop many, many times because it had erratic behavior, and it needed to be tested to see if it was airworthy.

"We were anxious to fly. The men weren't because many of them had been in combat and so forth, so Petey [E. Marie Pedersen] and I were kept busy. We flew, flew, flew all the time, and we liked it.

"So this particular aircraft was up for test, and none of the guys would fly it. They said, 'No way! No way am I flying that bird!' So they asked us. Petey looked at me, and I looked at her, and we flipped a coin. I won, or lost, depending on how you look at it. So I went through all the airplane's records, everything they had done to it, and I noticed that this airplane had really been wracked around. All the ground crew were around me saying, 'What kind of flowers would you like at your funeral?' Very encouraging!

"I got in and checked it on the ground as thoroughly as I could. I made sure all the controls were connected up properly, because often they weren't, and that could kill you.

"I taxied out, and on the way up I was doing gradual turns and climbing turns. I realized the airplane was very sluggish. It did not respond the way an AT-6 normally would.

"I went on up to about 10,000 feet. I had done a series of stalls on the way up, but I wondered how this thing would act in a spin. I cleared the area, stalled the aircraft, and kicked in left rudder, pulled back on the stick, and went into a spin to the left.

"Well, we were always taught in an AT-6 never to go over one revolution in a spin, because it would really wind up like a top. When spinning the AT-6 we'd let it go into one turn, and then we'd immediately recover. As I was coming up to the recovery, I kicked in opposite controls to recover, and the airplane just went right on spinning, and I thought, Uh oh!

"I then tried to reenter, like we had been taught, and the spin just kept gettin' tighter and tighter and tighter, going its own little merry way. I thought, Holy Nelly! What do I do now? The forces were unbelievable.

"There's a hatch on this thing. In order to jump out you have to pull this hatch up, but the forces were so strong that I couldn't get my hand up above chest level. I couldn't get my hand even to the latch.

"As they say, my life passed in front of my eyes. I remembered things from when I was four years old. But then a voice in my ear, from one of my instructors, said, 'If you ever get into a condition like that where the airplane won't respond, take both hands and put them on the stick and pretend that you're whipping a big bowl of mashed potatoes and go clear around. Sweep out the cockpit.' You're never supposed to use aileron in a recovery from a spin because it could snap the wing, but I had nothing to lose, so I went all the way around just wiping out the cockpit and the airplane responded. Oh boy! How wonderful!

"But now I was going at such a tremendous speed toward earth that in order to slow it up, I could not bring the stick back fast or I would still have ripped the wings off. I had to inch it back—inch, inch, inch, ever so little—to try to reduce the speed and bring it under control. When I recovered, I was 500 feet off the ground.

"So I started back up again, and I thought, I wonder if it'd do that to the right? The eternal problem solver, I was going to do a thorough job so that when I got back I could tell the engineering people exactly what was wrong with this airplane. So up I went, back up to 10,000 feet, and all of a sudden this little voice said, 'Why don't you stop when you're ahead?' That seemed a reasonable idea, so I just trimmed off, got my composure back, and came back into the traffic pattern and landed.

"I had another interesting experience. When we knew we were going to be deactivated, we wanted to fly, fly, fly because we knew this was it. We wouldn't have any more opportunities to get this kind of training in this kind of aircraft. The Army had some brand new P-40s, and I wanted the experience of flying that P-40. So I went to the major in charge, and I said, 'What do I have to do to fly that P-40?' He said, 'Get in line, there are generals ahead of you!' I said, 'Okay, but in the meantime, what could I do?' So he handed me the tech manual and told me to read it.

"Petey and I sat down at every lunch period and poured over the tech manual. Well, when we thought we were ready, we took the blindfold test—they would put a blindfold on you, sit you in the cockpit, and you had to touch every knob, control, and lever and even the circuit breakers and tell what they were (I think I missed two circuit breakers)—and passed. So I wanted to fly it.

"It wasn't too long after that the major called and asked if we two gals would like to check out in a P-40.

Margaret "Maggie" Gee in her A-2 leather flight jacket and goggles. Gee became the second Chinese-American female service pilot when she graduated with WASP Class 44-W-9.

And we said, 'Wowee!' So Petey took one and I took the other, and boy, what an experience.

"The P-40 has a long in-line engine. Whenever a P-40 taxied out to take off, they stopped all air traffic because the engine had a habit of overheating, so the minute the P-40 got into takeoff position they didn't want it to have to wait. They gave us clearance to take off right away. That nose was so long, and when I opened up that throttle and started down that runway, the force actually pushed me back in my seat.

"Anyway, we flew the P-40s, and then we landed beautifully, so our check-out pilots told us we were checked out. It was only two days later that they called up and said they had a P-40 to be tested, and Petey says, 'Not me!' Well I wasn't going to be chicken, so I went over, and the mechanics didn't have it quite ready. That made me a little bit nervous because the later they got it ready, the more certain it would be that I would have to land after dark.

"The airplane needed to be 'slow timed.' That means I had to take the airplane up and fly it at slow speed for an hour to break in a new engine. It was late in the afternoon when they finally got it all ready to go, and this was only my second time in the airplane. I took off and went upstairs.

"I trimmed off and was slow-timin' it, when all of a sudden I looked out and boy, it was gettin' dark. Pretty soon lights started to come on, and I was thinking, Oh no! The second time I'm going to land this airplane I'm going to land it at night? Well I didn't have any choice, I had to come in and land it at night and that was scary! I don't like night flying anyway!

"The next day at lunch, this red-headed major who was a real hotshot pilot came over, and he said, 'Boy, lady, you're somethin'; we don't even allow our tactical pilots to land a P-40 at night!' And I said, 'Well sir, what was I to do? I didn't have a choice, did I? I couldn't keep flying all night. I would have run out of gas!'"

Rita (Davoly) Webster: "Jean [(Hoopes) Parker] went up solo to practice recovery from a spin. As the plane was spinning down, she took the stick and pushed it forward. Her sleeve caught on the hook of the seatbelt and undid the latch. The seatbelt came off, and she started to fly out of the airplane. She was half out of the plane, but was still holding onto the stick. Of course, as she did that she was pulling back on the stick, so the nose of the airplane started coming up, and she thought, My God, this thing is going to stall again.

"To prevent the stall, she popped the stick forward again and fell completely out of the plane. Luckily, she had her parachute on and she landed safely. I don't remember what happened to the airplane. It probably crashed someplace.

"Later, when she was close to getting her license, the instructor said, 'You have to go up and complete a spin.' After falling out of the plane during that earlier spin, she didn't want to try spins again. Fortunately, this instructor was just as nice as he could be. He was just like a father. I can still see him sitting under the wing with Jean, talking and talking and talking to her. He finally talked her into going up.

"So she went up and all of us stood there and watched her. She went round and round and recovered beautifully. The next thing you know she came in and landed."

Genevieve (Landman) Rausch: "One of my close calls was on a night flight. I was 150 feet below the altitude I was supposed to be at. So I start to pull up. The stars are suddenly gone. I look out to the left and I see a red light. I look out to the right and I see a green light. I had pulled up under the belly of a B-17! And I wasn't killed. The pilot of the B-17 never saw me, but he pulled off one way and I went the other. So we had our close calls. And that was one of my close calls."

And, finally, it was sometimes safer to be up in a plane than down on the ground. Frances Grimes and Margaret Cook had a head-on collision—on a baseball field. Frances lost two front teeth and Margaret had to have eleven stitches in her ear.

Mr. Jenkinson, one of the WASPs' favorite instructors. ***"Dottie" Davis.*** **Below, planes on the field just before a night flying mission.** ***Vivian Fagan.*** **Previous page,above, on the flightline and in the plexiglass cockpits of their aircraft, WASPs were constantly exposed to the sun, so the girls sometimes resorted to unusual methods to protect themselves.** ***Jeanne Robertson.*** **Previous page, below, Fifinella can be found on all sorts of memorabilia. At reunions, you can purchase necklaces, patches, watches, pins, and T-shirts with the image of the little aviatrix.** *© Disney Enterprises, Inc.; photo by Hans Halberstadt*

Genevieve (Landman) Rausch, Class 44-W-5. As a WASP, she was stationed at Moore Army Air Base and at Alamogordo Army Air Base, where she towed targets and flew as a lookout in the plexiglass nose of bombers that were on rescue missions. *Hans Halberstadt.* Right, what is it about pilots and their leather jackets? The Fifinella patch on Lillian Ruth Dixon's well-aged A-2 flight jacket. *© Disney Enterprises, Inc.; photo by Hans Halberstadt*

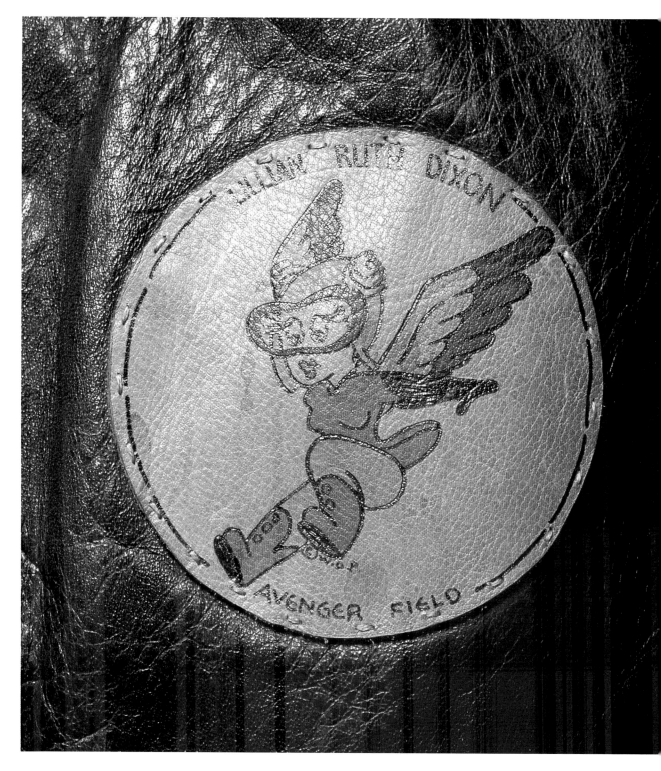

The log book is only one of a WASP's cherished documents. *Hans Halberstadt.* Left, dog tags were for identifying the pilot if something tragic should happen. Thirty-eight WASPs were killed in flying accidents caused by pilot error, instructor error, mechanical error, and even weather. Some WASPs became quite superstitious and would never fly without their good-luck charms. *Hans Halberstadt*

"Micky" (Tuttle) Axton stands outside the cockpit of a Cessna UC-78 twin-engine trainer. *"Micky" Axton.* Below, Dorothea (Johnson) Moorman and Dora (Dougherty) Strother in the window of a Boeing B-17 at Grand Island Army Air Field, Nebraska. Both Moorman and Dougherty were checked out as first pilot on the B-17. *Special Collections, Texas Woman's University.* Next page, WASPs Evelyn (Stewart) Jackson, Rita (Davoly) Webster, and Carol (Webb) Cook of Class 43-W-6 in front of a B-26 Marauder. *Rita (Davoly) Webster*

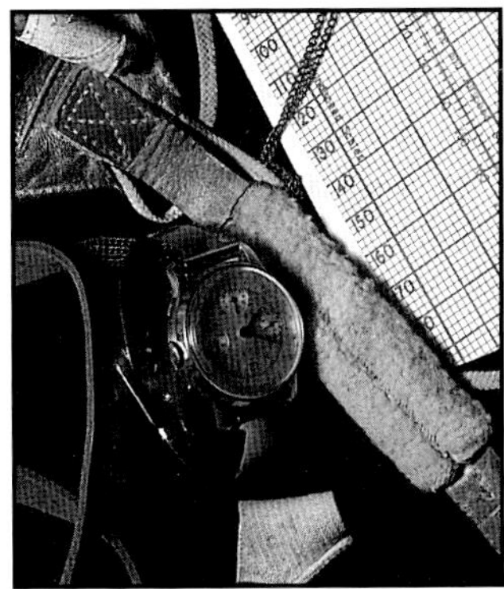

Chapter 6

"Goin' Back to Where I Come From"

The WASPs are Disbanded and Go On With Their Lives

For what is ultimately a triumphal story, the tale of the WASPs takes a pretty nasty turn at this point. The WASPs had been doing their jobs, happily. They had been awaiting the day when they would be militarized so they would not have to feel so insecure about their standing. Jackie Cochran had been actively working to get them militarized. General "Hap" Arnold was on her side, but since there was a war on and he had been recovering from a heart attack, he was a wee bit busy and not of much help. The important players—the secretary of war, the president, and many military leaders—were *for* militarization. But they also were a bit busy and wished the whole issue would resolve itself. "Militarize them—under the WACs if necessary—just don't bother me with the details," might describe their attitude.

The Fight For Militarization

Jackie Cochran was a detail person. She feared militarization under the WACs for personal reasons: she didn't like Oveta Culp Hobby and felt Hobby had mismanaged the WACs. Cochran also had two compelling professional reasons for keeping the WASPs separate from the WACs: WACs had to be over twenty years old (many important and necessary WASPs were between eighteen and twenty) and WACs couldn't have any children under the age of fourteen (again, many WASPs had children under fourteen). Finally, the WASPs were flyers—not typists or nurses or cooks, but flyers. And Cochran didn't want the WASPs' skills to be squandered.

For a number of reasons, the champions on Cochran's side weren't very loud in voicing their support. But the other side, the nasty side, had a number of loudmouths. The loudest was Drew Pearson of the Washington *Times-Herald.*

While researching and doing interviews for this book, I started out thinking of these women as "Glamour Girls" and in the most reverent way. They were young and strong and beautiful and courageous. They had stamina and proved themselves time and again to be good at their jobs. It was grueling, dangerous work, yet they still managed to run a comb through their hair and put on some lipstick as they were taxiing in. Now that's glamour.

Drew Pearson, however, used the term "Glamour Girls" as an epithet. He must have decided that the issue of the WASPs would be his claim to fame. And he had no use for Jackie Cochran, either. In June 1944, a week before the House of Representatives was

Flying necessities: dog tags, watch, E-6B computer, and helmet with gosport. The gosport was a way for the instructor to communicate with the student, but it was a one-way device. The students were to be seen and not heard. ***Hans Halberstadt***

Goin' Back to Where I Come From

I'm goin' back to where I come from
Where the honeysuckly smells so sweet
It darn near makes you sick.
I usta think my life was hum-drum,
But I sure have learned a lesson that is bound to stick.
There ain't no use in my pretendin',
But the city just ain't no place
For a gal like me to end in.

I crawled away from every check ride,
Hurdled all the tees and stages,
Got with instruments and gages.
RONs were might pleasant
And our navigating efforts were a sight to see.
DEW DE DEW DEW DEW DEW DEW DEW DEW DEW
DO DO DO.

There ain't no use in my pretendin'
That the Army is the proper place,
For a gal like me to end in.
I'm going back to where I come from,
But I'll have my silver wings and Santiago Blues.
DEW DE DEW DEW DEW DEW DEW DEW DEW DEW
DO DO DO.

When I grow old and have a grandson,
I'll tell him how I flew and watch his eyes bug out.
And you can bet that he'll believe me,
And he'll do the same dern thing
When he grows up, no doubt.

That's how it goes. That's how it should be.
Cause he got it from his grandma...HE WAS BORN TO FLY!
DEW DE DEW DEW DEW DEW DEW DEW DEW DEW
DO DO DO.

Betty Archibald and Juanita Bolish, WASPs at Romulus Army Air Field, discuss an aeronautical chart on a P-39 Airacobra fighter. WASPs logged sixty million miles, some as chauffeurs and gofers! They were occasionally sent to the Gulf of Mexico to pick up lobsters for dinner.
USAF (neg. no. A 29684 AC)

In October 1944, the WASPs were sent letters from Jackie Cochran and "Hap" Arnold breaking the news that the WASPs were to be disbanded on December 20, 1944.

to vote on WASP militarization, he wrote the following:

"In the last week, the shapely pilot [Jackie Cochran] has seen her coveted commission come closer and closer. One of the highest placed generals, it seems, gazed into her eyes and since then has taken her cause célèbre very much to heart. . . . She's such an attractive composition of windblown bob, smiling eyes, and outdoor skin, nobody blames him."

Even for the era, his tone was patronizing and insulting.

He and other writers and publications like *Time* magazine turned public opinion against the WASPs. In a May 29, 1944, *Time* article titled "Unnecessary and Undesirable," the writer said that the WASP experiment had been expensive and that there were men out there who could have been trained more quickly and cheaply.

Al Williams of the Washington *Daily News* wrote that Barbara Jane (Erickson) London's Air Medal and the feat she accomplished to be awarded it were mere publicity stunts. And one more poison-pen article from Drew Pearson talked about "Hap" Arnold "sidetracking the law by continuing to use the WASPs." He exaggerated the amount of money spent on training and once again implied hanky-panky going on in the relationship between Cochran and Arnold.

Secretary of War Stimson spoke up on the side of the WASPs, stating in the May 4, 1944, New York *Times* that "'neither the existence nor the militarization of the Wasps [sic] will keep out of the Army Air Forces a single instructor or partially trained civilian pilot who desires to become a service pilot or cadet and can meet the applicable standards of the Army Air Forces."

When the issue of militarization came up for a vote, public opinion, the Veteran's Administration, the American Legion, and civilian pilots (who feared for their jobs after the war) were strong voices against the WASPs, and the issue was lost. Those who were *for* militarization had spoken up too late.

Disbanded

Cochran then took a last desperate step. She released a very long, very detailed statement to the public and to General Arnold. It included all the facts about the WASPs: their history, activities, achievements, and the goings-on in Congress over militarization. She ended the report by asking for "simple justice." She wanted the WASPs to be militarized or the program to be scrapped.

Her timing was fatal. The year before, there was a shortage of pilots. Planes were stacked up at factories. The civilian male pilots that now spoke up against the WASPs had been rejected for a number of reasons, such as health problems, and women seemed to be, and proved to be, the solution.

By the time Cochran's report was released, the situation was a little different. Ironically, because of the work of the WASPs (that is, ferrying and training), the pilot shortage was not as critical as it had been. "Hap" Arnold grabbed on to the "ultimatum" aspect of the report as a way to make the issue go away. And so it was decided to disband, deactivate, and dispose of this experimental and successful program to have women fly for the military.

In October 1944, the WASPs were sent letters from Cochran and Arnold breaking the news that the WASPs were to be disbanded on December 20, 1944. They were shocked.

One person who was especially shocked to receive her letters was Nancy Love. She had supported Cochran, somewhat, in her bid for militarization because she realized it was best for the program in the long run. All along, though, she thought her girls were in a different category. She thought that the training school might eventually be shut down, which would be fine by her, but she thought that the original WAFS would be allowed to fly until the end of the war. They had been formed with a different set of goals and standards. They were never supposed to be militarized. They had required only minimal training and were only supposed to ferry planes. But she was wrong and the WAFS were to be sent home too.

Love felt that Cochran's "grand schemes" had swept her girls up in a conflict in which they had no desire to engage. Among the WAFS, Cochran's activities were seen as meddling.

Barbara Jane (Erickson) London: "Our group [the WAFS and WASPs] was just an absolute melting pot of different types of people. And every one of them is going to have a different view of what these three years were. It depends a lot on when they came in, why they came in, and where they were stationed. I talk to some of the girls in the later classes who think Cochran gave them the world. Well, she did in a way; they never would have flown without her and that opportunity. But the very pattern of what was done with that whole program is what put us out of business.

"So you can look at it two ways. It was great for those individual girls who might not have ever flown. But we started taking girls who were eighteen years old with only thirty-five hours and building up a monstrous, huge program. The program should have been reined in a little bit sooner, and then maybe the rest of us who were already there could have stayed. Jackie did not get her way of getting us militarized, and she refused to have us associated with the WACs and Oveta Culp Hobby. Her idea was, 'Either I get my way or they go home.' So home we went."

Betty (Huyler) Gillies felt that Cochran's ego—wanting to be of higher rank that Colonel Hobby and wanting

Many WASPs attended an officer training program, the school of applied tactics, in Orlando, Florida. This school taught them everything they would need to know to be Army Air Forces officers, in anticipation of the Wasps being militarized. By mid-1944, about half of the WASPs had undergone this training. *Special Collections, Texas Woman's University*

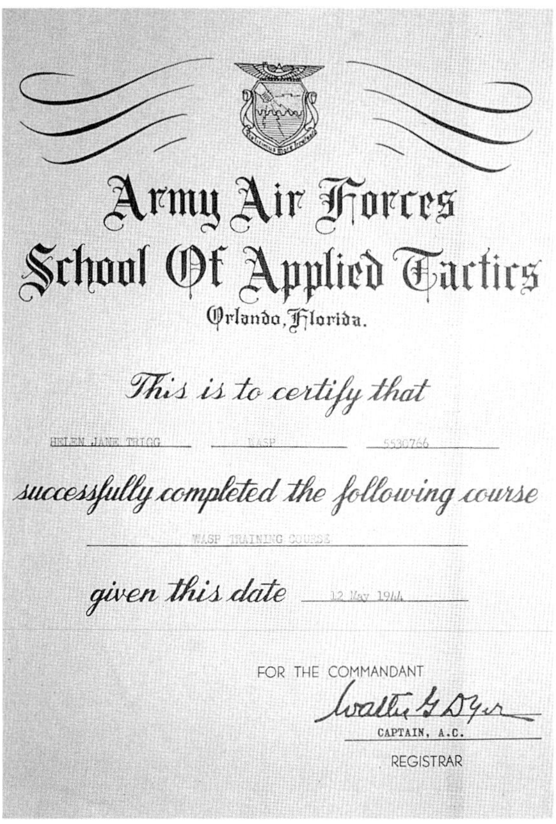

Army Air Forces
School Of Applied Tactics
Orlando, Florida.

This is to certify that

HELEN JANE TRIGG WASP 5530766

successfully completed the following course

WASP TRAINING COURSE

given this date 12 May 1944

FOR THE COMMANDANT

Walter G. Dyer
CAPTAIN, A.C.
REGISTRAR

the WASPs for a feather in her own cap—was at fault for their deactivation. She and Barbara Jane (Erickson) London were heartbroken to have to quit flying while over fifty planes were on the field at Long Beach waiting to be ferried. Gillies and the other ferry pilots wrote to the Pentagon and volunteered to continue to ferry planes for one dollar a year. Their offer was turned down.

To the WASPs, though, Jackie Cochran was Athena, goddess of war, fighting for their honor, and she lost.

The "Lost Last Class"

Speaking of lost, what happened in all the hullabaloo to the women who had been accepted for the last classes? Class 45-W-1 was sent home without flying a single military plane. Class 44-W-10 graduated on December 7, 1944, and had only a little over a week to be WASPs.

"Cappy" Morrison: "I was in the last class [44-W-10], and why they let us graduate nobody knows. They knew when we were in primary that we would be deactivated and there would be no more classes. Yet they let us graduate and get our wings. I will be eternally grateful for that.

"There were gals that came after us who had sold their houses and didn't get the word about deactivation. They appeared in Sweetwater ready to go on to their classes only to be told to go home. 'Go home to what? I sold it!' So they were *really* lost. But we called ourselves the 'Lost Last Class.'"

Everyone called them the "Lost Last Class."

Ruth (Glaser) Guhsé just barely made it into Class 44-W-10. "Originally I received notice to report to the June 1944 class, but received a telegram telling me to report earlier in May. By the grace of the Powers that Be, I did get in the last class. I'm forever grateful to have had the experience of flying military planes. It was one of the happiest periods of my life."

Vivian (Hicks) Fagan: "When we found out we were going to be disbanded, we were so anxious to get as much high-horsepower time as we could that we'd nab some of the return combat pilots and they'd fly copilot for us. We'd make a deal: 'We'll play golf with you on Sunday if you'll fly copilot for us on Saturday so we can log more time.'"

As of one minute past midnight on December 20, 1944, 1,074 WASPs were officially just women. They were supposed to be given transportation home, or at least officially as close to home as possible. Some bases were grateful to have had them, sorry to see them go, and glad to be able to offer them transportation home. Other bases only saw them out the gates.

Emotionally, this was devastating for the girls.

Lois (Hollingsworth) Ziler: "I just couldn't imagine how they were going to get along without us!"

"Maggie" Gee said she felt empty, that it didn't feel right coming home when the war wasn't over. Genevieve (Landman) Rausch was just blue. She went home to her mother in shock.

Marjory (Foster) Munn: "It was almost like a funeral, it was a shock. What do we do now? We wondered what kind of jobs we could get flying."

They wondered what they had done wrong.

Ironically, by now, public opinion and the newspapers (except Drew Pearson) were in favor of the WASPs. But it was too late. So they went home and went on with their lives.

The bases where the WASPs had served submitted final reports on their performance. A history of the WASPs was gathered by the Army Air Forces, the Training Command, and the Air Transport Command. The conclusion was sort of surprising considering the ignominious way the WASPs were sent home. They found that the women had been an asset at every base and that they had been the victims of competition and bias. In fact, it was a glowing report on their service to the country. The medical section of the report said they were healthy specimens, if unusual in that they never menstruated (remember, the WASPs had adopted a policy of

WASP Evelyn Sharp in the cockpit of a Douglas C-47. *USAF (neg. no. B 24844 AC)*

Betty (Huyler) Gillies and the other ferry pilots wrote to the Pentagon and volunteered to continue to ferry planes for one dollar a year. Their offer was turned down.

"Don't tell, and certainly don't complain!"). The report was filed away as classified. It was an awkward end for all concerned, and the country was still at war. So everyone forgot that the WASPs had even existed and went on to win the war and celebrate.

Luckily we don't have to end the story of the fly girls on this sad note. Most WASPs went on to have very interesting lives. Their experience in the program was heartbreaking at the end, but their hearts healed and it ultimately gave them the confidence to go on and do many great things.

"B. J." Williams: "One of the few jobs we *could* get was flying surplus aircraft that were sitting dormant on various airfields to airport operators who wanted them. The men were still off flying in the war and those old planes could be had for a song, so that's what a lot of us did when we first got out. It was extremely dangerous work. In some of those aircraft, you'd go to use a control and you'd pull it right out of its mount. It was just awful. I knew somebody who was killed trying to fly those worn-out airplanes.

"This gal was flying a surplus aircraft, and the operator wanted her to go down below the border and do a pickup. She didn't know what the cargo was, but he had that ship very overloaded. When an aircraft is overloaded, balance is critical. If not balanced properly, the plane's like a Mack truck with no brakes when you get into rough weather or anything. It's just impossible. And she crashed.

"I flew a surplus plane once, and it was the most horrendous experience. I said to myself, 'You went through a war situation and you came out unscathed. Why are you doing this when you know better?' So I quit.

"After I quit, I got my commercial license as a flight instructor. I had the flight instructor's rating and the Link Trainer instructor's rating, so I got a job to set up an instrument school in 1946 and 1947.

"One of my students was an executive with the Young and Rubicam ad agency. He liked my style and

By 1944, many in the media were now against militarization of the WASPs, and turned public opinion against them. ***Special Collections, Texas Woman's University***

"One of the few jobs we could get was flying surplus aircraft that were sitting dormant on various airfields to airport operators who wanted them.... It was extremely dangerous work. In some of those aircraft, you'd go to use a control and you'd pull it right out of its mount. It was just awful.

—Betty Jane "B. J." Williams, Class 44-W-6

asked me if I had ever thought about going into television. This was in the infancy of television, so I had to ask what it was. Once he explained it to me, I couldn't shut out the creative forces. I came up with an idea for a weather show. He wanted to know why. I said farmers, pilots, and everyone else wants to know about the weather because it affects what they wear to work, etc. Then I had this concept of putting an aviation program on television that would be educational, but also entertaining. Well, CBS was then trying to perfect color, and they said to me, 'We can't spend too much money on this. Can you do a program from an airport so we won't have to build a new set?' 'Perfect,' I said. 'Sure!'

"Well, we did it. We used all sorts of camera techniques and special split-screen effects never seen before, and it turned out to be quite a show."

Williams ended up back on active duty in the Air Force, but they weren't allowing women to fly, so she was a television producer. She retired as a lieutenant colonel.

Barbara Jane (Erickson) London: "I tried to get in the airlines when I got out of the military. We were as qualified as a lot of guys, but they offered us jobs as stews, not as pilots. My husband and I met up with some people and we formed our own aviation company here in Long Beach. I also worked with Betty [Gillies] in the Powder Puff Derby from 1949 until the early sixties. We raced every year for eighteen or nineteen years. I only missed two years, the two years my kids were born. But I flew while I was pregnant, until I couldn't get the stick back.

"I've been so fortunate. Here I am almost seventy-three years old, and I have everything. I've got two gorgeous kids. Of course, the kids were born and raised in an airplane. We never went anyplace that we didn't dump them in the back seat of an airplane to fly to grandma's. We didn't drive.

"All my daughter, Terry, wanted was to be a pilot. She soloed on her sixteenth birthday, got her license on her seventeenth birthday, and she was twenty-six or twenty-seven when she finally got hired as the first woman pilot for Western Airlines. There were only about ten women airline pilots at that time. And that's all she really wanted to do. She has been an airline pilot for seventeen years.

"I've had a marvelous life. So I think it was just a series of best days. I could drop dead tomorrow; I've had it all."

Marjory (Foster) Munn: "I became an aircraft communicator for about a year. You're based at airports and you receive calls from airplanes and they might ask for the weather or other information, and that was interesting. Then I was an aircraft inspector for the Army at Washington National Airport, and I got to see the president and 'Hap' Arnold and all the visiting dignitaries. Then that job folded so I applied for a job with Pan American and became an airline stewardess."

Betty (Huyler) Gillies test-flew the FRI Interceptor for Grumman Aircraft and competed in and ran the All Woman Transcontinental Air Race for many years. This race was called the Powder Puff Derby.

Muriel (Rath) Reynolds, who had wanted to fly because she wanted to see the world, got a job teaching physical education in Shanghai, China, for a year and a half before Mao Tse Tung came marching through. On her way home she stopped in Hong Kong, Rangoon, Thailand, New Delhi, Europe, and London.

"Cappy" Morrison: "After I left the WASP I went into the Navy. But the war ended while I was in boot camp, and they didn't know what to do with all of us women, so they offered us either mess detail in Washington, D.C., or the Hospital Corps. So I joined the Hospital Corps, and that was okay. Then I joined the Air Force. While I was on active duty I was with Aerospace Research. I tested the ejection seats for the B-47. I also rode in the centrifuge, testing the g-forces. One day I felt a pain in my chest, and I asked the doctor about it. He said, 'Don't worry about it. It's just your sternum poking into your chest. It'll go away after a while.'

"One idiot doctor who was doing an arterial study would come off the centrifuge dripping blood. He had this catheter in an artery and he was squirtin' blood all over the place. So we did some stupid things."

Vivian (Hicks) Fagan: "I just couldn't stay grounded so I went back to eastern Washington where I got an airplane and started instructing. I was giving lessons, and finally, after about a year, the city council in Lind, Washington, wanted me to come there and start a flying school for returned military personnel that could fly and could do things under the GI bill. It was a nice field. It was a little tough to get the school started, but I did and then it worked out fine. I was there for several years.

"When I came to Hawaii in 1949, I applied for a copilot's job with Aloha Airlines. I had all the qualifications, but they turned me down because I was a woman. They could be very honest about it then. They thought that nobody would fly with a woman pilot, so instead they hired me to train their pilots on instruments. Well, times have changed."

"Dot" (Swain) Lewis and "Winnie" Wood tell about Lewis' unusual activities after deactivation.

"Winnie" Wood: "We did the All Women's Air Show in Miami and 'Kaddy' [Katherine (Landry) Steele] said, 'Get Winnie to be operation's manager, because everybody will get mad at her and she'll get mad at everybody else, but nobody will hold a grudge.' So we did it and that was the first Powder Puff Derby in Miami.

"Then Dot started this awful, dangerous air show act. It was one of the funniest things I've ever seen, but it also scared the beejeezus out of me, if you'll pardon my saying so. I was sitting on the stands, and the commentator said, 'We would like anybody who would like to learn to fly to come down.' So here comes this little old lady out of the grandstand. And it was Dot. She had on these terrible baggy stockings and this long black dress, and she comes down. He says, 'Now here's the instruction book.' So here she is pretending to be a first-time flyer and gets in that Cub, all alone with just the book. She took off like she'd never flown before, all over the place. She did things in that Cub, which no fool would ever have done. I'm serious. And it was the scariest thing I ever saw, it really was."

Lewis: "The commentator would say, 'Now lower the wing.' I'd lower the wrong wing, and then I'd come around. I was low.

Wood: "She was far too low."

Lewis: "I was about twenty feet above the ground."

Wood: "From the grandstand you could see her."

Lewis: "I held the stick with my knees, so I could read the book."

In 1946 a few of the gals had their first reunion. William Piper had these ex-WASPs fly ninety-two Cubs from Lockhaven, Pennsylvania, to Cleveland, Ohio, for the National Air Races. They flew in formation and landed at their destination with nary a mishap. ***Special Collections, Texas Woman's University***

Wood: "She flew by the grandstand reading the book! I thought I'd die."

Lewis: "And then the book fell out the window, and then *everything* went crazy! It was really funny."

Wood: "It was terrible!"

"Kay" (Menges) Brick kept up with aviation. She got her instructor rating and then went into air racing. She was instrumental in the All Woman Transcontinental Air Race and stayed active in the Ninety-Nines (the International Organization of Woman Pilots).

Lois (Hollingsworth) Ziler and Lois (Hailey) Brooks went back to El Paso, Texas, and ran a ground school there for many years.

Jeanne (Bennett) Robertson became a very accomplished artist in Hawaii. Along with Tweet Coleman, she has set up a scholarship fund to help women achieve a career in aviation. She gives the proceeds from two of her watercolor prints to this fund.

"Maggie" Gee found that when she ran for president of the Chinese Student group at the University of California—Berkeley there was no stopping her. Her confidence and maturity were way beyond the other

Gene (Shaffer) FitzPatrick still gives flight lessons in her Piper Cherokee. (FitzPatrick gave the author her first lesson!) *Hans Halberstadt.* Below left, Debbie Woodson, Gene (Shaffer) FitzPatrick's granddaughter, in FitzPatrick's A-2 leather flight jacket. WASPs were issued flight jackets but had to purchase them for a fairly substantial sum if they wanted to keep the jackets after the WASPs were deactivated. *Hans Halberstadt.* Below right, proud possessions of the WASPs. *Hans Halberstadt.* Next page, "Micky" (Tuttle) Axton is a colonel in the Confederate Air Force. Axton still flies every chance she gets and speaks about her experiences as a WASP at every opportunity. Many of the former WASPs are still flying. Here she is, in September 1991, flying *Fifi,* the only B-29 Superfortress still flying in the world. *Boeing photo courtesy of "Micky" Axton*

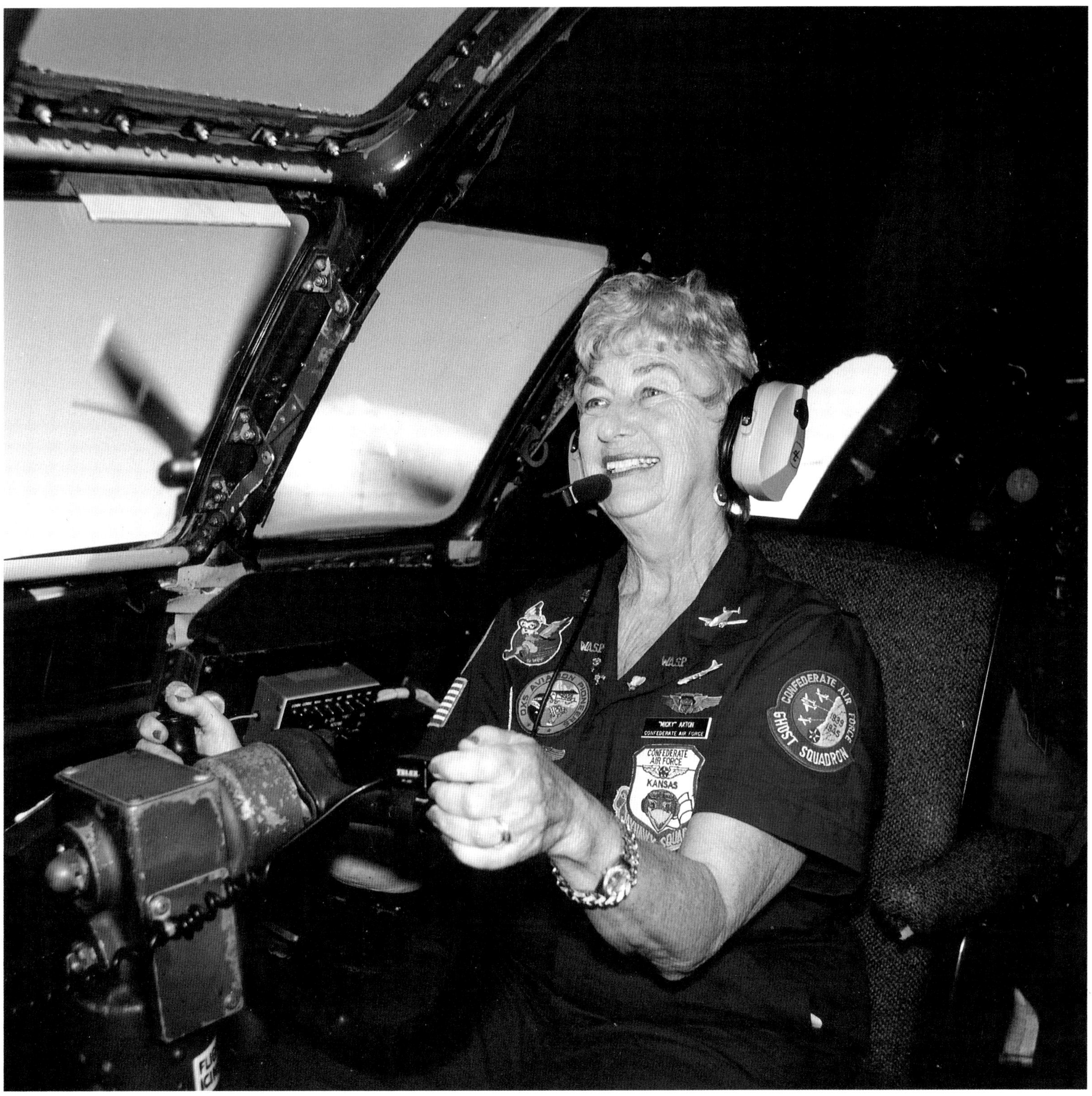
W.A.S.P.
W.A.S.P.
OX5 AVIATION PIONEERS
"MICKY" AXTON
CONFEDERATE AIR FORCE
CONFEDERATE AIR FORCE
KANSAS
CONFEDERATE AIR FORCE
GHOST SQUADRON

"By the grace of the Powers that Be, I did get in the last class. I'm forever grateful to have had the experience of flying military planes. It was one of the happiest periods of my life."

—Ruth (Glaser) Guhsé, Class 44-W-10

Jackie Cochran's Final Report

Reprinted below is the cover letter to the final report by Jackie Cochran on the WASP program. She named names, counted numbers, and still came up short. She was heartbroken when the WASPs were deactivated and sent home. They were given no word of thanks, and the whole program was filed away as classified and forgotten. Letter courtesy of Texas Woman's University

HEADQUARTERS, ARMY AIR FORCES
WASHINGTON 25, D. C.

SUBJECT: Final Report on Women Pilot Progress
TO: Commanding General, Army Air Forces

The requested report on the women pilot program is transmitted herewith. Of necessity, it omits comparative study of experience abroad in various countries with women pilots, due to unavailability of most of the material to date; that information, including therein the experience of American women pilots who served in England, will be included in a supplemental report in due course. The report transmitted herewith eliminates detailed supporting data, all of which is being assembled as a part of the historical report being prepared by the Historical Division of the AAF. Statistical data in the accompanying report has been either furnished or verified by the Statistical Control Division.

The outstanding facts and the conclusions and recommendations of the Director of Women Pilots are briefly summarized as follows:

FACTS

More than 25,000 women applied for women pilot training. Eighteen hundred and thirty (1,830) were accepted. 30.7% were eliminated during training for flying deficiency and another 2.5% for other reasons, with consequent lower elimination rate than among male cadet pilots. 8% of those accepted resigned and 1,074 graduated, or 58.7% of the total. Of the 1,074 who graduated, 900 remained at time of inactivation, or 83.6% of the graduates, to which should be added 16 of the original WAFS employed who were still with the program at time of inactivation.

The women pilots, subsequent to graduation from the training program, flew approximately 60 million miles for the Army Air Forces; the fatalities were 38, or one to about 16,000 hours of flying. Both the accident rate and the fatality rate compared favorably with the rates for male pilots in similar work.

The WASP, according to the overwhelming opinion of station commanders where they were on duty, were as efficient and effective as the male pilots in most classes of duties; and were better than the men in some duties, as for example towing of targets for gunnery practice. Almost uniformly the WASP were reported eager to learn, willing to work, and well behaved. The WASPs did ferrying, target towing, tracking and searchlight missions, simulated strafing, smoke laying and other chemical missions, radio control flying, basic instrumentation instruction, engineering test flying, administrative and utility flying. The WASPs flew during operational duties nearly every type of airplane used by the AAF, from the small primary trainer to the Superfortress (B-29), including the Mustang, Thunderbolt, B-17, B-26, and C-54.

The WASPs, according to the medical surveys, had as much endurance and were no more subject to fatigue and flew as regularly and for as long hours as the male pilots in similar work. Aptitude and psychological tests, including the

students'. She became a physicist and works at Lawrence Livermore Lab in California. She says she was the only woman to work at the lab for many years; her experience as a WASP helped her cope with this situation.

Rita (Davoly) Webster also worked ferrying those old junked planes. "After I left the service, I did get a job at an airport in New Jersey, in Sommerville. It was a very nice field that this Norwegian man had built, and he was going to start a flying school. And so he bought some surplus trainers from the Army, some PT-17s. They were staked out in an open field in Oklahoma for God knows how many years, and I got the job of ferrying them from that field to New Jersey. Everybody I talk to now says, 'You were out of your mind. Those things were not safe.' Anyhow, I got home okay, but the planes really weren't safe. I checked them the best I could, and I asked the mechanic there if he had checked them. He said, 'Yes.' So, I just trusted them.

"But really, it was fun. I was up there all by myself, looking down at these little cars; you don't see the people, just the cars. You're up there and you trim the plane and put your feet up and eat an apple. It's just like you're floating in the air.

"In those days, companies used to give out calendars, which nobody does anymore. A lot of the companies had a picture of their factory or their manufacturing plant on this calendar, and so a couple of times I went out with the photographer and we'd do aerial photography or aerial mappings. We weren't supposed to fly lower than 3,000 feet over the city, but we'd have to go out and find the manufacturing plant and then when we would get all set, the photographer would take the door off the plane, and hang out there with his camera. When we would get near the factory, I would sort of side-slip in and he would click, click, click. Then I would take off before anybody could get our number.

Stanine test, were found to be equally determinative and selective in the case of WASPs as in the case of males. The conclusion of the medical studies is, "It is no longer a matter of speculation that graduate WASPs were adapted physically, mentally, and psychologically to the type of flying assigned."

CONCLUSIONS

1. Women can meet the standard WD-AGO Form 64 physical examination for flying; and those meeting the proper height and weight requirements can be trained, approximately as quickly and as economically as men in the same age group, to fly all types of planes safely, efficiently, and regularly.

2. The best women pilot material is in the lower age brackets, down to 18 years.

3. It follows from conclusion 1 above that women can effectively release male pilots for other duties; and they have done so with the WASP program.

4. Physiology peculiar to women is not a handicap to flying or dependable performance of duty in a properly selected group.

5. The psychological, aptitude, and other tests used in the case of male pilots have approximately the same usefulness in the case of women pilots.

6. The flying safety record of women pilots approximates that of male pilots in the same type of work, whether training or operational. The elimination rate for women in training as pilots is approximately the same as for the flying cadets in the same age groups.

7. Women pilots have as much stamina and endurance and are no more subject to operational or flying fatigue than male pilots doing similar work. Women pilots can safely fly as many hours per month as male pilots.

8. Even limiting the selection of women pilots to the age and height groups named below, and also discounting for all factors incident to the fact that the WASP program was comparatively small and therefore somewhat more selective than even the aviation cadet program, an effective women's air force of many scores of thousands of good dependable pilots could be built up in the case of need from the nearly 13 million young women of our country between the ages of 18 and 28, about 6 million of whom are single.

RECOMMENDATIONS

1. Any future women pilot program should be militarized from the beginning.

2. For general economy and efficiency, the upper age limit should be 27 or 28 years for women to be trained as pilots for subsequent operational flying duties.

3. All pilots in any future program should pass through a standard training course before being assigned to operational flying duty.

4. The minimum height for women accepted for service as pilots with the Army Air Forces, with the present types of planes in use, should be 64 inches, with a minimum weight of 110 pounds. Above these limits the weight allowance in relationship to height should be the same as for men, less about 7 pounds.

5. If at any time in the future, the War Department takes a favorable position with respect to legislation to grant veterans' rights to various civilian organizations which have served with the armed forces, all WASP who completed the program in good standing should be included, and the next of kin of WASP who died in the line of duty should receive compensation comparable to that which would have been received if the WASP had been on military status with insurance privileges and benefits.

JACQUELINE COCHRAN
Director of Women Pilots.

"On another job, I was sent up to Maine to photograph a forest with infrared film. We went in the fall when the leaves were beginning to turn, and by the colors on this infrared film they could tell what kind of lumber was in that forest."

Genevieve (Landman) Rausch took a job with an aviation magazine. She got to fly a different plane every month and do a pilot's report on it.

"Micky" (Tuttle) Axton is very active in the Confederate Air Force and speaks about her experiences in the WASP every chance she gets.

When Florence (Emig) Wheeler got out of the WASP, she went back to her family in California. She says one of the real delights in her life is that she then taught her dad to fly. He had been the one who was so crazy about aviation and had really propelled her into it, so she was happy to share that feeling with him of "leaving the earth behind."

Gene (Shaffer) FitzPatrick gives lessons and flies every chance she gets. "Here I am about fifty years later, still instructing. I didn't do it the whole time; I took twenty years off to raise the kids and all that kind of stuff. But now it beats staying home with grandkids. You might as well do what you like to do. I like to fly; it's fun."

Florence (Emig) Wheeler expressed the sentiments of almost all of them at this stage in their lives. "When it was over, my feeling was get on with my life. History is history. It is good to remember our WASP experiences and to appreciate them, but what is present is more important, and what is future is much more important."

"When I came to Hawaii in 1949, I applied for a copilot's job with Aloha Airlines. I had all the qualifications, but they turned me down because I was a woman. They could be very honest about it then. They thought that nobody would fly with a woman pilot, so instead they hired me to train their pilots on instruments. Well, times have changed."

—Vivian (Hicks) Fagan, Class 44-W-7

AVENGER FIELD
SWEETWATER
HOME OF THE WASP'S 1942 - 194

Chapter 7

"Buckle Down Fifinella"

One Last Mission: Military Recognition

After deactivation, most of the WASPs got married and had children and never said a word about what "mommy did in the war." Before they were deactivated, two WASPs—Katherine "Kay" Dussaq, Class 44-W-1, and Clara Jo (Marsh) Stember, Class 44-W-3—started an organization to keep track of the WASPs: The Order of the Fifinella. One of their original goals was to help find jobs for the women, but mostly it turned out to be a way to keep in touch with others who had shared a secret, bittersweet experience. (Speaking of bittersweet, Dussaq was killed in a crash while she was on her way to talk to Nancy Love about future plans for the Air Transport Command women pilots.)

The WASPs would get together and have reunions occasionally, but most of the ladies went on to other things. But in 1972 they had a thirty-year reunion at Sweetwater, Texas. By then, most of their children were raised and the ladies were getting a little older and perhaps a little nostalgic, and so a large crowd of them showed up in Sweetwater. They marched in a parade and caught up on old times. A grand time was had by all. One of the subjects of discussion was that sore one: militarization. But most of them were resigned to their experience: "It's over, we've led good lives, just forget about it."

Later, they began to feel a new emotion about their experience: anger. In 1976, the Air Force decided to train women to fly, and the Pentagon released a proud statement to the public referring to the "first women to fly for the military."

Well, that was it! The WASPs got angry. "Fine! Use us and discard us. Don't pay us. Don't respect us. But don't sit there and pretend we never existed!" And they buckled down.

They recruited a couple of warriors to help them. Colonel Bruce Arnold (son of "Hap") vowed to see the wishes of his father, the militarization of the WASPs, accomplished. Senator Barry Goldwater had great respect for the WASPs and wanted their contribution recognized. He had flown with the WASPs during World War II when he, too, was a pilot in the Ferry Command. (Jackie Cochran had used herself up in 1944 fighting for militarization and stayed out of this fight.)

Round one: Senator Goldwater and Colonel Arnold put the issue before the Senate, and it passed. Piece of cake! Then on to the House of Representatives, where the real work began. The American Legion and Veteran's Administration, just like in 1944, got involved and lobbied against militarization. Since most of the members of congress were veterans, this was a mighty powerful lobby. Their premise was that if the WASPs were militarized, then every civilian organization that existed during World War II would ask to be militarized: the Civil Air Patrol, the Merchant Marines, and so on. The lobbyists raised fears about how much it would cost when all these civilian organizations came forward

Buckle Down, Fifinella
(Tune: "Buckle Down Windsock!")

Buckle down, Fifinella, buckle down,
You can win, Fifinella, if you'll buckle down,
You can really fly, if you'll only try,
Take it way up high and bring it down.

Six to go Fifinella, don't be slow,
Stay an eager beaver, you'll be in the show.
Don't get in a spin, take it on the chin,
And you're bound to win,
If you will only buckle down.

If you fight, your luck will not retreat,
If you work, you'll overcome defeat,
Buckle down, Fifinella, buckle down,
Don't you frown, Fifinella,
You'll get off the ground,
We'll count every day and we'll make it pay,
For we're here to stay,
Because we're gonna buckle down!

The entrance to Avenger Field, Sweetwater, Texas, today. ***Hans Halberstadt***

Many people who are not World War II buffs, don't recognize this mascot, or know that women flew in World War II. The WASPs did not talk about their experiences for many years. Many of their children did not even know that "Mom flew in the war." *© Disney Enterprises, Inc.; photo by Hans Halberstadt*

with hat in one hand, the other hand outstretched.

The WASPs got to work. They had done their homework and replied that they *were* a de facto military organization. The women had applied to the program with the expectation of being militarized. They had been trained in military procedures and had lived by them. They had worn uniforms and side arms, they had saluted and marched, they had gone to the School of Applied Tactics at Orlando for officer training, and they had died for their country.

Dora (Dougherty) Strother (one of the two who checked out in the B-29, a Ph.D., the chief of human factors testing at Bell Helicopter, and a lieutenant colonel in the USAF Reserve) testified to the record of the WASPs, their service, their safety record, and their professionalism.

This time, they also worked on getting public support. Dorothy "Dottie" Davis was living in San Francisco and had been asked to help out by getting petitions signed. She sat out in front of restaurants and was very politely told, "No, they hadn't heard of the WASP and had no time to sign a petition to support White Anglo-Saxon Protestants who couldn't get into the military." So "Dottie" wrote up a fact sheet about the WASPs, but had little success when she tried to get people to read it.

Then the movie *Star Wars* was released in the theater. The lines for the movie stretched around the block, and Davis saw these people as a captive audience for her cause. She passed out the fact sheet to the people waiting in line. They were happy to have something to read, and once they understood who she was and what she was asking, they happily signed the petition. After all, she was asking that the "force be with the WASPs." The Air Force that is. Her efforts paid off; she gathered thousands of signatures and these were sent to Washington, D.C., to illustrate public support.

Public support and a stunning presentation by Dora (Dougherty) Strother added to the WASPs cause, but their success was sealed by a technical error that had been made during the war. When WASP Helen (Porter) Sheffer learned that she was to be deactivated in 1944, she was the only WASP stationed at Strother Field in Kansas. Porter was lonely and decided to resign instead of waiting for deactivation. The base commander was fond of her, and of WASPs in general, and was sorry to see her go. He gave her a regulation Army Honorable Discharge certificate. She thanked him, but she did not correct his misunderstanding of her status. Sheffer kept that paper with her all those years, and when someone with the House Military Affairs Committee remarked that there was no proof that the WASPs had been a de facto military organization, she quietly handed him her Army discharge.

Proof? Proof!

During the seventies, the military was having some growing pains, or actually shrinking pains. America had gone from a draft to an all-volunteer military, and the military was trying to recruit more people. The female population was being wooed, and the Pentagon worried that a defeat of the WASPs bid might look bad to all those potential G.I. Josephinas. So the WASPs won.

In 1977, President Jimmy Carter signed the WASPs on as military. They would not receive retroactive pay, death insurance, or gold stars for the windows of the families who lost a daughter in service to their country, but at least some recognition that they had existed, that they had performed a valuable service to their country, and that some had been killed while doing so.

Barbara Jane (Erickson) London: "It gave the families of the girls that were killed a feeling that they died for their country. Six of my girls were killed. I had to go six times and tell their mothers that their daughters weren't coming home, and I was only twenty-two!

"I think that's what really hurt during the war, is that we were put in the position of telling them that they did not get a flag or any other military recognition. And that was a shame."

On a more cheerful note, Jeanne (Bennett) Robertson was thrilled when the WASPs were militarized: "One of the main reasons it was done is that some of our women were having a hard time financially. Through this they get some veteran's benefits, and they can get medical care at Veteran's Administration facilities. And I can be buried in a military grave, which just *thrills* me to pieces."

Nancy Love had wanted to do a job for her country. Her way might have been better in the short term. The girls would have flown until the war was over. No conflict, no stress, just ferrying—and then home to husbands and family.

Jackie Cochran had wanted women to be an equal part of the Air Force, doing all the jobs the men had done (except combat). She had gone about this her own way. You might argue that she made some errors. Perhaps it had been a mistake to allow the women to be brought in as civilians at first with the hope that they would be militarized after proving themselves. In the end, the women had a lower rate of accidents per 100,000 hours flown than the men. They had stamina and guts. Their record would prove they were worthy of being "wingtip to wingtip" with their "brothers in the sky."

Perhaps it had been a mistake not to allow the women to be militarized under the WACs, but none of the WASPs had wanted be part of the WAC.

Jackie Cochran had not prevented Nancy Love and Betty (Huyler) Gillies from delivering the B-17 bomber to England (a mission that might have opened up the possibilities of women ferrying beyond the contiguous United States), but she would have tried to had she not been ill at the time. Cochran was concerned about individual achievement. If the two had successfully delivered the plane to Britain, Love and Gillies would have gotten the glory. If the two had gone down in the drink, though, it probably would have been seen as proof that women (in general) weren't good pilots. Cochran knew that individual achievement reflected on the individual, whereas individual failure reflected on the group.

Cochran's schemes had been grand. She had wanted to get women pilots flying for their country. She had failed, in a very specific sense. The program had been discarded, and the women had been sent home with no recognition for a job well done. When I talked to my contemporaries about this project, they said, "I didn't know there were women pilots in World War II!"

But finally, I feel the program was a success and that it succeeded because of what some would consider Jackie Cochran's "mistakes." The 25,000 women who applied had their horizons broadened. They thought, Hey, maybe I can do this! when they had never thought beyond hometown and marriage before. The 1,830 women who were accepted tried to accomplish something extraordinary and

By 1972, their children were grown, they may have retired from careers, and they had more time on their hands. The WASPs were ready to remember their glory days as "fly girls," so many of them gathered for the reunion in 1972 in Sweetwater, Texas. The town welcomed the women with open arms.
Jeanne Robertson

Marguerite "Ty" (Hughes) Killen, Class 44-W-7, wearing her Zoot Suit.
Hans Halberstadt

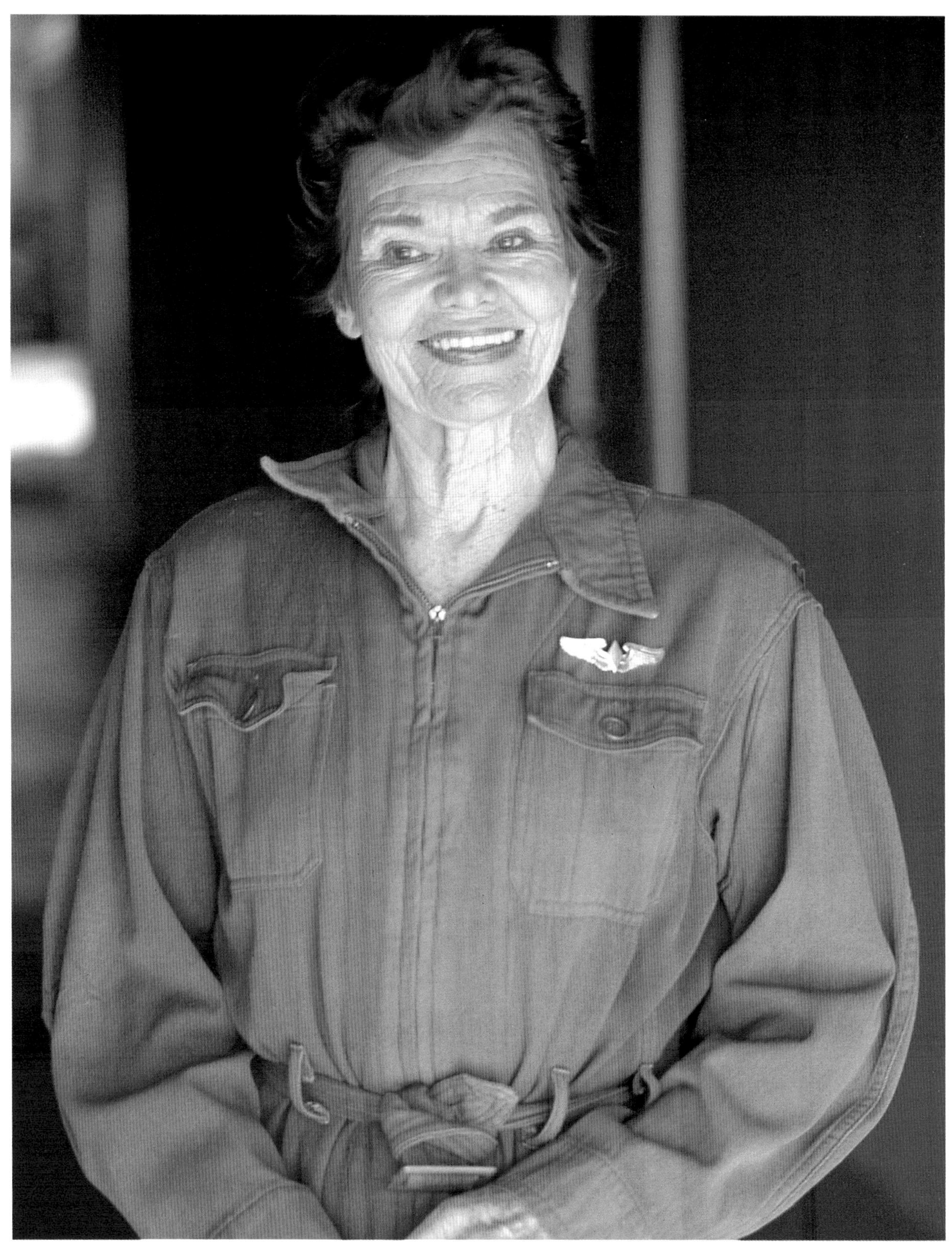

During the seventies, the military was having some growing pains, or actually shrinking pains. America had gone from a draft to an all-volunteer military . . . the female population was being wooed, and the Pentagon worried that a defeat of the WASPs bid might look bad to all those potential G.I. Josephinas. So the WASPs won.

should look at that as an achievement. Their names are on the plaques at Avenger Field. The 1,074 women who graduated, whether they flew for two years or one week, did change the way we look at women pilots.

In every case, the experience changed a life—sometimes for the worse. Helen Richey was one of the Americans who flew with the ATA in Britain and then came back home and flew as a WASP. She committed suicide after the war.

"B. J." Williams said that after she got out she felt like a fish out of water. None of them wanted to give up flying. But she also said, "It was a pioneer program and whenever you are pioneering, you are going to run up against these kinds of obstacles. If everything were easy, life would be boring."

But for the most part the experience was for the best.

Vivian (Hicks) Fagan: "No regrets. We were doing what we wanted to do."

The WASPs I spoke with were grateful for the chance to serve their country, grateful for the opportunity to fly all those delicious planes, and grateful for the lifelong friends they made.

Jeanne (Bennett) Robertson, Class 43-W-4, in the cockpit of a restored AT-6 in November 1993. Robertson is an artist and lives in Hawaii. She has set up a scholarship program to help young women learn to fly. *Left,* Jeanne (Bennett) Robertson in the cockpit of an AT-6 at Avenger Field, May 1943. *Jeanne Robertson*

Mementos of "Dottie" Davis' best day. "Dottie" Davis was part of the grass roots effort to get military recognition for the WASPs. Davis passed around an informational flyer to people waiting in line to see the movie *Star Wars* and managed to gather thousands of signatures on a petition to militarize the WASPs. Davis' next best day was in 1977 when President Jimmy Carter officially militarized the WASPs. *"Dottie" Davis*

"Kay" (Menges) Brick: "After fifty years we have stayed friends, and you just never lose that comradeship. We don't feel fifty years older."

Lois (Hollingsworth) Ziler: "The years drop away and you're girls again. We go back to maiden names."

"Maggie" Gee: "We're all good friends. It was such a short part of our lives and we all went our own directions, but I feel very comfortable with them. I feel like I can go to some town and call them up and go to their house. It's a network, and we can count on each other."

They had a reunion in 1946, and William Piper saved for them ninety-two little yellow Cubs that needed delivery. The WASPs got to fly them, in formation, to the National Air races at Cleveland, Ohio. The Cubs all arrived in perfect condition—and some of the women hadn't flown in a year and a half.

They still go to reunions: their fiftieth was in 1992 in San Antonio. They all said it would probably be the last big get-together. They said they were getting old. Well, not in my book, literally and figuratively. They are young at heart, vibrant, funny ladies with great stories to tell.

Women in the military today know the story of the WASPs, know they were pioneers, and think of them as role models. At the dedication of a memorial statue in Sweetwater I met a young women who had driven from Colorado all by herself to meet her heroes. She wore a Zoot Suit and a turban.

Rita (Davoly) Webster: "Now we're getting more recognition, now that we're dying off like flies. But at the time we were a hush-hush operation."

The WASPs have divergent views about women in the military today.

Vivian (Hicks) Fagan: "I hope that we never have a war again, but I am glad that now the girls can go in and be military pilots and fly the big wings and have the experiences we had."

Barbara Jane (Erickson) London: "I think it's fantastic that they are getting opportunities like we used to get. There's a DC-10 out in San Bernardino that is called the only unmanned DC-10 in the Air Force because the crew is entirely female."

Although Mary Jane (Lind) Sellers is delighted that women are doing so much for the military today, she would hate to have a daughter of hers put in a position where she might be taken prisoner by an enemy.

Alyce (Stevens) Rohrer: "If I had been asked, or if I'd been allowed, to fly in combat back then, I would have done it. I don't see why a woman who wants to do that shouldn't. But I do think that women in combat on the ground present a different problem.

"We as human beings have thousands of years of development behind us. Women have always had to produce the babies, and they've always had to be protected by the males while they did it. That protective instinct on the part of the male is bred into us. I can see that if women were allowed in combat, that it might cause problems because no matter how well-trained a soldier would be, his first thought would be to protect the woman beside him, and that might be dangerous in certain cases. So I can see why some people are hesitant about it. A man's life in my way of thinking is every bit as precious as a woman's, but his attitude would be to sacrifice himself for her. So maybe women shouldn't be in combat. I'm not sure."

Jeanne (Bennett) Robertson: "I have some mixed feelings on women in the military. I didn't experience any of the harassment that they talk about. I'm sure there was some harassment, somewhere, but I had a wedding ring, and that was respected. We tended to overlook comments. We pretended not to hear or just ignored the meaning of them. And maybe that wasn't good, but that was the way we handled it. Today, women are much more knowledgeable; we were naive. And I think when women go into the military they should go with their eyes open and be ready to do the equivalent of what men do or they shouldn't go in."

Many of the WASPs feel the same way Jeanne (Bennett) Robertson does about sexual harassment. They dealt with unwanted male attention by not dealing with it; they

"The years drop away and you're girls again. We go back to maiden names."
—Lois (Hollingsworth) Ziler, Class 43-W-3

In May 1993 at Avenger Field, a memorial was dedicated to the women who came there to train in 1943 and 1944. The centerpiece of the memorial is a statue showing a trainee in her coveralls. The names of the trainees and graduates are engraved on black granite plaques, and the names of those who were killed are indicated by a gold star. During World War II, the families of soldiers who gave their lives could display a gold star in their window—it was a small but vital consolation for the family. The families of WASPs who were killed could not display the star because their WASP daughters had not been officially inducted into the military. It is only fitting that these women who gave their lives in service to the United States finally have their gold star. *Hans Halberstadt*

Bernice "Bee" (Falk) Haydu, Class 44-W-7, with her two granddaughters in May 1993. Haydu was stationed at Pecos Army Air Base in Pecos, Texas. *Hans Halberstadt*

ignored it. In 1943, this was probably a good short-term solution to the problem. But in the 1990s, women in the military need to consider long-term solutions. The WASPs realize that their situation was different from that of today, and that theirs may not be the best advice.

Elvira (Griggs) Cardin has a theory that she was never hassled because she had talent and confidence. And she feels that this holds true for women pilots today. She met Kelly Hamilton and another gal who was a pilot for the Navy at one of the WASP reunions, and they both said that they had experienced no harassment. They agreed with Elvira that if you're good at your job, you'll get treated with respect.

The WASPs are surprised and honored to be considered role models.

"Micky" (Tuttle) Axton: "I spoke at a graduation ceremony for Navy pilots. There were three girls in the graduating class I spoke to. It meant a lot to them, they told me, to have a woman pilot give them their graduation talk. And it really meant a lot to me to be asked."

In 1993 at Sweetwater there was a get-together of WASPs, and the keynote speaker at a dinner honoring them was Janet Reno, attorney general of the United

After deactivation, Vivian (Hicks) Fagan started a flying school in Washington State, went on to train pilots for Hawaiian Air Lines, and still flies as much as she can. Below, left to right: Leonora "Nonnie" (Horton) Anderson (Class 43-W-7), Betty Jane "B. J." Williams (Class 44-W-6), and Genevieve (Landman) Rausch (Class 44-W-5), meet for the first time in almost fifty years at the 1993 dedication of the WASP statue in Sweetwater. ***Hans Halberstadt***

States. She gave a very moving speech, and handkerchiefs were being discreetly used all over the place.

Reno was there because her aunt, "Winnie" Wood had been a WASP. After deactivation, her aunt had come back to Miami with a number of her WASP friends. Reno and her friends took one look at these tanned, slim, tall, beautiful young women pilots and decided to adopt the WASPs as their role models. They fought over which one "owned" Doris Gee, Class 44-W-1, or which one "owned" "Winnie" Wood. They all won, though, because Wood and the other WASPs took on the responsibility of being role models to these girls. Reno said that fear of the look of disapproval from one of these WASPs was enough to keep them in line. She attributed her success in life to their influence and guidance and spoke of feeling their guidance during the worst days of the Waco situation. (In April 1993, David Koresh and his Branch Davidians were holed up in a compound in Waco, Texas, until a controversial raid by the Bureau of Alcohol, Tobacco, and Firearms agents precipitated a fiery and fatal end for most

WASP Pat Young with her son, Lieutenant Colonel Jerry Young. He is part of an organization called K.O.W. (Kids of WASPs). They are so darned proud of their moms, aunts, and honorary moms that they are starting to come to the reunions and join in listening to the stories. ***Hans Halberstadt***

of the cult members in the compound.) She called on the young adults in the audience that day to take on the responsibility of being role models to the young people around them, and I hope we all heard her. Some of us now look to her as a role model.

Florence (Emig) Wheeler: "Her comments were not about how great we were or about the wonderful things we did. Instead she made the point that our leadership was being identified. She said that we WASPs were her role models. That I appreciated, but her main point was that we need to have role models and guidance for our young people. Every last one of us at that dinner, whether we were WASPs or not, had a duty to be conscious of trying to get our young people to be responsible citizens. Yeah, Reno."

When the WASPs were deactivated, Joyce (Sherwood) Secciani, Class 43-W-3, whittled a little statue of a WASP. The statue figure wore a Zoot Suit and helmet and carried a parachute. Her head was down and her expression was tragic. The inscription read: "Mission Completed."

In May 1993 at Avenger Field, a statue of a WASP was unveiled. She wears her Zoot Suit and helmet. But unlike the little WASP that Secciani had carved, this one's head is raised toward the sky and her expression is exuberant. "Dot" (Swain) Lewis was the sculptor of this statue, and it represents the ultimate victory of a courageous group of women, of "Glamour Girls," of "Fly Girls," of WASPs.

Vivian (Gilchrist) Nemhauser, Class 44-W-3, (right) poses for a picture with Allison Dillard. Dillard is a big fan of the WASPs and tries to attend WASP events so that she can talk with her role models. Imitation as flattery, she dresses up in a Zoot Suit, and asks for suggestions on making her outfit even more authentic. *Hans Halberstadt.* Left, "Micky" (Tuttle) Axton at a Navy pilots' graduation ceremony in December 1990. She was the first woman asked to be a guest speaker at such a ceremony. *"Micky" Axton*

Violet "Vi" (Thurn) Cowden, Class 43-W-4, at the memorial at Avenger Field, May 1993. Vi was stationed at Love Field in Dallas, Texas. *Hans Halberstadt.* Next page, Ethel (Meyer) Finley, Class 43-W-5, is currently the president of the WASPs. She did a magnificent job arranging the memorial dedication in Sweetwater. *Hans Halberstadt*

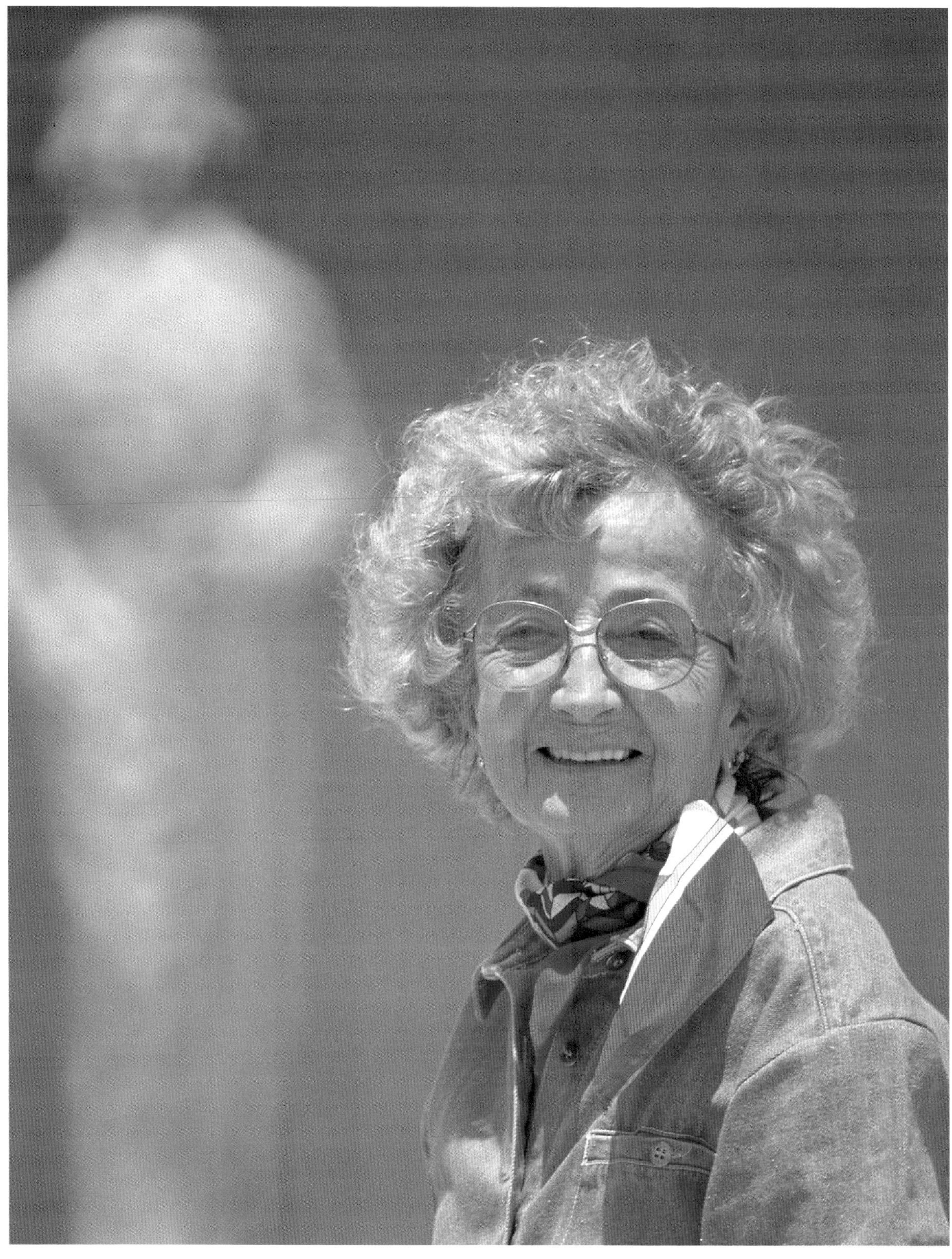

WASP

Muriel (Rath) Reynolds, at the dedication of a new WASP exhibit at the American Airpower Heritage Museum in Midland, Texas, May 1993. *Hans Halberstadt*

"I was taxiing once, when I suddenly found myself flying behind a B-17, three feet off the ground. . . . There I was trying to keep that AT-6 flying. If I didn't keep the engine going I would be flipped over backwards. I couldn't move forward. I couldn't move backward."

—Muriel (Rath) Reynolds, Class 44-W-7

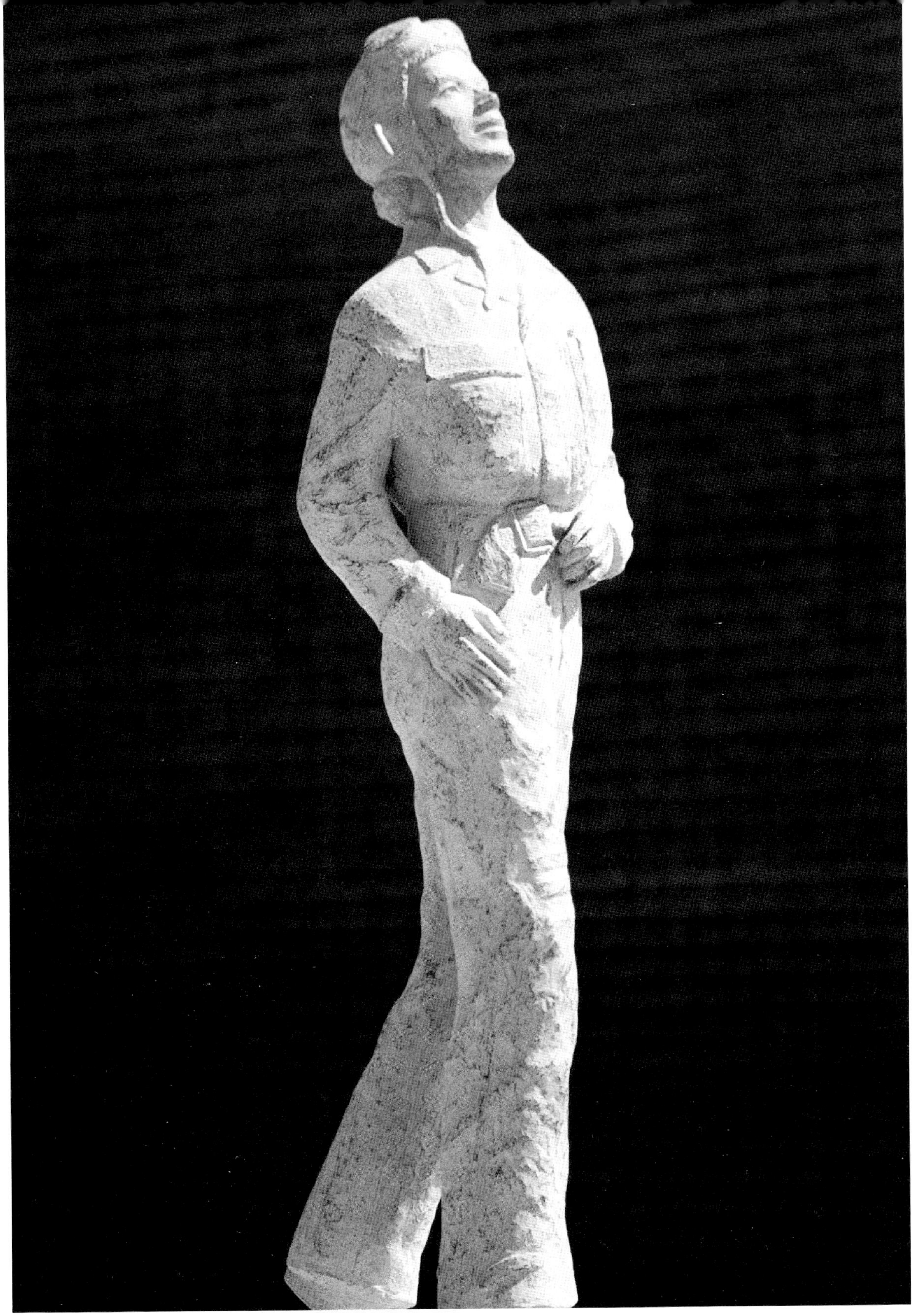

43-W-5 GRADUATES
MAPES, FRANCES D.
McCLAIN, RUTH A.
McENROE, KATHRYN
OLDENBURG, MARGARET*
POCCIANITI, W. LEE
POWELL, MARY
RHOADS, DORIS
RICHARDS, ELIZABETH
RICHEY, JEANNE D'ARC
ROSENTHAL, BERNICE D.
SCHMITT, PATRICIA
SELBY, MARJORIE J.
SIMMONS, JEANETTE C.
SINK, MARGARET W.
SWETITCH, THERESA
HAGEMANN, RUTH
HAGUE, HELEN
HARDMAN, GERALDINE
HARTSON, MARY *
HICKS, BARBARA
HILL, GERALDINE P.
HILLER, MARY
HUNTER, CELIA
JONES, CARYL L.
KARLSON, ANN M.
KEKIC, ANNABELLE
KURTEN, ELENOR
LEDBETTER, JULIE E.
LINDLEY, RUTH
LIVINGSTON, WINIFRED
LOVEJOY, ALICE *
MacLANE, HARRIET N.
MARKLE, PAULINE
McCLELLAN, ANN A.
McCORMICK, JILL S.
McINTYRE, FLOELLA
MEYER, ETHEL M.
MITCHELL, CHARLOTTE
MODISETTE, EDNA
MOHRMAN, JEAN M.
MOREHEAD, WILMA
MUNDT, ROBERTA E.
MYERS, JO
NILES, CHARLOTTE
PARKER, MARY
PATEMAN, YVONNE C.
PITZ, JOSEPHINE
POPELL, MARJORIE T.
PORTER, HELEN B.
RAMSEY, NADINE
RAY, MARGARET
RICHEY, HELEN
ROCHOW, DAWN Y.
SANFORD, MARJORIE
SCHWARTZ, SYLVIA
SCOTT, JANE S.
SHEA, BETTY
SLADE, SHIRLEY
STARK, KATHRYN S.
STEGEMAN, MARION
STERKEL, LILLIAN
STREETER, VIRGINIA
THOMAS, JANE
TURNER, HELEN
URBAN, HARRIET L.
WILSON, VIRGINIA C.
TRAINEES

The names on the plaques are the names the ladies went by when they were WASPs. *Hans Halberstadt.* Left, the memorial statue for the WASPs was dedicated in May 1993. She stands in the same wishing well at Avenger Field into which so many WASPs were tossed after their first solo flight. *Hans Halberstadt*

WASP WWII 43-4
DOROTHEA M. MOORMAN

"Bee" (Falk) Haydu, Janet Reno, and "Dot" (Swain) Lewis. Left, Janet Reno, Attorney General of the United States, presented a speech in Sweetwater to honor the WASPs. Her aunt, "Winnie" Wood, was a WASP and was an important role model for Ms. Reno. Previous page, Dorothea (Johnson) Moorman, Class 43-W-4, at Avenger Field, May 1993. *Hans Halberstadt.*
© Disney Enterprises, Inc.

The next generation. The granddaughter of "Bee" (Falk) Haydu. She'll be able to fly anything that the military builds, if she so desires, thanks to the accomplishments of her grandmother and the other WASPs. Below, left to right: "Dot" (Swain) Lewis (the sculptor of the statue) Ethel (Meyer) Finley, Attorney General Janet Reno, and Governor of Texas Ann Richards unveiling the statue. At this occasion there were lots of speeches by politicians, a BBQ, a fly-over by a B-1B from Randolph Field, and rides for the WASPs in vintage planes provided by the Confederate Air Force. It was a wonderful day. *Hans Halberstadt.* Next page, More than 1,800 women with at least thirty-five hours of flying experience reported for training in Sweetwater and learned to fly the Army way. They loved being able to fly military aircraft such as this B-17 Flying Fortress. *USAF (neg. no. 160449AC)*

PISTOL PAC
MAMA

They loved their baymates. They loved their instructors. They loved their lives and will always be young at heart.
"Dottie" Davis and Jeanne Robertson

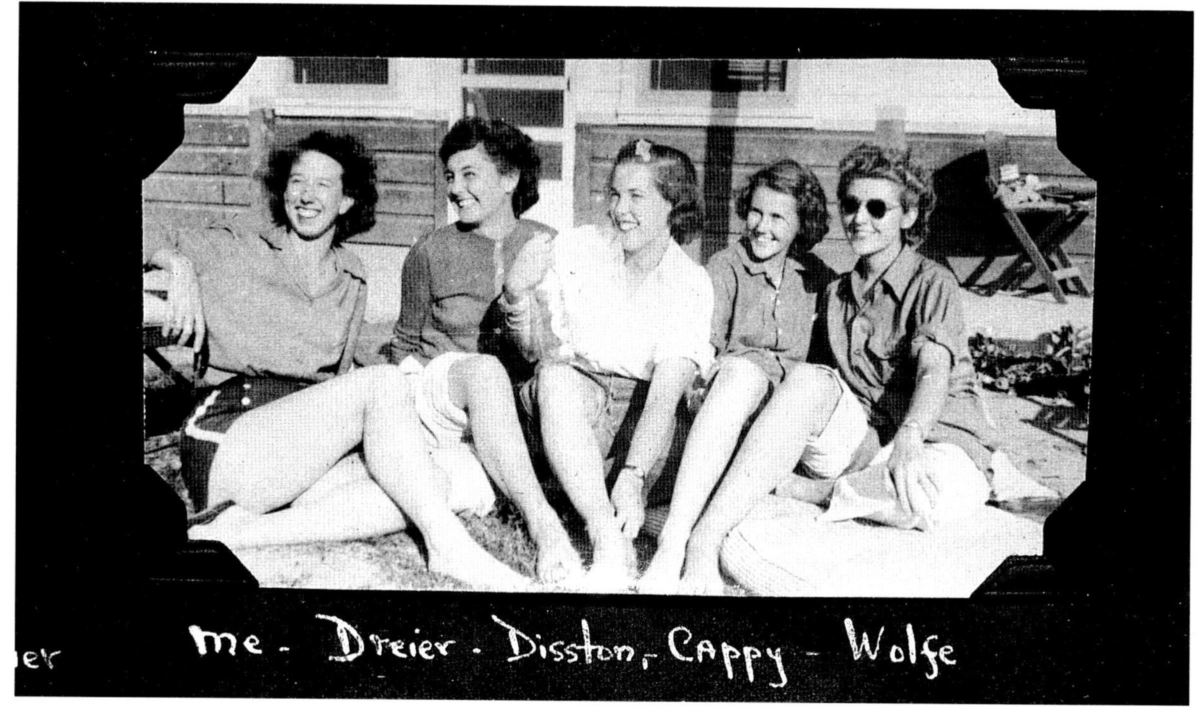

Index